a Year's Journey *with* God

Also by Jennifer Rees Larcombe

Journey into God's Heart
Turning Point
Unexpected Healing

JENNIFER REES LARCOMBE

a Year's Journey with God

HODDER

Unless indicated otherwise, Scripture quotations are taken from
the Holy Bible, New International Version.
Copyright © 1973, 1978, 1984 by Biblica (formerly International Bible Society).
Used by permission. All rights reserved.

Details of other Bible translations featured are printed at the back of the book.

First published in Great Britain in 2010 by Hodder & Stoughton
An Hachette UK company

This paperback edition first published in 2013

2

Copyright © Jennifer Rees Larcombe, 2010

A CIP catalogue record for this title is available from the British Library

ISBN 978 0 340 99501 3
eBook ISBN 978 1 444 70225 5

Typeset in Sabon MT by Palimpsest Book Production Limited,
Falkirk, Stirlingshire

Printed and bound in the UK by Clays Ltd, St Ives plc

Hodder & Stoughton policy is to use papers that are natural, renewable and recyclable
products and made from wood grown in sustainable forests. The logging and
manufacturing processes are expected to conform to the environmental
regulations of the country of origin.

Hodder & Stoughton Ltd
338 Euston Road
London NW1 3BH

www.hodderfaith.com

To Jenny Cooper, with thanks for her faithful
and patient proofreading and reference checking

Introduction

The verses and ideas that I've shared in this book have sustained me during many years of journeying with God. Some have felt like miners' lamps in underground darkness, but I've danced with the joy of others on my mountain tops. They are just ordinary little thoughts that God made special to me, and I'm praying He'll do the same for you. Many of them spring from my own experiences; others are things that I've felt God saying to me through the countryside, my dogs, my garden or my grandchildren. I've also shared my love for the old hymns that we don't often sing these days, and background details about the people who wrote them. Friends have kindly allowed me to share poems that I've enjoyed, and I'm particularly grateful to Russ Parker for letting me include some of his gloriously robust material.

God's love and compassion are 'new every morning' (Lamentation 3:22–23), so you could read this book chronologically by calendar date; or you might prefer to follow themes such as Prayer, Intimacy with God, Angels or Inner Healing. You may share my love for exploring Bible characters, or, if life is seeming sad or tough, you might want to stick to days that talk about Handling Hard Times or Surviving a Faith Crisis.

Why not make this book a record of your own personal journey through this year by jotting down special prayer requests in the margin? Later, when you look back, you can add in the date when you received the answer. Perhaps you might also like to note down any resolves or promises you make to the Lord so you can keep a permanent record of them. Underline, add your own comments or parallel verses, *be messy*, leave your own footprints on this map.

I hope this book will sit by your bed throughout the year; I'll be praying for you every day as you journey through it; even if I don't know your name – God does! My longing is that, by the time you reach the end, you will have gone deeper than ever before into the heart of God.

Do it with Jesus

Forgetting what is behind, and straining towards what is ahead, I press on towards the goal to win the prize for which God has called me heavenwards in Christ Jesus.

Phil. 3:13–14

How are you feeling about stepping out into this New Year? Perhaps you're 'straining towards what is ahead' like an Olympic sprinter, full of hope and confidence? Or you could be limping up to the start, exhausted by Christmas and crippled by endless problems. You might even be hanging back, dreading some of the forthcoming events in your brand-new diary, or unable to face life without someone you have recently lost.

As I was writing that, an email popped into my inbox from my friend in Australia. She finished by saying, 'Oh well, here's another year to do with Jesus.' I like that! It feels like a large injection of faith.

We've got to 'do' this year, however we feel about its shadowy uncertainties, and it *is* uncertain for all of us – even if we've planned it out to the last detail. Life on this planet is always unpredictable. Yet one thing is rock-solid sure: we don't have to face the future alone; we can 'do it with Jesus'.

His promise to us rings out like a glorious peal of church bells, ringing in the New Year: 'Do not be afraid . . . for the LORD your God goes with you; he will never leave you nor forsake you' (Deut. 31:6).

Thank you, Lord, that nothing is going to happen this year that you and I can't handle together. Amen.

Dry and drooping

*I will bless my people and their homes around my holy hill. And in
the proper season I will send the showers they need. There will be
showers of blessing.*

Ezek. 34:25–26, NLT

Today I took down my Christmas decorations and packed them away
in the attic for next year. It felt sad but good all at the same time. My
pot plants had been badly neglected during the whirl of Christmas,
and one poor cyclamen was in a bad way – soil dry, flowers flopping
– so I plunged it into tepid water and hoped for the best. An hour
later it was transformed! It made me realise that the last few days have
dried me out too. I love the run-up to Christmas and often feel very
close to the Lord, but there is something about the actual week of
celebration itself that seems to pull me away from Him and dries me
up – then flops me down spiritually, just like my cyclamen. It is almost
as if I switch Him off while I enjoy myself with all those 'naughty
but nice' treats and a surfeit of telly. Today I suddenly felt lonely for
Him and I badly needed those 'showers' Ezekiel was talking about.

Even when we have 'switched Him off' we only have to plunge
ourselves back into his presence to be revived and refreshed once again.
In his devotional work 'Morning and Evening', Charles Haddon
Spurgeon (1834–1892) put it like this: 'Look up today, O parched plant,
and open thy leaves and flowers for a heavenly watering.'

Lord, I feel I've lost you a bit recently; please bring my spirit back to
life again.

The gift of myself

I appeal to you therefore, brethren, and beg of you in view of (all) the mercies of God, to make a decisive dedication of your bodies (presenting all your members and faculties) as a living sacrifice, holy (devoted, consecrated) and well pleasing to God, which is your reasonable (rational, intelligent) service and spiritual worship.

Rom. 12:1, AMP

Whenever I went to a service over Christmas I always hoped we would sing my favourite carol, 'In the bleak midwinter' by Christina Rossetti (1830–1894), which finishes, 'If I were a shepherd I would bring a lamb, If I were a wise man I would do my part, Yet what I can I give Him, give my heart.' Now singing that one will have to wait for another year, I guess, but another of my favourite hymns will do in the meantime, 'When I survey the wondrous cross' by Isaac Watts (1674–1748): 'Were the whole realm of nature mine, that were an offering far too small; love so amazing, so divine, demands [shall have] my soul, my life, my all.' As the spiritual sogginess of Christmas gradually recedes, this is a great time of year for resolutions and a fresh giving of ourselves and our lives to God. This week someone sent me this lovely poem, written by a neighbour of mine, Ann Clifton:

Lord, I surrender all my gifts, to take into this year,
That I may use them in your will, to bring the Saviour near.
The gifts you give are not my own – they're yours to take away,
Or let remain, if you should choose, to use for you each day.

And so my gifts I dedicate that I may serve you here.
May all the glory go to you – my King, my Saviour dear.

Jesus loves the real me

Jesus called in a loud voice, 'Lazarus, come out!' The dead man came out, his hands and feet wrapped with strips of linen, and a cloth around his face. Jesus said to them, 'Take off the grave clothes and let him go.'

John 11:43–44

Who am I really – and why am I so afraid to let others see the real me? Sometimes, the 'real me' can get lost inside layers of other people's expectations. We tried to gain our parents' love by becoming the kind of person they seemed to admire, and later in life the desire for approval became a kind of addiction. Some Christians act like clones of those they admire and wish they were like, talking in the same way and copying clothes and hair styles.

Actually Jesus likes the 'real me', warts and all! He is the only person any of us should be trying to imitate. Today, He may be saying to someone, 'Come out of that tomb you're hiding in and let's get all those wrappings off you; I created you the way you are – not how other people think you should be!'

The words translated as 'let him go' also mean 'forgive him'. Sometimes the way to be free of all those binding bandages is to forgive the people who tried to control us and make us fulfil their goals, rather than affirming the person God had created us to be.

Lord, I've always been a bit ashamed of the secret me I hide inside. Help me realise you actually love the real me!

Barbed wire and cobwebs

To all who mourn in Israel, he will give a crown of beauty for ashes, a joyous blessing instead of mourning, festive praise instead of despair.
Isa. 61:3, NLT

One of my favourite dog walks began with a gap in the hedge which led onto a trail round the edge of a wide, open field which sweeps down the side of a hill; the magnificent view from the top made the breath-robbing climb well worthwhile. One morning last summer I found 'my gap' firmly closed by four rows of brutal barbed wire. I'd always known my trail was not an official footpath, but I kept to the very edge and never let the dogs stray onto any crops. So I've muttered angrily to myself about the farmer every time I've passed that blocked-up gap. Today was different. Overnight we had been enveloped in freezing fog; the sun was just breaking through on the far side of the barbed wire. Each cruel spike was decorated by stalks of haw frost, glittering like diamonds. Intricately patterned spiders' webs hung suspended between the rows of wire, encrusted with frozen 'diamonds', while the stalks of last year's grass, nettles and docks added to the glorious pattern. It was one of those moments you want to preserve in a bottle, carefully corked up for ever. As I walked on, savouring my 'moment', I thought of all the times in life when my goals and desires have been blocked by circumstances or the meanness of other people; how often I've boiled with frustration until I suddenly saw how God had covered these obstacles with his own particular brand of loveliness, transforming them into something utterly beautiful.

Lord, I guess that this year I'll hit all kinds of blocked goals and infuriating stoppages; help me let you transform them for me.

Accepting His will

Your will be done.

Matt. 6:3

We so often pray those words in a kind of fatalistic resignation: 'Oh well, have it your own way; after all, you're bigger than I am.' There is an old hymn that the poet William Cowper wrote back in the 1700s which, at first sight, seems full of this kind of weary resignation:

O Lord, my best desire fulfil,
and help me to resign
Life, health, and comfort, to Thy will,
and make Thy pleasure mine.

Actually he is saying, 'My greatest desire is to do and be what you desire. I long for my goals to mingle with your goals, whatever that actually means for my life; then we'll both be happy.' He had grasped a fact that many of us miss, namely that it is *always* God's will to bless us in the richest possible way through everything we experience. This morning I discovered this gloriously vigorous poem written by Russ Parker, which, for me, sums up the huge pleasure of living life God's way:

O Holy Spirit of the living God, in my life be wild and free;
Uphold me and upset me, strengthen me and weaken me,
Stop me and stir me, waken me and rest me,
Teach me and test me, make me more like Christ,
Make me fully human, whether it be the cross or the crown
May your mercy and your might flood me and fill me
So that I long for God all the more.

From *Wild Spirit of the Living God*
(Eagle, 2007)

Stop nagging!

The earnest prayer of a righteous person has great power and produces wonderful results.

Jas 5:16, NLT

Some people claim that it is earnest, daily prayer that achieves miraculous results. I have to confess that recently I was so worried about one of my grandchildren that I began nagging God incessantly for her healing. When prayer is not partnered with trust it degenerates into a form of worrying, and God used my two dogs to show me what He feels about that. One has been my companion for so long that she trusts me implicitly. Phoebe has learnt that I never forget to feed and walk her because I love her, so if I'm running late for one of those two important events of her day she simply lies down peacefully and waits until I am ready. The other is a blind spaniel who has only been with me a few months and has not yet had time to prove my love and commitment, so when she feels hungry she panics, whining and yapping infuriatingly. When I am busy in another room, counselling or praying with someone, there is nothing I can do about it, but she is convinced I've completely forgotten her. The difference is that one dog trusts my love and the other has not yet learnt to do so. I suddenly realised that God might find my endless nagging just as distressing. When we realise how deeply He loves us we know for sure that He can turn everything that touches our lives – even the hard things – into gifts and blessings.

Lord, I am so sorry I nag you instead of committing my request to you, trusting that you will answer in your way and at your time.

The first snowdrop

Don't shuffle along, eyes to the ground, absorbed with the things right in front of you. Look up, and be alert to what is going on around Christ . . . See things from his perspective. Your old life is dead. Your new life, which is your real life . . . is with Christ in God.

Col. 3:2–3, *The Message*

Last night we had a terrible storm. By morning I found the roof had leaked, ruining two ceilings, and the wind had felled my favourite tree. As I stomped out with the dogs my resolve to praise the Lord and remember His promises was sorely tried! My house was a sodden mess and the fallen tree had devastated the garden and demolished the fence. I wondered bleakly how I was ever going to pay for all this damage – just when my bank account still hadn't recovered from Christmas.

I felt weak and helpless and very much alone, until suddenly, in an obscure corner of the garden, almost obliterated by soggy dead leaves, I saw one solitary snowdrop waving triumphantly at me from the gloom. I could so easily have missed this small token of all the summer flowers to come. As I set off through the gate to the woods, I remembered some verses I'd written out and stuck up on my kitchen wall recently: 'The one who looked like a man touched me and gave me strength. "Do not be afraid . . ." he said. "Peace! Be strong now; be strong." When he spoke to me, I was strengthened' (Dan. 10:18–19).

'I need you to touch me like that, Lord,' I prayed. 'Make me as strong as that snowdrop. It looks so fragile and helpless but you created it strong enough to push up through the mud and then to withstand last night's wind and rain.'

. . . if we are faithless, he will remain faithful.

(2 Tim. 2:13)

Sunrise

Through the heartfelt mercies of our God,
God's Sunrise will break in upon us,
Shining on those in the darkness,
those sitting in the shadow of death,
Then showing us the way, one foot at a time,
down the path of peace.

Luke 1:78–79, *The Message*

Walking the dogs has been sheer misery during this last week, with nothing but grey gloom, icy rain and mud. This morning at last, the sun rose gloriously, piercing the shrouds of freezing fog, so I decided to walk the dogs down a footpath I had never explored before. I must have been walking due east because the winter sun was so low in the sky, and so gloriously bright that it totally blinded me. I couldn't see where I was going as I groped along, one step at a time, hoping I wouldn't fall into a ditch or trip over a fallen log. It felt a bit like life: when you walk towards the radiance of the Son of God the rest of the world is dimmed. When He is our focus we can only take one step at a time.

> *The sun of righteousness will dawn on those who honor my name, healing radiating from its wings.*
>
> (Mal. 4:2, *The Message*)

Father God, this year may I always walk towards your Son, the Light of the World, and may I reflect His radiance to others I meet along the way.

The eye of faith

My lover speaks to me, 'The winter is over ... the flowers are in bloom. Figs are beginning to ripen; the air is fragrant with blossoming vines. Come then, my love; my darling, come with me.'

Song of Songs 2:10, 13, GNB

My poor garden looks so bare and bleak at this time of year that sometimes it is hard to believe in springtime at all!

When I lived in a town and didn't have a garden, I loved walking in the park. One bitingly cold day, when no one else seemed brave enough to be out, I noticed an old lady standing under the bare, damp branches of a cherry tree. She was still for so long that I thought she must be ill – or frozen solid.

'I'm fine,' she assured me. 'I was just picturing all that pink blossom that's *going to be* on this tree soon. And just think of all the daffs waiting to push through all that mud.' What an exceptional person; most eighty-year-olds would have been moaning about the cold! But isn't that what faith really is, 'being sure of what we hope for and certain of what we do not see' (Heb. 11:1)? Sometimes we pray long and hard for a situation, or a person, to change but nothing seems to happen, so we begin to doubt God's promises – and His love. The old lady in the park refused to see the bleak deadness around her; instead she thought of pink cherry blossom.

Sometimes we have to do the same – by choosing to believe that God can change situations and people eventually, just as He brings back the spring.

Lord, you seem so far away right now, and I feel low and weary deep inside. Please help me to go on trusting you, just a little bit longer.

No grace in advance

I am still confident of this:
I will see the goodness of the LORD
in the land of the living.
Wait for the LORD;
be strong and take heart
and wait for the LORD.

Ps. 27:13–14

Have you ever found yourself thinking, 'If God ever let that particular situation hit me, I know I simply wouldn't be able to cope'? You would, of course, when the time came, because God gives us His grace when those terrible situations hit us, but He never gives grace in advance! If you try to picture how you would react if that dreaded phone call woke you at night or if the police arrived at your door with terrible news, you would most probably imagine yourself living through the agony in your own strength. The way God's protective love and care wraps us round with unimaginable tenderness takes most of us completely by surprise.

Peter and Sue were both teachers; one evening at house group they asked for prayer. They were about to take a group of thirty ten-year-olds to France for a week.

'I'm totally dreading it,' Sue admitted. 'I just get so worried we might lose a child.' Five days later we heard that one of the boys in their care had been drowned. Apparently it was not their fault, and they were coping magnificently with the situation. When they finally returned to house group they were obviously shaken – but also radiant as they told us how God's presence had carried them through every awful minute.

God never gives strength for tomorrow, or for the next hour, but only for the strain of the minute.

Oswald Chambers (1874–1917),
My Utmost for His Highest (1935)

How big is your God?

And Mary said: 'My soul magnifies the LORD. And my spirit has rejoiced in God my Saviour.

Luke 1:46–47, KJV

Back in the 1980s I was always irritated by a song we often sang in church with the refrain, 'We will magnify'. It made me feel so cross I kept my mouth tight shut and refused to sing. 'How could we possibly make God any bigger than He is already?' I used to mutter under my breath. Then one day we went to supper with a friend who owns a powerful telescope. As we looked up at the full moon I realised that his magnifying lenses were not making the moon itself any larger, they simply made it seem bigger to *me*! Ever since that evening I've really enjoyed singing that song!

Most of us worship a very little God indeed, limiting Him by our own small faith and huge ignorance of what the Bible tells us about Him. What a difference it would make to the way we think and act if, every day, we asked the Holy Spirit to act like those magnifying lenses and increase our vision of God as we take time to gaze at Him. David's concept of God was enormous, perhaps because he spent so much time with Him. This is his prayer:

> *One thing I ask of the LORD . . .*
> *that I may dwell in the house of the LORD*
> *all the days of my life,*
> *to gaze upon the beauty of the LORD . . .*

(Ps. 27:4)

What is worship?

Be filled with the Holy Spirit, singing psalms and hymns and spiritual songs among yourselves, and making music to the LORD in your hearts. And give thanks for everything to God the Father in the name of our LORD Jesus Christ.

Eph. 5:18–20, NLT

What does worship mean to you? For many of us Christians it is the part of a service when we express our love for God by singing hymns or songs. Others find it more satisfying to praise and honour the Lord by putting their feelings towards Him into spoken words or by using liturgy written by others. Some people just like to sit silently in His presence – perhaps focusing on a candle flame, or on something beautiful that He has created. Some kneel or lie flat on their faces while others dance and leap like King David. It really doesn't matter what our outward bodies are doing while we worship; Paul reminds us that the music of worship happens internally, in our hearts.

Worshipping is a very different activity from 'saying our prayers', which is often more about asking Him to do things for us or others. However we prefer to express it, worship is reaching out in love towards Him and letting Him know how much we value and appreciate Him for who He is, and not just for what He can do for us.

Please, Lord, make me a good worshipper.

Arms to cuddle sad people

Praise be to the . . . Father of compassion and the God of all comfort,
who comforts us in all our troubles, so that we can comfort those in
any trouble with the comfort we ourselves have received from God.

2 Cor. 1:3–4

Today's gloomy grey fog reminds me of a January afternoon many
years ago when I was waiting at the school gate. As the children erupted
like a flock of noisy starlings from the Infant department, I noticed
my five-year-old, Justyn, trudging slowly behind the others, his white,
tear-stained face shadowed by the grey hood of his duffel coat.

'What went wrong?' I asked anxiously.

'Everything,' was his doleful reply. 'My sums wouldn't come right,
the teacher was cross, and no one loved me all day.'

His six-year-old sister said reprovingly, 'That's not true! Jesus loved
you and He's always with you, even in the toilet.'

I will never forget Justyn's profound reply. 'Yes, but He hasn't got
arms any more to cuddle sad people.'

St Teresa of Avila would have agreed with that statement! She once
said, 'He has no hands now, but ours.' The Father of compassion needs
to borrow our hands and arms in order to comfort 'sad people'.

When I'm in need of some TLC I always seem to gravitate towards
people who know what suffering feels like from the inside, because
the best comforters are always those who have first received God's
comfort themselves.

So does God 'arrange' horrible experiences to teach us to be compassionate to others? No way! God's desire is first to comfort us, simply
because He loves us, and then because we know the joy of His comfort
we long for Him to use our arms to cuddle other sad people.

Lord, transform my agony into healing grace for others.

Leanne Payne (From *Listening Prayer*
(Baker Publishing Group, 1994)

Seed-sowers

*A farmer went out to sow his seed. As he was scattering the seed,
some fell along the path, and the birds came and ate it up . . . Still
other seed fell on good soil, where it produced a crop.*

Matt. 13:3, 8

Standing in the checkout queue yesterday, I started chatting to a
harassed-looking woman who told me her daughter was in hospital.
'I'll stick up some prayers for her,' I promised. 'I really believe it makes
a difference.' We are all seed-sowers! Every time we mention our faith
in a conversation, even indirectly by saying we go to church, we sow
a seed in someone's mind. Often our remark doesn't seem to register,
or they might even react with a sneer or an argument. All the same,
it is vital that we pray for the protection of that seed. Our prayers
can't change the rocky, hard heart of the person we spoke to but prayer
can protect the seed and keep it from being 'pecked up' by the enemy.
Our continuing prayers help the seed to germinate and tiny roots begin
to work their way round the stones. One day, perhaps years later,
during a time of worry or sadness, a tiny shoot will appear, causing
that person to begin seeking for the God they met in us.

Paul sowed many seeds in Thessalonica during the very short time
he visited that city. After persecution drove him out, he worried that
the 'birds' would soon eat up those seeds (1 Thess. 3:5–7); but, no,
when he sent Timothy to visit them the seeds had produced a lovely
harvest and a new church was flourishing. It had been protected because
he 'remembered them constantly in his prayers' (1 Thess. 1:2).

Men can be moved for God by prayer alone.

Hudson Taylor (1832–1905)

ELOHIM . . . Creator God most high

In the beginning God created the heavens and the earth.

The heavens declare the glory of God; the skies proclaim the work of his hands.

Gen. 1:1, Ps. 19:1

God has so many different names; I thought it might be fun to spend a few days looking at some of them.

'Elohim' shows us just what a great God we serve. He was the one who created everything. Whether we believe He did it in seven days or millions of years, we must concede that behind all the intricacies of nature there has to be an intelligent creator. His creation delights and amazes us when we watch those stunning TV documentaries. No previous generation has ever been able to appreciate them as fully as we can with all our modern technology.

But far more amazing is the fact that the God whose spirit 'brooded like a bird above the watery abyss . . . bottomless emptiness . . . inky blackness' (Gen. 1:2, *The Message*) is the God who loves me (and you) enough to die in order to win our everlasting friendship. The one who 'created all things visible and invisible, whether thrones or powers or rulers or authorities' (Col. 1:15–16), and is still 'sustaining all things by his powerful word' (Heb. 1:3), is the one who knows how many hairs grow on our heads! He has also pledged to care for us tenderly right into our old age (Isa. 46:4).

Since we are loved individually and passionately by such a powerful God, why on Earth do I get worried so ridiculously often?

Lord, help me to remember that problems are the nasty things I see when I take my eyes off you.

EL OLAM . . . The everlasting God

The LORD is the everlasting God . . . He will not grow tired or weary, and his understanding no-one can fathom.

Isa. 40:28

'The older you get, the more people you lose! It's all loss after loss once you hit fifty.' When I first heard my friend say that, I replied, 'That's an odd thing to say when you have such a full, satisfying life!' He was happily married with three delightful teenage sons – a leading consultant who headed up a department of a London teaching hospital – as well as being an elder of our church.

'These days we hate facing reality!' he replied. 'But the truth is that twenty years from now I will have retired and lost all my work contacts, my sons will have left home, my wife may have died, left me or developed dementia; the church will probably want a younger man in my role and many of my friends and neighbours will have died. Our lives on this Earth are terrifyingly brief! Only God stays the same.' David wasn't depressed; he was simply stating facts, but I was relieved when he added, 'It's a good job God is everlasting!' *The Message* paraphrases today's verse like this: 'GOD doesn't come and go. God *lasts* . . . And he knows *everything*, inside and out.'

Lord, when I lose people I love, help me remember that you promised, 'Never will I leave you; never will I forsake you.'

(Heb. 13:5)

EL ROI . . . The living one who sees me

Hagar used another name to refer to the LORD, who had spoken to her. She said, 'You are the God who sees me.' She also said, 'Have I truly seen the One who sees me?'

Gen. 16:13, NLT

The sheer wonder and poignancy that I sense in Hagar's name for God always reduces me to tears. In her day, slaves had no rights; their masters had power of life and death over them. She had even forfeited her master's provision and protection by running away. She was a mere woman in a male-dominated world, and a foreigner far from home. At that time she was worth less than nothing, and she was also dying of exhaustion, lost in a desert, all because of her own arrogant stupidity (Gen. 16:4).

Her master and mistress, Abraham and Sarah, had treated her appallingly. They had both stepped right out of God's will by trying to achieve a son by Hagar instead of waiting for God's time, and Sarah had been so harsh and cruel that Hagar had dashed off impulsively, heading for her old home in Egypt. When the desert defeated her she didn't even dare to pray to the God she must often have seen her master worshipping. Perhaps she did not feel worthy? Yet God came to her aid in person. (The phrase 'Angel of the Lord' means God Himself – the pre-incarnate Christ).

Whenever I have an attack of feeling worthless or a total failure, I remind myself of Hagar and her realisation that God could see her and cared about her when no one else on Earth loved her or knew where she was.

Lord, however badly I may mess things up, you are my El-Roi, who is miraculously able to give me your undivided attention.

JEHOVAH MACCADDESHEM . . . The Lord who sanctifies me

I am the LORD, who makes you holy.

Exod. 31:13

In my first flush of teenage religious fervour I vowed to live a perfect, sin-free life. The resolve lasted almost a whole morning! I fell (violently) from grace well before lunch and was probably unbearably grumpy for the rest of the day. After a few more tries (and failures), I consulted a wonderful old saint called Lindsay Glegg. He answered me by scribbling a few words on a piece of paper and told me to stick them up on my bedroom wall. They stayed there for years and helped me profoundly.

> *Don't try and live a holy life for that will crush you by its immensity; rather think of a series of holy moments, each one lived for God – then one day you will realise that you have lived a holy life without effort. Concentrate on Jesus rather than on your own efforts because it is His job to sanctify us.*

Great advice, that, but when you read this name of God in context you have to admit that this holiness doesn't just happen automatically. We have to deliberately make room for God in our lives. The Jews were commanded to do this each week by keeping the Sabbath; we have our Sundays, but so many of us dash out of church to get on with DIY, socialising, sport or hobbies. All these things are good, and we need to keep fit and enjoy recreation, but sometimes they crowd out time just to BE, to read Christian books or pray things over with God at greater length.

Lord, forgive me for the sin of Sabbath-breaking.

JEHOVAH YAHWEH ... The great I AM – I will be what I will be

And God said to Moses ... say ... I AM *has sent me to you.*

Exod. 3:14, NKJV

Jehovah Yahweh is the Old Testament's most important name for God, and it is used 6,800 times. God called Himself by this name during an argument He was having with Moses. God asked this eighty-year-old fugitive to go back to Egypt and lead a nation of slaves to freedom – and it is hardly surprising that Moses was horrified! He felt totally inadequate for the job and was sure the slaves would share his low opinion! After he had thought up every possible excuse, God thundered at Him, 'Tell them I AM sent you.' In other words, 'If you've got me with you, what else could you possibly need?'

When the soldiers came to arrest Jesus in Gethsemane He asked them who they were looking for; they replied, 'Jesus of Nazareth.' When Jesus answered by using this name, 'I AM', they staggered backwards, felled to the ground by the impact of the most powerful name in the universe (John 18:6). They could never have dragged Him away to His death unless He had allowed them to do so.

For hundreds of years the name 'Yahweh' was held in such reverence that the Jews did not even dare to speak it out loud. How different it is for us now we have been given permission to call Him 'Abba' – Daddy!

Next time you face a person or situation you fear, remember to invoke that great name and remember that His power completely surrounds you.

JEHOVAH SHAMMAH . . . The Lord who is present

The LORD is there.

Ezek. 48:35

When God first used the name 'Jehovah-Shammah', Jerusalem and the whole land of Israel lay in desolate ruins. As a result of their persistent disobedience, the Jews had been driven into captivity in Babylon. God had not abandoned them, however, and He used this name as He finished giving detailed instructions to Ezekiel about how the land would be divided up among the tribes when they resettled there. Jerusalem and the newly built temple would be the pivotal point of their lives because He would be there in that spot where He has placed His name for all time. In other words, He was saying, 'Remember, when you finally get back home, I will be right there in the centre of your families, your daily lives and your worship.'

At one of the lowest points in my life, when I felt I was losing most of what I valued most, I tripped over and landed in a pond full of liquid cow dung. It felt just as if life had become a similar stinking mess! As I wallowed about, cursing God for allowing everything to go wrong, I suddenly felt overwhelmed by His presence and love. I didn't hear a voice but I sensed He was saying, 'Ask me into the centre of this mess with you and let me take control.' The outer circumstances did not improve for at least six years but inside I had His peace and a deep sense of well-being, simply because He was in the centre.

Lord, help me to keep you, Jehovah-Shammah, right in the centre of my entire life, today and for always.

Where are you, Jehovah Shammah?

Who is among you who [reverently] fears the LORD, who obeys the voice of His Servant, yet who walks in darkness and deep trouble and has no shining splendor [in his heart]? Let him rely on, trust in, and be confident in the name of the LORD, and let him lean upon and be supported by his God.

Isa. 50:10, AMP

Some people feel wonderfully carried by God when their lives suddenly crash down around their ears; when mine disintegrated I felt nothing at all – there was certainly no 'shining splendour' in my heart! I don't remember being conscious of God at all; for weeks I just went through the motions of living, rather like a mindless robot.

Emma was one of those people who felt euphoric at first: 'I don't think I ever felt closer to God than I did after my husband died,' she told me. 'Then about six months later He suddenly seemed to disappear completely. One night in the bath I was so desperate I said, "Where have you gone, God, just when I need you most?" He didn't reply but I had this feeling that He wanted me to *know* He was there even if I couldn't feel His presence – to believe it in my head, regardless of feelings. After all, He promised we would always have His presence with us (Heb. 13:5) but He never promised we would always *feel* His presence.'

I want to trust in and be confident in the name of JEHOVAH SHAMMAH . . . The Lord who is present. Help me to lean on you and rely on you today, whether I feel you with me or not.

JEHOVAH JIREH . . . My provider

So Abraham called that place 'The LORD Will Provide'

Gen. 22:14

Abraham gave God this name, probably with a huge sigh of relief! God had provided for him – just in time!

'Well He doesn't provide for *me*!' someone may be thinking, after receiving a 'no' to their prayers. Confusing! I've had some bad faith-wobbles, too, over prayers I felt God was ignoring, but I've come to realise that prayer has to be linked with the conviction that God *will* give us what we ask for when the time is right – but *only* if it is the best option for us. I look back at some of my most earnest prayers – and shudder when I realise how disastrous it would have been if God had granted my request!

The day my husband was interviewed for the headship of a large primary school I paced and prayed – and fasted. I knew how he would love the job and how perfectly suited he was to do it brilliantly. I was shattered when he came home disappointed. God had let us down! A few months later, just when my husband should have been taking over all the responsibilities and long hours involved in a major headship, I was disabled by a brain virus and confined to a wheelchair. Tony could never have coped with that job on top of caring for me and our six children.

One of the hardest things in our secret prayer life is to accept with joy and not with grief the answers to our deepest prayers. It was a long time before I discovered that whatever came was the answer. I had expected something so different that I did not recognise it when it came. He doesn't explain; He trusts us not to be offended, that's all.

Amy Carmichael (1867–1951)

JEHOVAH ROHI . . . The Lord my shepherd

The LORD is my shepherd; I have all that I need.

Ps. 23:1, NLT

Imagine David, the lonely shepherd boy, lying by his campfire one night with his head on the woolly side of his favourite old sheep. Suppose he began composing the kind of song the old sheep might sing – if only sheep *could* sing . . .

'David is my shepherd, so I'm a lucky old sheep; he always gives me everything I need. He knows I hate dry, scorched grass, so he leads me to where the lush green grass grows; and when my old legs get tired he always finds me a nice bit of shade for a snooze. He knows those fizzy mountain streams give me tummy ache, so he finds still pools for me. When we have to go through the Dark Ravine, with all those slimy green rocks and menacing shadows, he knows I always get the shivers, so he walks extra close, talking to me all the way. With him beside me how could I possibly be scared? He knows all about those nasty little snakes that hide in the grass, so when we arrive at a new patch of pasture, he walks all over it first, whacking them with his rod and staff so they can't bite my nose while I feed. I know he won't go off and leave me; he'll see me through to the end of my life, and if he eats me up for his supper one day, well I'll become part of him, and stay with him for ever.'

When David had baa-ed and laughed his way through that, on behalf of his old sheep, perhaps he suddenly thought, 'If I care about my sheep as much as that, surely God is going to be an even better shepherd to me.'

Thank you, Lord, for always being there for me.

JEHOVAH SABBAOTH . . . The Lord of heaven's armies

Say to my servant David, 'This is what the LORD of Heaven's Armies has declared: I took you from tending sheep . . . and selected you to be the leader of my people . . . I have been with you wherever you have gone, and I have destroyed all your enemies before your eyes.

2 Sam. 7:8–9, NLT

I love the way David always brought God into whatever he happened to be doing. When he was looking after his flock he related to God as a shepherd, but when he became a successful soldier he often addressed God by today's name. It was like saying, 'God is my commander-in-chief; I just obey orders.'

He called God by other military names as well. In his song of triumph after escaping from Saul he said, 'The LORD is . . . my fortress and my deliverer . . . my rock, in whom I take refuge, my shield . . . my stronghold, my refuge and my saviour – from violent men you save me' (2 Sam. 22:2–3).

Could you invent some names for God, derived from things in your own personal world? Mine could be: 'You are my duvet, wrapping me round with your love. You are my Satellite Navigational System, guiding me through life. You are my bath full of warm water, cleaning away the dirt of the day. You are my big armchair, taking all my weight as I sink down into you and relax.' Can you think of some more?

I'm so glad that you are the Lord of Heaven's Armies. You are greater and more powerful than any forces that could ever come against me, both human and spiritual.

EL SHADDAI . . . God Almighty

He who dwells in the secret place of the Most High shall abide under the shadow of the Almighty.

Ps. 91:1, NKJV

God first called Himself by this name when He told an old man of ninety-nine, whose wife wasn't much younger, that they were going to be the parents of a son (Gen. 17:1). Only God Almighty can do the impossible! David also called God by this name when he, too, was facing an impossible situation. God had told David that he was going to be king, and then turned him into a superstar overnight by helping him to slay Goliath. When he had married a princess and become a highly successful army general, his career seemed set fair – until King Saul became irrationally jealous. He separated David from his wife, sacked him from his job and drove him into exile in the desert; then he proceeded to hunt him and his followers, relentlessly, for years. Yet David still believed God would keep His promise and do the impossible.

Finding shade in the Judean desert is something you only dream about, and it would also have been difficult to find enough cover for David's rapidly increasing gang of guerrilla fighters. Perhaps it was when he and his men were crouching among some rocks, praying Saul's soldiers would not see them, that the seed-idea for this psalm first came to David. Maybe he whispered to the others, 'God is like a cool, secret hiding place. The Almighty is God of the impossible; we'll hide in Him until He has sorted all this confusing mess out for us.' And of course, eventually God did just that!

Hide me, O my saviour, hide, till the storm of life is past.

Charles Wesley (1707–1788)

JEHOVAH NISSI . . . The Lord our banner

Moses built an altar and called it The LORD is my Banner.

Exod. 17:15

By a series of amazing miracles God had managed to get the Jewish slaves out of Egypt, but He needed them to get to know and trust Him before He took them into the Promised Land. So, instead of leading them by the direct route, which would only have taken a matter of days, He led them into the terrible, dry desert of Sinai. They soon ran out of food and water but God proved His ability to provide all they needed – in spite of their grumbles and doubts. As they trudged on through the endless sand they had no idea they were being spied on from the craggy rocks above their heads. A fierce tribe of Bedouin were far from pleased to see them. Without warning they attacked the rear of the convoy, slaughtering the stragglers. Joshua had to lead some very raw recruits into battle while Moses prayed all day, with hands held high. The enemy had just been utterly routed when Moses spoke out today's name for God.

When a general led his army into battle he always had a banner flying over his head so his soldiers could follow wherever he went. The Lord had definitely been their banner of triumph that day. A verse that has helped me through many nasty skirmishes is Isaiah 59:19 in the King James Version: 'When the enemy shall come in like a flood, the Spirit of the LORD shall lift up a standard against him.'

Lord, temptation surges at me like a tidal wave; my enemies are my own wrong goals, negative thinking and doubts. Help me to follow your banner into battle so I emerge victorious.

ADONAI . . . My great Lord

Thomas said to him, 'My LORD and my God!'

John 20:28

'Adonai' is my favourite name for God; in fact I often use it when I pray. It is much more personal and intimate than some of His other names, and yet it retains the sense of awe and reverence we would feel if we bowed down in front of the throne of the greatest and most powerful monarch in the world. Actually that is exactly what we *are* doing whenever we use this name. Yet there is that glorious 'MY' in front of the 'great Lord'. It helps us to see God not just as the great architect of the universal, but as MY OWN PERSONAL Lord and Master; my Owner, Boss, Pastor, Ruler, King – in fact everything I need.

In the days when a husband owned his wife, body and soul, she would have addressed him as 'Adonai', seeing him as her material provider and protector as well as the source of her emotional happiness and fulfilment. She would also have derived her social status from him – if her husband was poor or spendthrift she went down into the gutter with him, but if he was rich and respected she basked in his reflected glory. God refers to Himself as our husband (Isa. 54:5). I suspect it was something like 'Adonai' that Thomas murmured when he bowed down on the dusty floor in front of Jesus in that upper room (John 20:26–28). Before, he had called Jesus 'Rabboni', which meant 'teacher', but this was totally different. Suddenly this sceptical man realised that the carpenter from the backwoods of Galilee was God Himself, and demanded his lifelong allegiance.

I bow my whole self before you today, my great God.

Treasure-seekers: Jesus is our wisdom

Christ, in whom are hidden all the treasures of wisdom and knowledge.
Col. 2:2–3

When we have a major decision to make, or we are not sure how to solve some conflict in the family or at work, the one thing we long for is wisdom. Most of us dash straight off to the wisest person we know and ask their advice. Good idea, up to a point – but if we happen to know several wise people we'll probably find they each advise something different and we'll be left more confused than ever. It is far easier just to go directly to the Bank of Wisdom Himself and draw out what we need.

That might sound a bit simplistic, if you are going through a time of major confusion and you just can't seem to hear God's voice at all. Your thoughts won't stay still for a moment as you wonder, 'Should I do this? Or suppose I tried that . . .?' Once, when I was going through a major Confusion Attack like that, my brain seemed to crash like an overloaded computer! I realised I just had to stop asking God 'What shall I do . . .?' and simply focus on Jesus instead. My brain needed a rest, so I just sat still and started telling Him which of His qualities I valued most and which of the stories about Him in the Gospels I love best. Over the following days, as I concentrated on connecting with Him like that, He was gradually able to download the right solutions, in stages, at the exact time that I needed them.

Thank you, Jesus, for your promise to lavish on me all wisdom and understanding

(Eph. 1:7–8)

How kind He is!

How kind the LORD is! How good he is! So merciful, this God of ours! The LORD protects those of childlike faith.

Ps. 116:5–6, NLT

My mother loved the word 'kind'. She had a little saying which became a recurring family joke: 'Be kind to each other,' and if she wanted to pay someone the highest possible compliment, she would say they were 'so kind'.

She was brought up on the old King James Version of the Bible, but one Christmas I gave her a present of the Living Bible, which was first published in 1971. She loved it and used it daily for the rest of her life. Just after she died I was flipping through it one day, fascinated by all her markings and the little notes she had written in the margins. Every time she had come across the word 'kind' she must have underlined it, and one of the last things she ever said to me was, 'How kind the Lord is.'

When I looked up 'kind' in my thesaurus, and saw how many shades of meaning the word has, I realised the list gives a wonderfully rich picture of the Lord's character:

Affectionate; altruistic; compassionate; congenial; considerate; courteous; friendly; generous; gentle; good; good-natured; gracious; helpful; indulgent; kind-hearted; kindly; lenient; loving; mild; philanthropic; sympathetic; tender-hearted; thoughtful; understanding.

LORD, today, please help me to 'clothe myself with kindness'.

(Col. 3:12)

'Say the kind thing'

When she speaks, her words are wise, and she gives instructions with kindness.

In her tongue is the law of kindness.

Prov. 31:26a, NLT, 26b, KJV

My mother's mother *also* loved the word 'kind', and she too had a catchphrase her family often quoted: 'Say the kind thing.' One of her favourite Bible passages was Proverbs 31, which describes the virtuous woman. This remarkable lady organised a huge household (v. 15) and also worked hard running her own business (vv. 16 and 24). She was brilliant at managing her staff, not to mention her husband and children (v. 28)! My granny maintained that this was because she kept her tongue under control by the 'law of kindness'. Perhaps she identified with this woman because she too ran a large household, with her seven children and three maids. They all loved and respected her simply because she was always so kind. Even when she told someone off, she did it so kindly they were invariably left feeling valued and appreciated – as well as being determined to do better in future.

Unkind words can do profound damage, especially to children. Words stick in their minds, often for a lifetime – distorting the way they feel about themselves and destroying their confidence. On the other hand, a kindly, appreciative comment builds up and can even change the course of someone's life.

Please, Lord, may every word I speak today be subject to your law of kindness. Give me wisdom to speak the truth kindly and may I use my tongue to bless others.

The well-kept secret

I will be glad and rejoice in your unfailing love, for you have seen my troubles, and you care about the anguish of my soul.

Ps. 31:7, NLT

It was always fun to pop in and see Mrs Shoesmith – an elderly lady who lived alone. She was a wonderful listener and loved to hear about the funny little things the children said and did. I always came away from her home smiling. When she died I told her daughter how she used to cheer me up and make me feel good about life.

'Did you realise she suffered from depression for years?' her daughter asked. 'Not to mention the awful pain she was in with her arthritis.' Then she showed me a prayer Mrs Shoesmith had copied out in her copperplate handwriting and stuck inside the cover of her Bible.

O God . . . Help us to bring happiness and peace to others, even when our own hearts are in turmoil. Save us from spreading grief and sorrow, depression and despair. May we never sell our courage to buy sympathy. May we never sell another's good name to buy pity for ourselves.

Show us that it is more enriching to show courage than to receive sympathy, even when no-one suspects that there is anything to be courageous about. O Lord deliver us from yielding to melancholy moods that depress others; from the sullenness of temper that drives the sunshine from other faces; from the refusal to do battle with gloom and by that refusal to make life harder for others. Through Jesus Christ our Lord, Amen.

Dr Leslie Weatherhead (1893–1976) (From *A Private House of Prayer*, Hodder & Stoughton, 1958)

Love that will not let me go

O Love that wilt not let me go,
I rest my weary soul in thee; I give thee back the life I owe,
That in thine ocean depths its flow May richer, fuller be.

O light that follow'st all my way,
I yield my flick'ring torch to thee; My heart restores its borrowed ray,
That in thy sunshine's blaze its day May brighter, fairer be.

O Joy that seekest me through pain,
I cannot close my heart to thee; I trace the rainbow through the rain,
And feel the promise is not vain, That morn shall tearless be.

O Cross that liftest up my head,
I dare not ask to fly from thee; I lay in dust life's glory dead,
and from the ground there blossoms red Life that shall endless be.

George Matheson (1842–1906)

This beautiful hymn was written in exactly five minutes, by a man whose heart had just been broken. George Matheson was born with a brilliant mind trapped inside a frail body. Against all odds he made it to Edinburgh University and eventually became one of Scotland's greatest theologians. He was engaged to a girl he adored when he discovered he was rapidly going blind; she could not face the thought of being married to a handicapped husband so she gave him back his ring. George was devastated; all he had left in the world was his devoted sister, with whom he lived, but on her wedding day he felt he had lost her too, and was completely alone. It was that very day he scrawled this hymn on a piece of paper. He always maintained the words were 'dictated to me by some inward voice'.

Thank you, Lord, that you have loved me with 'an everlasting love'.
(Jer. 31:3)

The real heroes

'I tell you the truth, whatever you did for one of the least of these brothers of mine, you did for me'.

'Your Father, who sees what is done in secret, will reward you.'

Matt. 25:40, Matt. 6:6

Yesterday I visited a friend and her baby. She had recently swapped a successful career for motherhood and a life consisting of changing disgusting nappies, with little sleep and endless washing. Perhaps her reward comes from all those toothless smiles? Then I went on to visit another friend who had also given up a career to care for someone she loves. Her mother is ninety and, like the baby, she also needs round-the-clock care, but the old lady never smiles, she only grumbles.

'I think they've written me off at church now I can't get out to things easily,' admitted my friend, but behind her remark lay an abyss of loneliness. There must be thousands of people who spend their lives hidden and forgotten because they love a relative too much to abandon them. Few of us notice or affirm them. This life just isn't fair, but Jesus promises to put everything right in the next! He said, 'Many who are first will be last, and many who are last will be first' (Matt. 19:30) and 'Great is your reward in heaven' (Matt. 5:12). Perhaps we think, 'I could do so much good in this world if only I were free to go out and do it!' Yet, so long as we are sure we are doing what God wants us to do, our reward will be the same whether we are Shaftesbury and Wilberforce or a carer focusing our life on just one complaining old lady.

Lord, help me to do something kind for someone today that only you notice.

Leaning on a spider's web

Jesus looked at him and loved him. 'One thing you lack,' he said.

Mark 10:21

'A perfect young man!' I guess that is how most people described the 'rich young ruler' who asked Jesus what he could do to ensure his salvation. He was a good man, prosperous and already in charge of the local synagogue. As Jesus looked intently and searchingly into his face He saw all that he was, and all he could become. However, He also saw there was something in this man's life that had become dangerously important to him. Money was his god: it made him feel safe, valuable and fulfilled, and he derived his comfort and happiness from the things he could buy.

Yet, in spite of seeing this major weakness, Jesus still loved him. When Mark uses the phrase 'looked at him and loved him', he describes a very intense and particular kind of love which deeply desires the other person's greatest happiness and well-being.

It may not be wealth that you worship, but has something, or someone, else become the centre of your existence?

When Jesus looks deep into us He loves us so much that He knows we are heading for disaster when we look to people, finance, career or physical fitness to make our lives safe, successful and satisfying. Nothing and no one lasts; our only hope of perfect security is to depend on Him first and foremost. This young man chose to put his trust in a lesser god.

'What he trusts in is fragile; what he relies on is a spider's web. He leans on his web, but it gives way; he clings to it, but it does not hold' (Job 8:14–15). Are you leaning on a spider's web?

The red light

So then, let us purify ourselves from everything that makes body or soul unclean, and let us be completely holy by living in awe of God. For the sadness that is used by God brings a change of heart that leads to salvation – and there is no regret in that!

2 Cor. 7:1, 10, GNB

Guilt is not fashionable these days, perhaps because we no longer live 'in awe of God'. We prefer to focus on His loving tenderness rather than His holiness and wrath. Knowing we are loved is vital but we can so easily overstep the mark and become too 'pally' with God. When we break one of His rules we think, 'He's so loving; He won't mind.' Actually He *does mind*, because unconfessed sin eventually kills our relationship with Him while repentance brings instant forgiveness and restoration.

I was having coffee with a group of not-yet-Christian neighbours when I overhead one say, 'Guilt is such a self-indulgent, destructive emotion!' But is it? Perhaps it can be for people who hold on to guilt by refusing to forgive themselves for something they have done. Then it definitely becomes destructive of peace, happiness and relationships. Unfortunately I've met a lot of Christians who misuse guilt like this, punishing themselves instead of realising that Jesus has paid the penalty for them.

God designed guilt to feel so unpleasant that it prods us into doing something to relieve it. It is like the red warning light that comes on to warn me when my car needs to be taken to the garage *urgently*. Too many of us, these days, ignore our 'red warning lights'.

Please, Lord, help me to become ultra-sensitive to guilt, which is really your gift to me, there to keep me walking close to your heels.

Clouds

He was taken up before their very eyes, and a cloud hid him from their sight.

Acts 1:9

The disciples must have felt so lonely and desolate when Jesus disappeared into the clouds and they could no longer see or touch Him. A similar cloud had separated Him from them once before – on the Mount of Transfiguration, when He talked with Moses and Elijah. Peter had made one of his usual silly remarks and suddenly they lost Jesus completely in a billowing bright cloud (Matt. 17:1–8). They'd been so terrified that they fell on their faces and didn't move until they looked up and saw 'no man, save Jesus only' (Matt. 17:8, KJV). Clouds separate us from the sun, and also from Jesus at times. These clouds are the harrowing experiences that hit our lives, making us doubt God's power to intervene in response to our prayers. Our faith grows most rapidly, however, when, in spite of the clouds, we go on believing that He is good, that He loves us and that He is one hundred per cent there for us. That is when we learn to 'walk by faith, not by sight' (2 Cor. 5:7, KJV).

When we can't see Jesus because of some horrible cloud, most of us couldn't care less about growing our faith; we just want to get out of the cloud! It is not until afterwards that we realise that, to God, our faith was more valuable than anything else (1 Pet. 1:7), because faith is the only ladder by which we can reach God. We can't do it intellectually or by good deeds – just by faith alone.

Thank you, Lord, that it is often in the clouds that we 'see no man save Jesus only'.

The best is yet to come!

We know that when these bodies of ours are taken down like tents and folded away, they will be replaced by resurrection bodies in heaven . . . Sometimes we can hardly wait to move . . . Compared to what's coming, living conditions around here seem like a stopover in an unfurnished shack, and we're tired of it! The Spirit of God whets our appetite by giving us a taste of what's ahead. He puts a little of heaven in our hearts so that we'll never settle for less.

2 Cor. 5:1–5, *The Message*

Samuel Rutherford, a Scottish professor in the 1600s, said, 'If this earth were heaven, then heaven were not heaven.' So many of us try to create heaven for ourselves on earth and the thought of death appals us.

I love the way Paul held his life in an open hand when he wrote, 'For to me, to live is Christ and to die is gain' (Phil. 1:21).

When my friend Rhoda was diagnosed with liver cancer, her church began to pray for her so earnestly you would think death was the worst thing that could ever happen to a Christian, rather than the very best! Her reaction was, 'We all have to go sometime and I so long to be with the Lord.' The day before her death I was sitting next to her while she literally gazed into heaven. 'Oh, Jen,' she whispered, 'it's all so beautiful.' She died with a radiant smile on her face, reaching out both hands towards someone only she could see.

Of course it is sad to leave behind the people we love, but the one we trust to take us to heaven is the one we can trust to take care of them for us on earth.

FEBRUARY 8

Blocked goals

We make it our goal to please him.

2 Cor. 5:9

What would you say is the main goal that drives you on through life? To be successful, have a comfortable home, help people? We usually form these goals in childhood, maybe because we want to copy our parents, to please them or to be as different from them as possible: 'I'm not going to be a slob like my mum; I'll always look stylishly beautiful.'

When we give our lives to Jesus our goals often change: 'I want to have a wonderful Christian marriage . . . raise my children to become strong Christians . . . have a powerful ministry in the church . . .' These are good goals but the problem is that they can all be blocked by other people. For example, if our husband leaves us the wonderful Christian marriage we wanted disintegrates; our children may not choose to become Christians and our church may not recognise our ministry. When others block our goals, very powerful emotions spring up inside us. Anger: 'How dare they do this after all I've done!' Guilt: 'I failed!' Anxiety: 'Help, what do I do now?' Hopelessness: 'I might as well give up; I'm useless.'

These rogue emotions are uncomfortable bedfellows and the reason they plague us is that our goals were good, but not the best. If Paul's goal had been to be popular or to be free to go on with his church planting, he would have felt miserable stuck in prison, but his goal was not blocked because he had chosen the best of all – simply to do his best to please God every minute of every day he lived. No one has the power to block that goal.

Lord, help me remember I only have an audience of one!

The 'bit of plastic'

Everything that goes into a life of pleasing God has been miraculously given to us by getting to know, personally and intimately, the One who invited us to God. The best invitation we ever received!

2 Pet. 1:3, *The Message*

When we have made it our goal to please God, we can soon get discouraged, for example when someone irritates or criticises us and we retaliate with words – or thoughts – that we know won't please God at all! Or we fall into our 'little besetting sin' *yet again* and have to ask forgiveness for the millionth time. What a relief to realise we don't have to achieve our goal by our own efforts! It is not that we have to try to imitate all the qualities that made God so pleased with Jesus (Luke 3:22); when we invite Him to live in us He makes His patience, strength, gentleness, etc. available for us to use instead of our own.

A multibillionaire had a son who, at eighteen, wanted to go off round the world to see if he could be independent and live by his own resources. His father agreed to let him go for three years but gave him a bank card, saying, 'If you need anything, just use this to access my bank account,' which, of course, was limitless. Three years later the body of a vagrant was found in a filthy squat, the unused bank card still in his pocket. Our Father has made limitless 'funds' available to us for the asking, but the trouble is, either we forget, or we're too proud to use our 'bit of plastic'.

What do you need to draw from the bank of heaven today? Patience, self-control, peace, love or wisdom? They are all there waiting, and your pin number is: J.E.S.U.S.

Word of a gentleman

When God wanted to guarantee his promises, he gave his word, a rock-solid guarantee – God can't break his word. And because his word cannot change, the promise is likewise unchangeable. We who have run for our very lives to God have every reason to grab the promised hope with both hands and never let go. It's an unbreakable spiritual lifeline, reaching past all appearances right to the very presence of God.

Heb. 6:17–19, *The Message*

My aunt recently lent me her audio collection of Victorian novels. It fascinated me to see how differently people thought and acted 150 years ago. For one thing, a promise was held as sacred in those days, and the word of a gentleman was trusted implicitly. Now we break promises whenever it suits us, so we find it much harder to believe that God keeps His word.

When I tried to count just how many of His promises the Bible contains I had to give up; they are innumerable – and He never ever breaks them. Yet we all have this built-in niggle which says, 'He may keep His promise to others but He won't to me!' We are crippled by fears, and forget He promised us peace (John 14:27); we worry about dying, and ignore His promise of everlasting life (John 3:16); we torture ourselves with worry about finances or arrangements for our old age, and disregard His promise to supply all our needs (Phil. 4:19). All God's amazing provisions for us are sitting there waiting for us to access them, just by turning to Him in faith. He hears our 'HELP' before we get past the first 'H'!

Lord, my faith seems so small and weak at present; I *want* to believe your promises but there is a part of me that doubts. Please pour yourself into my struggling side.

Don't cling to the dust

I am completely discouraged, I lie in the dust. Revive me by your word.

My soul clings to the dust; Revive me according to Your word.

My soul cleaves to the dust; Revive me according to Your word.

Ps. 119:25, LB, NKJV, NASB

I'm suffering from post-flu blues, and various other dismal problems are bombarding me from every side. Anyone but the Lord would be getting bored with all my negative whingeing!

This morning, in the middle of my usual grumbling prayers, this verse from Psalm 119 'hit me in the eye'. It felt like God's word – just for me; it talks about lying in the dust, clinging to the dust and finally cleaving, or getting stuck in it. Slowly I began to realise that, although I have a lot to be discouraged about, while I continue to lie in the dust, deliberately clinging to it, I am going to stay there – permanently! The psalmist says it is God's word that will revive me, and that means His promises. So I wrote down a few that seemed particularly relevant to my present predicaments, and stuck them up firmly on the kitchen wall near my kettle. No more whingeing! I'm going to repeat those promises and thank Him that He *always* keeps them.

Discouragements hit us all; they are inevitable, but we have the option to let them keep us in the dust or to choose to believe what He says He will do for us!

And because of His glory and excellence, He has given us great and precious promises. These are the promises that enable you to share His divine nature and escape the world's corruption caused by human desires. In view of all this, make every effort to respond to God's promises.

(2 Pet. 1:4–5, NLT)

FEBRUARY 12

Spindly seedlings

My Father is the gardener.

John 15:16

For the last few years I've been inviting people to spend Quiet Days in my garden, during the spring and summer. They come just to be with God and take time out with Him. I love to see them enjoying the flowers – but flowers don't just 'happen'; cultivating them takes time and a lot of effort. Right now my greenhouse is full of trays containing rows of tiny seedlings. They have to be watered, kept warm, pricked out, potted on and then finally planted out in the beds. That won't be the end of it, either; they have to be fed, protected from slugs, given still more water and 'dead-headed' regularly.

At the moment it is hard to believe that these spindly little things, lolling weakly on fragile stems, could ever possibly turn into enormous banks of colour and foliage. They won't, of course, without my constant daily care.

Other people, looking at us right now, may well consider us 'weak, spindly little Christians and no use to God at all'; but when He looks at us He doesn't just see us as we are now. He has glorious plans for our lives (Jer. 29:11), and He has the power to turn those plans into reality, if we are willing to let Him. He is committed to watching over us day by day, even more diligently than I watch my seedlings!

Please, Lord, deliver me from the limiting effects of my own opinion of myself! I know, and you know, and the Devil knows that I'm a puny, stunted little specimen, but with a 'Gardener' like you to tend me, I could develop into something miraculously beautiful for your pleasure.

Send me

Then I heard the voice of the LORD saying, 'Whom shall I send? And who will go for us?' And I said, 'Here am I. Send me!'

Isa. 6:8

Many of us start the day by praying, 'Lord, use me to help others today.' Russ Parker has made something beautiful out of that simple request:

Being there

Wild Spirit of the living God,
Make me cool waters
In someone else's parched land;
A sheltered place for the fallen
A haven for the wounded;
A safe place for the frightened
A highway for the wanderer;
A still place for the fugitive
A home for the weary;
A strong place for the feeble
And a hill for the ones
Who want to see further,
Wild Spirit of the living God,
Give me a listening heart
Instead of an informed mind
So that I meet someone else's need
Rather than my own,
Through Jesus Christ my Lord, Amen.

(From Wild Spirit of the Living God)

Lord, I may not be a poet or a highly revered saint, but please use my life today.

Red roses

The LORD says, 'I was ready to respond, but no one asked for help. I was ready to be found, but no one was looking for me. I said, "Here I am, here I am!" . . . All day long I opened my arms to a rebellious people. But they follow their own evil paths . . .'

Isa. 65:1–2, NLT

The original St Valentine, who was a Roman, was martyred on 14 February 269 because he refused to give up his Christian faith. Quite how his name became linked with our celebration of romance is anyone's guess!

When my son was seventeen he fell passionately in love. On Valentine's Day he blew his entire savings on a huge bunch of red roses and cycled off to present them. Unfortunately it was snowing heavily that day, and his beloved lived three miles up a long steep hill. When I saw his cold, bedraggled figure returning two hours later with the sodden bouquet still strapped to the back of his bike I could have cried for him. She had refused them!

Nothing hurts any of us more than loving someone with everything we've got but having our love completely rejected. God has to live with that agony all the time. John tells us, 'God is love' (1 John 4:8). Love just pours out of Him – He can't stop Himself; but the one thing Love longs for is for that Love to be accepted and returned. God could have programmed humans so that they loved Him automatically, but that would not have been real love, so He gave us the gift of choice. We can choose to receive His love and return it, or we have the right to turn our backs and totally reject Him.

Lord, today I choose, as St Valentine did, to love you more than life itself.

'Beam me up, Scotty'

When I said, 'My foot is slipping,' your love, O LORD, supported me. When anxiety was great within me, your consolation brought joy to my soul.

Ps. 94:18

Kim's eyes were full of fear as we talked after church. She'd left work after bullying had caused a breakdown but had recently started a new job. 'It's happening again!' she said, fighting back tears. 'Gareth, my line manager, is being so critical and aggressive; I can't seem to do anything right. I'm so scared I keep making mistakes.' I promised to pray, but privately didn't expect she would keep that job. Then one day she emailed me.

'I read that story about Moses and all those poisonous snakes, and how he put a bronze snake up on a pole. Anyone who was bitten only had to look at it to be OK (Num. 21:8). Well, I suddenly realised that every time Gareth 'bites' me with his nastiness, I could look up at Jesus on the cross, so He could give me His comfort and strength. Somehow I feel as if I'm being lifted right up above Gareth's anger and my fear. It's really working and because I'm more confident I'm working much better.'

As Christians we live on two different levels. We have the power to switch instantly, and secretly, from our ordinary everyday life on Earth into the supernatural realm – and then back again – without anyone knowing. When we are in the middle of a 'blue moment', a painful situation or major stress, we can say the equivalent of 'Beam me up, Scotty' and be right there standing safe and comforted in the presence of the Almighty.

Lord, I know you never promised me a trouble-free life, but thank you for making your consolation always available to me.

'Rejoice in the Lord Himself'

Give ear to my words, O LORD, consider my sighing. Listen to my cry for help . . . But let all who take refuge in you be glad; let them ever sing for joy.

Spread your protection over them, that those who love your name may rejoice in you.

Ps. 5:1–2 and 11

These words are said to have been written by King David, at perhaps the worst moment of his life. The son he totally adored had turned the nation against him in order to steal his crown. David, who was an old man by then, was hiding in the wilderness, like a fugitive, in danger of his life. No wonder he was 'sighing' and 'crying' for God's help!

Yet he goes on to talk about 'being glad and rejoicing', but surely that is totally impossible for any of us in the middle of a painful crisis? There is nothing so maddening as being told, 'Just praise the Lord, dear,' when we are punch-drunk with problems. No, David is not telling us to rejoice in our circumstances – remember, he 'sighed' and 'cried' about those. He is saying we can rejoice in God Himself, just because of who He is and what He is like. David had no idea if God was going to spare his life or give him victory over his enemies, but his joy in the Lord did not depend on whether the Lord rescued him or not; his joy came from knowing God could be trusted to do what was best for everyone concerned, however personally difficult that might be at the time.

May my meditation be pleasing to him, as I rejoice in the LORD.
(Ps. 104:34)

Don't forget!

Praise the LORD, O my soul, and forget not all his benefits.

Ps. 103:2

'Benefits' is *not* a word I like! For eight years when I was a registered disabled person, struggling to bring up six children from a wheelchair, I had to collect my 'state benefits' every week. They helped us to survive financially but they made me feel like a leech on society. Fortunately, the psalmist was not saying, 'Forget not all His charity handouts'; he was urging us not to forget all God's kindnesses.

I'm not sure I could have made it through those wheelchair years without the 'kindnesses' my friend Marjorie showered on me and my children. She always turned up unexpectedly on the doorstep when we needed help most, baked us home-made bread and rang each morning to ask how she should pray for us that day. When my grown-up children visit we always remind one another of all Marjorie did for us.

Because I so easily forget God's little kindnesses I've started writing a list of them in my journal each day. It amazes me just how many there are! Not being grateful to God for His benefits is obviously a sin of pride. God protected King Hezekiah miraculously when invasion threatened and healed him when he became seriously ill. 'But Hezekiah was too proud to show gratitude for what the LORD had done for him, and Judah and Jerusalem suffered for it. Finally, however, Hezekiah and the people of Jerusalem humbled themselves, and so the LORD did not punish the people until after Hezekiah's death' (2 Chr. 32:24–26, GNB).

Lord, I guess remembering your benefits helps me to realise the sheer futility of thinking I can run my own life without you.

The reasons for our existence

God, who through Christ changed us from enemies into his friends and gave us the task of making others his friends also . . . Here we are, then, speaking for Christ, as though God himself were making his appeal through us. We plead on Christ's behalf: let God change you from enemies into his friends!

2 Cor. 5:18, 20, GNB

I love the simplicity of these verses; they spell out so plainly the two reasons why we exist. First and foremost, we were created to be God's friends; not just His servants (John 15:15) but His close companions. Secondly, He has given us the job of drawing others into the same close relationship of love and trust. It really is as simple as that!

People so often say, 'I don't have a ministry,' but actually we all have! When someone obviously enjoys living close to God there is something so attractive and unusual about them that other people can't help being curious. In a world where everyone is desperately hunting for love, peace and happiness, they watch anyone who seems to have discovered the source of these things very carefully indeed. 'Speaking for Christ, as though God was making His appeal through us' doesn't mean we have to stand on a soapbox and preach in our local shopping centre. It isn't even the good things they see us doing that impress them; they want to know if being friends with God really will provide them with the love, peace and happiness that they crave. If they see that our involvement in church activities is nothing more to us than a boring duty or a way of making us feel pleased with ourselves for our 'do-gooding', they will turn away and look for satisfaction somewhere else.

Please make me a good advert.

The P.O.M.S.

Restore to me the joy of your salvation and grant me a willing spirit, to sustain me.

Ps. 51:12

'Self-pity is Satanic': when I read that phrase, written by Oswald Chambers in *My Utmost for His Highest* (20 August), I thought, 'That's putting it a bit too strongly!' But is it? We are often full of enthusiasm when we take on a new role at church: helping with the children's work; visiting the old folks; organising the holiday club. The devil hates us to help others, so he blows some P.O.M. germs over us. It isn't long before we are suffering from an attack of Poor Old Me Syndrome. We start thinking, 'No one ever bothers to thank me for all I do!' 'Here I am flying round after everyone else, but they never seem to notice how tired I'm getting!'

Self-pity very quickly robs us of the enjoyment of serving Jesus, forcing our eyes off Him and onto ourselves, and it actually sounds so revoltingly ugly that it probably *does* come straight from hell. We think we are just taking care of ourselves and avoiding being used by everyone else as a doormat, and all the while our arch-enemy continues to blow his germs into our minds.

When King David wrote Psalm 51 he had lost his joy after messing up badly. He tells us how to have our lost joy restored: by having a 'willing spirit' instead, which is the total opposite of self-pity.

I'm sorry I'm feeling resentful and unappreciated; I realise this means I'm not actually doing what I do for you, Jesus, but wanting to be noticed or affirmed by people instead. Please give me a 'willing spirit' so I can serve you with joy.

Julian of Norwich

Whom have I in heaven but you? I desire you more than anything on earth. My health may fail, and my spirit may grow weak, but God remains the strength of my heart; he is mine forever.

Ps. 73:25–26, NLT

Julian of Norwich is definitely one of the people I'm looking forward to meeting! In 1373, when she was thirty, and probably already a nun, she met Jesus during a serious illness. He totally changed her life by giving her a series of visions and insights that she wrote down carefully once she had recovered. These became the first book in English ever to be written by a woman.

In Julian's day, people saw God as angry, punishing and threatening hell, but Julian met someone loving, gentle and forgiving – and fell in love with Him. After that all she wanted to do was be with Christ, so she went to live in a little one-roomed cell in the middle of busy, bustling Norwich. Her hut had three windows: through one her servant passed in her food, as she never went out; through another Julian could see the church, hear Mass and take communion; and the third window was always open to people who wanted to come and talk to her about the God of love she had discovered.

Here is my favourite quote from her work: 'Lord, in your kindness, give me yourself, for you are all I need.' Once, during the eight years I spent in a wheelchair, I was nagging Jesus yet again for healing and more gifts of the Spirit, the better to serve Him. I felt that He replied, 'All you need is me.'

God is our clothing, wrapping us and holding us in His love.
Julian of Norwich (1342–1416)

Gaps in the hedge

'Don't be afraid,' the prophet answered. 'Those who are with us are more than those who are with them.' And Elisha prayed, 'O LORD, open his eyes so that he may see.' Then the LORD opened the servant's eyes, and he looked and saw the hills full of horses and chariots of fire all round Elisha.

2 Kgs 6:16–17

Today I was walking down a country lane with the dogs when a terrible noise shattered the early-morning peace. A farm track runs parallel to the lane, hidden behind a high hedge; the noise was made by a tractor driving at high speed, pulling a rattling trailer. The hedge completely hid it from view but Stella, who is blind, must have thought a terrifying monster was roaring up behind her. She panicked completely and ran in agitated circles – her blindness prevented her from seeing any way of escape. She could not even hear my reassuring voice above the din. Phoebe, on the other hand, could see there was a hedge between her and danger, so she trotted happily on.

God has placed a hedge around mankind separating us from the invisible world of the supernatural which surrounds us. It is probably just as well; we might die of fright if we saw the evil spirits who watch us constantly, and if we could see the enormous warrior angels who guard us, we might start to worship them instead of their master, Jesus. Yet there are some people who are occasionally given the gift of seeing through gaps in this hedge. Elisha was one, but the Bible tells us about many who interpreted dreams, received messages from God through angels, and sensed supernatural danger.

Lord, I am ready for you to open the eyes of my spirit but only on occasions when what I see benefits your kingdom.

Does God have a face?

My heart says of you, 'Seek his face!' Your face, LORD, I will seek. Do not hide your face from me . . .

Ps. 27:8–9

At six every evening a little girl used to erupt from the front door of the house opposite ours. She whirled along the pavement, weaving between the streams of tired commuters, towards a tall man with a huge ginger beard. 'Daddy, my daddy!' she would shout as he crouched down and opened his arms wide. I loved to watch the way she would look up earnestly into his face from the circle of those arms as she told him her news. 'I found a caterpillar for you, and we've made sticky cakes for your tea.' All the time she talked, her little fingers would stroke the ginger shredded-wheat of his beard.

The Old Testament phrase 'enquire of God' could be translated from the Hebrew as 'stroke the Lord's beard'. Because God adores each of us He longs for the kind of intimacy that delighted my neighbour when his daughter gazed up into his face, chatting to him as she stroked his beard.

The Old Testament often mentions God's face, His smile and the way His eyes watch those He loves. Yet in those days God seemed so distant, powerful and mysterious, and most people were afraid of Him. God told Moses 'no-one can see me and live' (Exod. 33:20). Jesus came to Earth to show us what God is really like and the depth of His love for us. He told us, 'Anyone who has seen me has seen the Father' (John 14:9).

Lord, my human eyes can't see your face, but show me how to look into it by faith.

God's smile

The LORD bless you and keep you; the LORD make his face shine upon you and be gracious to you; the LORD turn his face towards you and give you peace.

Num. 6:24–26

As I was sitting in the park I noticed a family picnicking nearby. The toddler was obviously their first child – the longed-for son of his father's dreams. The man's beaming smile proudly followed the child wherever his unsteady legs carried him, and remained, doting, even when the child covered himself with ice cream!

People in the Bible often prayed that God's face would shine (smile) on them; perhaps they wanted God to look at them as a new and besotted father looks at his firstborn! And of course He *does*! He calls us the apple of His eye (Zech. 2.8) and His delighted smile follows us continuously (2 Chr. 16:9). If your own parents never looked at you like that, this might be difficult to believe, but the fact of it is repeated often throughout the whole Bible!

Yet we are also told that God turns His face away from people who deliberately disobey Him (Deut. 31:17). He never abandons His children but we can lose His smile – that sense of being close and comfortable with Him. One of my children behaved extremely badly once when Grandma came to tea. Later he came up to me and whispered, 'I'm sorry, Mummy, please make your face smiley again!'

I used to think I had to wait until I went to bed at night before bringing God a long list of all the things I'd done wrong that day. Now I've learnt it is more comfortable not to wait that long!

Lord, thank you for forgiving me instantly – and so often!

Another way of praying

As for me, I shall behold your face in righteousness; when I awake I shall be satisfied, beholding your likeness.

Ps. 17:15, NRSV

My friend Dave was born blind. When people urged him to pray for healing he used to smile and say, 'If the first thing I ever see is the face of Jesus – that's good enough for me!' Dave died recently and I often imagine him sitting there – gazing!

On his way to work in the fields an old French peasant used to slip into church and sit for a while, smiling up at the rafters. He did the same on his way home in the evening. Curious, the priest asked him what he was doing. 'I just look at Him and He looks at me,' was the simple reply.

The more you care about a person, the less important words are as a form of communication. My father and I were very close; we could spend all evening together by the fire without saying a word; we knew what the other was thinking by the expressions on our faces. To get that close to someone you do have to spend a lot of time with them. However rushed our lives are we need to sit for a few moments every day, like the old peasant, and look into the face of God. This is not just for our benefit either – He actually enjoys looking at us! He says to each of us:

Come then, my love, my darling, come with me. You are like a dove that hides in the crevice of a rock. Let me see your lovely face and hear your enchanting voice.

(Song of Songs 2:13b–14, GNB)

Avoiding his face

Surely then you will find delight in the Almighty and will lift up your face to God. You will pray to him, and he will hear you.

Job 22:26–27

There are times when the thought of looking into God's face is slightly discomforting, and other times when we are so hurt and angry that it is the very last thing we want to do. Whenever one of my children was deliberately not looking at me it was usually because they knew they had done something I wouldn't like, or I had done something they didn't like – such as refusing them sweets! When we start avoiding God's face it may be for the same two reasons!

Mary was dragged by a friend, rather unwillingly, to a workshop on 'Listening to God'. 'He never speaks to me, so what's the point of going?' she protested. After talking about listening, the speaker suggested everyone should sit and wait for God to speak. Mary sat fuming for an hour. 'What a waste of time!' she thought. 'And I can't even see the speaker with that great pillar in my way!' Just then Mary felt God was showing her that an unhealthy relationship had become a 'pillar' which was beginning to get in between her and God.

When God has allowed something to happen to us, or someone we love, or not answered our prayers in the way we expected, we are not always aware that we are avoiding His face. We just feel irritated by enthusiastic Christians; church seems boring, and prayer is too much effort. While we are 'looking the other way' we are actually in terrible danger.

For if we are faithful to the end, trusting God just as firmly as when we first believed, we will share in all that belongs to Christ.

(Heb. 3:14, NLT)

Unseen face

Some people brought a blind man and begged Jesus to touch him. He took the blind man by the hand and led him outside the village. When he had spat on the man's eyes and put his hands on him . . . his eyes were opened, his sight was restored.

Mark 8:22–26

'Your faith has healed you.' Jesus often said that, but I guess faith was easier when you could look up into that face and see the strength and compassion in the eyes of Jesus. This blind man didn't have that advantage. As he stood in the crowded marketplace, feeling the crowds jostling around him, all he could do was grope out towards a stranger's voice in the darkness. Suddenly, he felt his hand grasped and held tightly, but was he puzzled when he wasn't healed on the spot? Everyone was expecting that to happen. Murmurs of disappointment, even anger, must have followed the blind man as he stumbled away over the cobbles beside that stranger.

We don't know how far they walked, how long they spent together or what they talked about, but they were no longer strangers but friends by the time they reached the countryside. Even there, the healing was not instant but slow and gradual. Making friends with the blind man mattered more to Jesus than healing him, because relationship is always of paramount importance to Him.

Isn't it frustrating when you pray for something but nothing happens? Like this blind man we grope towards God by faith, feeling sure He must *want* to help, but the waiting feels endless! Yet something vital is happening between the point at which we begin to ask and the moment when our prayers are answered. He is teaching us to trust Him.

LORD, help me to 'walk by faith and not by sight' (2 Cor. 5:7, KJV).

The laughing face

If you obey my commands, you will remain in my love, just as I have obeyed my Father's commands and remain in his love. I have told you this so that my joy may be in you and that your joy may be complete.

John 15:10–11

One summer we went to Europe for our holiday – it was so wet that the only places where we could keep dry and financially solvent were the numerous, ornate churches. By the end of a fortnight I had looked into the face of Jesus thousands of times through icons, portraits, stained-glass windows or sculptures – but never once had He smiled back at me. The artists had all depicted him looking depressed, disapproving or downright cross!

I know Jesus was called the 'Man of Sorrows' and that He died in agony, but I am convinced He was also full of joy and laughed a lot. Some of the stories He told would have tickled the Jewish sense of humour and had people rolling on the ground! Humans are attracted to joy but we avoid people who are stern or miserable; those crowds would never have flocked after Jesus if He had looked like those religious portraits! The Pharisees might have approved of Him, and He might have attracted the academics of His day, but it was the ordinary working people, like Peter, whose hearts Jesus won, and the dropouts and no-hopers. One look at His face would have made them feel accepted and included instead of frowned-on and despised.

Joy is catching; my friend Liz is always laughing; being with her makes me feel better.

Jesus, as I look into your laughing face, help me to catch your joy so I can pass it on to others who need it so badly.

The disfigured face

I gave my back to those who struck me, and my cheeks to those who pulled out the beard; I did not hide my face from insult and spitting

Then they spat in his face and struck him with their fists.

Isa. 50:6, Matt. 26:67, NKJV

Heshbon's face looked grotesquely disfigured as he stood up to tell his story in our church. He had been a pastor in Kenya when terrorists attacked his village, burning his home and church and then forcing him to watch the murder of his wife and children. Finally they battered his face to a pulp with the butt ends of their rifles. As Heshbon told us how Jesus gave him His wonderful gift of peace-joy during the following months of imprisonment, his mutilated face shone with unearthly radiance.

The face of Jesus does not only have laughter lines but it also bears many ugly scars; Isaiah 52:14 (GNB) says: 'He was so disfigured that He hardly looked human.' His face will also be deeply lined by other kinds of suffering. He knows what it feels like to be rejected by the people you love, misunderstood by your family, betrayed, abandoned, blamed unfairly, misunderstood and excluded. He was single, lonely, poor, overworked, physically and verbally abused, taken for granted, publicly disgraced, beaten and apparently defeated. He understands, from personal experience, almost anything we go through – except, of course, the searing pain of guilt. Yet it was to spare us that worst of all emotions that He died in our place on the cross.

'Surely he hath borne our griefs, and carried our sorrows' (Isa. 53:4, KJV). Thank you that, at your cross, I can exchange my pain for your 'peace-joy'.

Reflecting His face

When Moses came down from Mount Sinai . . . he was not aware that his face was radiant because he had spoken with the LORD.

And we, who with unveiled faces all reflect the LORD's glory, are being transformed into his likeness with ever-increasing glory, which comes from the LORD.

Exod. 34:29, 2 Cor. 3:18

The other day I met a friend who had just returned from a silent retreat at a convent. Her face literally shone. 'Perhaps it's fresh air and monastic soap,' I thought, but as she talked about all that the Lord had done for her I realised her radiance came from inside. Like Moses, she had spent time alone with God and it *showed*!

The small boy who played Gabriel in a nativity play I attended last Christmas froze completely at the sight of the audience. His first line was 'Fear not!' but he was too afraid to say it! The entire cast prompted him but still he stood, green with terror. Then suddenly he caught sight of his dad, smiling encouragement at him from the front row. He caught that smile, as if it had been thrown like a ball. 'Fear not!' he bawled, beaming broadly; he was sharing his father's smile with everyone!

Lord, help me remember to keep looking up into your face, over the heads of all those who will surround me today. I know you love them, even the irritating ones. Let me catch your smile – and your attitude towards them, and reflect it back.

Switching from Martha to Mary

Jesus, the very thought of Thee With sweetness fills my breast;
But sweeter far Thy face to see, And in Thy presence rest.
. . . To those who fall, how kind Thou art! How good to those who
  seek.
But what to those who find? Ah, this Nor tongue nor pen can show;
The love of Jesus, what it is None but His loved ones know.

Bernard of Clairvaux (1090–1153)

Those beautiful words were written more than 850 years ago by a monk, Bernard of Clairvaux. I've often thought, 'If I lived in a cell in perpetual silence perhaps I could love Jesus with that kind of intensity.' The 'Martha' side of me, which loves to be busy serving the Lord in practical ways, has always warred against my 'Mary' side which longs for unlimited time to sit at the Lord's feet (Luke 10:38–42). Of course serving God is vital, but when what we do for Him becomes more important to us than our devotion to Him, then service becomes dangerous. However, when our love for Him is pre-eminent, service can be a way of expressing that love. St Teresa once commented, 'Our Lord is best served by a blend of both sisters!'

I recently discovered that Bernard of Clairvaux lived anything but a cloistered life. His wisdom kept him busy as an advisor and mediator to the political rulers of his day; so he must have learnt to switch frequently from Martha to Mary in order to enjoy the sweetness of his relationship with Jesus.

No amount of activity in the King's service will make up for the neglect of the King Himself.

Robert Murray M'Cheyne (1813–43)

The Michelin Man

You have stripped off your old sinful nature ... Put on your new nature, and be renewed as you learn to know your Creator and become like him.

Col. 3:9–10, NLT

Shyness was a major problem for me when I was young, trapping me in my own lonely world. Miraculously I was rescued by a knight in shining armour – who married me; and having him and our six children to hide behind did wonders for my confidence. Now I'm on my own again the shyness often returns, like a clammy cloud, whenever I have to walk into a room full of people.

Someone once told me, 'Don't try and fight shyness; just climb inside Jesus and let Him be the one people see.' Michelin Tyres advertise themselves by a little man covered completely in rolls of white latex rubber. You can't even see his face or hands. So now I often hide inside Jesus like that. St Paul had never heard of a Michelin Man but in Colossians 3:3 he says, 'Your life is now hidden with Christ in God.' Only yesterday, as I walked into a crowded church, I had to 'put on Jesus' and pray hard that all His qualities of love, joy, peace and kindness would flow out to the people I met. Humanly speaking I certainly had none of my own to offer! After chatting for a while to a highly successful and confident professional woman, she suddenly said, 'I wish I had your peace.' I smiled as I thought of myself standing outside the door just a short time before – panicking – before I put on my Michelin suit. So I let her in on my secret!

You are my hiding place; you will protect me from trouble and surround me with songs of victory.

(Ps. 32:7, NLT)

Handling VDPs

Any kingdom divided against itself will be ruined, and a house divided against itself will fall.

Luke 11:17

We all have our VDPs (very difficult people)! Recently a work colleague has been irritating me to bits; I've tried to swallow my anger but it kept boiling out all over her in most inappropriate ways, heaping guilt on top of my rage.

'This relationship is toxic! It has to end.' The day I made that decision, the sermon in church was on spiritual warfare. The preacher explained that Satan loves causing division. He began when he got Adam to blame Eve for 'making' him eat the forbidden fruit, which then divided them both from God. He put such an effective wedge between their sons that Cain murdered Abel, and he still plays the same 'Divide and rule' game today. He causes wars between nations and splits social, cultural and political groups – not to mention marriages, families and churches! It was what the preacher said next that made me sit bolt upright in my seat!

'When we are angry with someone we are actually joining forces with Satan – helping him to do his job. Once we realise what he is up to we can take action by diverting our anger right onto Satan himself, nullifying his evil plans by casting him out of the situation.' The preacher finished by pointing out that whenever Jesus met someone who was being controlled by Satan he never rebuked or reproached the person themselves. He invariably loved them and had compassion on them, and then confronted the evil indwelling them. Following Jesus means doing the same.

My colleague and I are working happily together now I can direct my irritation at the arch-divider himself.

Lord, open my eyes so I can see who my enemy really is!

❧

'Shut up to a miracle'

Moses answered the people, 'Do not be afraid. Stand firm and you
will see the deliverance the LORD *will bring you today. The Egyptians*
you see today you will never see again.

Exod. 14:13

I am writing this while staying with one of my daughters and her
family. She and her husband both serve the Lord full-time, but they
are facing a totally impossible and highly complicated situation which
affects their children and their ministry. We have discussed and prayed
over all their various options and solutions, only to realise they are all
impossible. Humanly speaking, there is no way out except through a
miraculous intervention from God Himself. As I prayed for them, during
a sleepless night, I remembered an old family friend, Revd Alan
Redpath. He would have described this situation as being 'shut up to
a miracle'. Moses knew what that felt like; after he had finally managed
to free several million slaves and their families, they became hopelessly
trapped by Pharaoh's pursuing army. Ahead lay the Red Sea, on either
side were high rocky mountains; there was no escape – only a miracle
could save them. When God said, 'Go forward,' it must have taken a
lot of courage to march straight into the sea! Of course the Lord made
the apparently impossible possible, but you never know that He will
until your toes touch the water!

St Teresa was 'shut up to a miracle' many times in her unusual life.
After her death these words were found scrawled inside the cover of
her breviary:

Let nothing trouble you, let nothing make you afraid.
All things pass away. God never changes.
Patience obtains everything. God alone is enough.

Beauty from darkness

*Let him who walks in the dark, who has no light, trust in the name of
the* LORD *and rely on his God.*

Isa. 50:10

William Cowper suffered recurring bouts of depression, but it was
during one of the worst, when he was in an asylum for the insane,
that he first met the risen Lord Jesus and gave his life to Him. No
wonder he later wrote, 'God moves in a mysterious way, His wonders
to perform!' He lived in the Buckinghamshire village of Olney, where
he became a close friend of John Newton, a clergyman who had
been the captain of a slave-trade ship until his conversion. They
both shared a passion for God and together they wrote some of
our best-loved hymns.

William's father prevented him from marrying the love of his life,
and his illness must have made life desperately hard, but amazingly
he wrote: 'help me to resign life, health, and comfort to Thy will
and make Thy pleasure mine.' Today we tend to think that God
ought to make our lives comfortable and restore failing health; if He
does not, we get angry and reject Him. Perhaps it was Cowper's
different attitude to God that made it possible for such beautiful
hymns to spring out of his suffering? Here are some extracts from
my favourite:

O for a closer walk with God . . .
Where is the blessedness I knew, When first I saw the Lord?
What peaceful hours I once enjoyed! How sweet their memory
  still!
But they have left an aching void The world can never fill.
I hate the sins that made Thee mourn And drove Thee from my
  breast.
The dearest idol I have known, Whate'er that idol be,
Help me to tear it from Thy throne, and worship only thee.

William Cowper (1731–1800)

Modern-day Job

*Satan replied to the LORD, 'Yes, but Job has good reason to fear God.
You have always put a wall of protection around him and his home
and his property. You have made him prosper in everything he does.
Look how rich he is! But reach out and take away everything he has,
and he will surely curse you to your face!'*

Job 1:9–11, NLT

'On my fiftieth birthday,' sighed Sylvia, 'I remember thinking, God is
blessing us lavishly in every direction; we were heavily involved in a
wonderful church; kids were doing well; Mike's business thriving. Then,
suddenly everything crashed! Our son was killed; our daughter's
husband left her; I got MS and the business nose-dived – we lost everything, including our home.

'God felt very close at first: people said I was "a wonderful example",
but after a bit I began to think, "How could God treat us like this?"
We'd prayed faithfully for our children yet God hadn't taken care of
them. We'd given all our energy and resources to serving Him, so why
dump us?

'Our friends knew *exactly* why! They said we were harbouring
unconfessed sin and leaving ourselves open to Satan's attack, or God
was punishing us, or testing our faith. I felt as if the God I'd always
loved and trusted had turned into a sadistic monster. When we talked
about how we felt, people at church said we were "pity-partying" or
being negative and bitter; we felt they had dumped us too!'

Reading the book of Job was the one thing that really helped
Sylvia. It did not answer her question, 'Why do bad things happen to
good people?', but it did encourage her to look at her experience
through a wide-angle lens.

My God, my God, why have you abandoned me?

(Ps. 22:1–2, NLT)

Love-hungry

'Did you notice my servant Job?' the LORD *asked . . . 'You persuaded me to let you attack him for no reason at all, but Job is still as faithful as ever.' Satan replied . . . 'suppose you hurt his body – he will curse you to your face!'*

Job 2:3–5, GNB

Job has just lost his ten children and all his possessions, and now Satan wants to hit him again. God must have felt torn apart by Satan's suggestion because it is terribly hard to watch someone you love suffering. We know God weeps for us when we hurt (John 11:35); He was also taking a huge risk. Satan might have been right: perhaps Job didn't really love God – but only the things God gave him?

God yearns for us to return His love, yet some of us just love the trappings of Christianity. We treat God like an impersonal insurance policy rather than our closest companion. We go to church to see our friends, for exciting worship or to find a role that will make us feel worth something. God must often feel like a multibillionaire who has been married only for His money!

I don't think I could relate to a God who sat in heaven thinking up horrible disasters to test my love, but I do believe He wants to use the bad times that hit us all – eventually. They face us with the choice of turning away from God in disillusion or moving nearer – clinging to Him for support. I know that when I've clung like that during my difficult experiences He has shown me such tenderness and personal care that my love for Him has grown more rapidly than ever before.

Lord, please help me love you for yourself alone and not just for the gifts you give.

Treasure trove

Job went and sat by the rubbish heap and took a piece of broken pottery to scrape his sores ... His wife said ...'Curse God and die!' He replied, 'When God sends us something good, we welcome it. How can we complain when he sends us trouble?' In spite of everything he suffered, Job said nothing against God.

Job 2:8–10, GNB

Poor Mrs Job, she was suffering too but her reactions were so different from Job's. In spite of all the rude things he said later, Job never quite let go of God – but she did. God gave us the gift of choice but it must break His heart when we choose to reject Him.

Have you ever felt as if your life has been chucked on the rubbish dump? I have – and it's a bleak experience. Right in the middle of a busy, fulfilling life, a brain virus left me facing permanent disability. At first I felt abandoned by God; it was not until later that I realised God wasn't wasting my life – He wanted to enrich it enormously. His priority is not our comfort or prosperity; it is our faith, which Peter says is 'of greater worth than gold' (1 Pet. 1:6–7). Job had lived a trouble-free life, respected, successful and healthy. He was in control of his life and scarcely needed to rely on God at all. Actually 'being in control' is only an illusion because human life is so fragile. God knows that our only hope of lasting security and happiness is to depend on Him in every single area of our lives. Health, success and prosperity increase our independence but God wanted Job to have God-dependence, the most precious treasure of all.

Even if I go through the deepest darkness, I will not be afraid, LORD, for you are with me.

(Ps. 23:4, GNB)

Anointed ears

I wish I had died in my mother's womb or died the moment I was born . . . I would be at rest now.

Job 3:11, 13, GNB

Job behaved so well – at first. Perhaps he felt the numb, unreal feeling that often follows a severe shock. Later he realised how much He had lost and grief set in with a vengeance. Pain like that needs to be talked out, but very few people are patient enough to listen without offering advice, looking shocked at our wild outbursts or trying to hurry us through our grief because it is making *them* feel uncomfortable! Real friends help most by listening quietly however many times we say the same thing! Job may well have been delighted to see his three friends when they arrived, but keeping quiet for that first week was the only thing they ever did to help him!

The whole scenario would have been so much easier for Job if only he could have seen into heaven and realised what was really going on. Satan and God both wanted to use his situation, Satan to destroy him and God to bless him. God also wanted to help the many thousands of suffering people who would read about Job in the years to come. Job was not a mere pawn in some game God and Satan were playing; he had the power to choose which of them won! Yet he had no idea what a VIP he was; he just felt totally trashed, sitting there in the ashes. Blinded by misery, he couldn't see God watching him with such tender compassion as He urged him to go on trusting – just a little bit longer.

Lord, I give you my ears; please anoint them for your service and make me a good listener.

Secret dread

What I feared has come upon me . . . I have no peace, no quietness; I have no rest, but only turmoil.

Job 3:25–26

Poor Job, he had certainly reached the 'fear' element in the tangle of emotions that goes to make up grief. Fear can range from a paralysing panic attack that hits so suddenly in the supermarket that you think you're about to die, through a slowly churning cement mixer in the stomach, to a loss of confidence that makes you feel you can't face people. Fear so often follows a major loss because we humans gain our sense of safety and security from our connections with people who matter to us, from our role, our appearance and our possessions. When one or, in Job's case, all of these things are yanked away we are left feeling as vulnerable as a snail without a shell.

It seems obvious from Job's outburst that he had been afraid of something for a long time. Perhaps it was illness, or worry about his children or, like many successful businessmen, he might have worried about losing his money. Whatever his fear had been, it was now a reality.

Do you have a secret dread? For years I told God I could cope with anything except the loss of my husband; I was terrified of that! When I *did* lose him I was devastated, but as I gradually emerged from a long tunnel of grief I realised God had helped me survive my worst fear. Discovering that He can do that gives you confidence to face anything the future may hold. God used the thing that Job feared most to bless him hugely. If your fear should become a reality, God is able to do exactly the same for you.

When anxiety was great within me, your consolation brought joy to my soul.

(Ps. 94:19)

Reasons and causes

'Think! Has a truly innocent person ever ended up on the scrapheap?
Do genuinely upright people ever lose out in the end?

Job 4:7, *The Message*

These are the words of one of Job's famous 'comforters'; he is telling
Job that all these disasters must have been his own fault because if he
had been a good person they would never have happened. He was
wrong, but, like so many of us humans, Eliphaz wanted to find a
reason for Job's misfortunes so he could avoid them himself.

I remember once standing outside the school gates with a group of
other horrified mums. Someone we all knew, whose son was in my
son's class, had died suddenly in the night.

'I told her she'd have a heart attack if she didn't lose weight,' said
one.

'And she smoked,' added another. 'Worked too hard, too – she did
three different jobs!' Their reactions infuriated me, yet, I suppose, we
are taught from babyhood the rule of cause and effect – 'If you touch
the fire you'll be burnt' – so we automatically look for a reason for
everything, forgetting that God never promises to make things fair in
this life, only in the next. Job understood that (19:25–27), but his
friends, like many of us, believed in God's justice 'here and now'.

This feeling of helplessness and confusion is like a clammy fog
wrapped round my head, Lord. I could cope so much better if only you
told me the reason for all that I'm going through. Yet I know you don't
always explain – this side of heaven. I'm trusting you to show me the
cause if there is something I can do to put it right; but if you never tell
me why, help me to trust you anyway!

Red-hot furnace

No! I can't be quiet! I am angry and bitter . . . Month after month I have nothing to live for; night after night brings me grief.

Job 7:11, 3, GNB

When we are going through difficult experiences we are often astounded, as well as embarrassed, by unexpected bouts of rage. They are usually directed at quite the wrong people, such as the kind friends who only want to help, and their shocked expressions only make us feel worse.

Job was angry with God (6:4, 8) and livid with his friends (6:14–15). Most of us are so afraid of anger that we hastily bury it, but pushing it down can actually cause physical, emotional and spiritual problems later on. When Martin Luther was upset about something, he went out and spread manure over his fields. That's a bit drastic for me, but vigorous exercise, bread-making or hammering nails certainly help to expend anger. Poor Job was too ill for anything like that (7:5), so he used words. A lot of them were flung in God's direction but, unwisely, Job also directed some at the friends who had hurt him. They simply did not understand and fought him back – causing him even more pain. Trying to justify ourselves often makes things worse! Even when you are in the right it is better to follow the example of Jesus, who told His Father how He felt – but never said a word to the people who were treating Him so unfairly (Matt. 27:14).

God is big enough to take all our anger; He let Job verbally punch and kick Him for a surprisingly long time. It is hiding anger that builds a wall to separate us from Him.

Lord, come into this red-hot furnace of pain inside me, and cool it down with your peace.

The black hole

Even if I summoned him [God] and he responded, I do not believe he would give me a hearing. He would crush me with a storm and multiply my wounds for no reason.

Job 9:16–17

Shock froze our house group into silence. Our good Christian smiles fell off, our mouths opened in surprise as Gareth poured out his pain in a far-from-positive tirade. His daughter was terminally ill, he had lost his job and his home was about to be repossessed. 'Either God's not powerful enough to help me, or He's so cruel He just doesn't care!'

Sadly, Gareth was peppered by the same kind of platitudes and reproaches that Job endured. All he would say was, 'It's hard enough "walking through the valley of the shadow", but when you suddenly can't believe God's there alongside any more, then you feel you've fallen down a black hole at the *bottom* of the valley!'

Mary, another friend of mine, also found herself in that 'black hole' soon after losing her baby. 'I knew God existed but I couldn't talk to Him; all my questions got in the way. I just couldn't believe He loved me, but I also knew I was totally lost if He didn't! In the end I just had to take His word for it, so I wrote out verses about His love and stuck them all over the place. I just had to keep on choosing to believe them by sheer willpower until my feelings and faith came back to life!'

Job's problem was that he had stopped believing in God's goodness, but it was harder for him than it is for us, because Jesus had not yet shown mankind what God is really like.

Lord, help me to doubt my doubts!

There is hope

At least there is hope for a tree: if it is cut down, it will sprout again, and its new shoots will not fail. Its roots may grow old in the ground and its stump die in the soil, yet at the scent of water it will bud and put forth shoots like a plant.

Job 14:7–9

The sermon was dull and I was fidgeting with pain, hunched in my wheelchair. So, to pass the dragging time, I was flipping backwards through the book of Job. 'My spirit is broken . . . My days have passed, my plans are shattered, and so are the desires of my heart' (Job 17:1, 11). 'Yes!' I thought. 'That's *exactly* how I feel!' Since a brain virus had destroyed so much of my life I felt, like Job, that I would never be happy or useful ever again. Then I reached chapter 14 and the words 'there is hope' jumped right out at me. At first I didn't realise Job was saying, 'Fallen trees have a hope of sprouting again but people don't get a second chance!' God just pulled the verse out of context to bless me and I remembered, as a child, making houses with my brother in an old apple tree. We loved that tree and cried when a storm felled it, but out of the stump a new tree grew whose apples taste wonderful.

In church that night my life felt like a fallen tree, fit only for firewood, but God reassured me that I was not on the scrapheap – He really did have a new life waiting ahead for me.

May the God of hope fill you with all joy and peace as you trust in him, so that you may overflow with hope by the power of the Holy Spirit.

(Rom. 15:13)

Passed with distinction!

I have treasured the words of his mouth more than my daily bread.

Job 23:12

What blesses me most about Job is his distress over the loss of intimacy with God. He seems to mind that far more than the loss of his
children or his money. He would have coped fine if only he could have
felt close to God; instead, his best friend seemed to be treating him
cruelly, and ignoring him without any explanation: 'I protest against
his violence, but no one is listening' (Job 19:7, GNB). Could Job's
extreme reaction to God's lengthy silence actually be the reason he
proved to Satan that he loved God above everything else? If Job had
not loved God deeply, would he have been in such anguish? In spite
of all of Job's whingeing, doubts and extremely rude remarks to God,
his core value was his devotion to the Lord, and in the end he passed
Satan's test with distinction.

All down the centuries God's friends have experienced the pain of
His occasional, unexplained periods of apparent absence. The mystics
christened it 'The Dark Night of the Soul'. 'Consolations' was the word
they used for that delightful sense of God's presence and the buzz we
get when prayers are answered. When we manage to go on pursuing
Him without these consolations it pleases the Lord enormously.

How much does God Himself actually matter to you? What differ-
ences would it make to your life if you discovered that God was a myth
and the Bible mere fiction?

> *Our restless spirits yearn for Thee,*
> *Where-e'er our changeful lot is cast;*
> *Glad, when Thy gracious smile we see;*
> *Blest when our faith can hold Thee fast.*
>
> Bernard of Clairvaux (1090–1153)

Sparklers

I know that my Redeemer lives, and that in the end he will stand upon the earth. And after my skin has been destroyed, yet in my flesh I will see God; I myself will see him with my own eyes – I, and not another. How my heart yearns within me!

Job 19:25–27

I find the book of Job rather dark and depressing, and perhaps most of us get sick of Job long before the end of the book. Wherever did he get his reputation for patience? He goes round and round in despairing circles, repeating himself endlessly. Yet every now and again a verse will explode into the gloomy narrative like fireworks on a dark night! God seems to give him tiny glimpses of what is really happening above the clouds of misery and, in spite of his wobbly faith, Job produces these little sparklers that have lit the way for so many of us ever since.

'Though he slay me, yet will I hope in him' (Job 13:15) is one of the most beautiful declarations of faith ever recorded, and so is his statement about the crucible of suffering: 'When He has tried me, I will come forth as refined gold [pure and luminous]' (Job 23:10, AMP).

When I had to tell my mother that my father had died suddenly, she responded, as thousands have done, by using Job's first sparkler: 'The LORD gave, and the LORD has taken away; Blessed be the name of the LORD' (Job 1:21, NKJV).

I believe God gives us all these little flashes of brilliant light to keep us plodding on faithfully through our dark tunnels, but we forget them so quickly if we don't write them down.

Lord, my tunnels felt very dark at the time but, looking back through my journals, I can see just how many sparklers you gave me – thank you!

Awesome interview

'Will the one who contends with the Almighty correct him? Let him who accuses God answer him!' Then Job answered the LORD: 'I am unworthy – how can I reply to you? I put my hand over my mouth.'

Job 40:2–4

Poor Job! He had been demanding this 'one to one' with God for months, but when his big moment came he couldn't say a word! I guess I'll be the same!

God's response to Job and his friends makes awe-inspiring reading – all four chapters of it (38–41), but nowhere does God answer any of Job's questions. He doesn't offer many solutions to the problem of suffering anywhere else in the Bible either. Perhaps He knows our human minds simply are not large enough to cope. We can never hope to reach God via the rickety ladder of our intellect – only by a leap of faith. God merely says to Job, and to the rest of us: 'If you once realised how powerful, all-knowing, all-seeing I am, you would forget all your fussy little questions and simply trust my firm intention to make everything that ever happens to you work for your maximum benefit' (Rom. 8:28). 'All you need is Me!'

Reading these sublime chapters can seriously stretch our perception of God's sheer magnificence. We glimpse the creator revelling in His universe, admiring the courage of a horse, laughing at the stupidity of an ostrich and helping the lioness stalk her prey. This same God knows how many hairs grow on your head (Matt. 10:30) and what you are about to say next (Ps. 139:4).

This is the awesome God who yearns for your personal love and friendship so much that He gave His life to win it!

Grand finale

After Job had prayed for his friends, the LORD made him prosperous again and gave him twice as much as he had before.

Job 42:10

When someone begins to emerge from a long journey of adjustment to some loss or upheaval, there comes a moment when happiness takes them by surprise. Often their outward circumstances have not changed as much as Job's did, but they realise they are changing on the inside.

When Job remembered the rude things he had said to God he cringed (Job 42:6), but, when he repented, God totally forgave. Doubting God's goodness and ability to care for all our needs is actually the sin that hurts God most. So, although doubts are natural during grief, they are still a sin we need to confess and renounce.

There is often another vital thing we need to do before we can successfully move on. During the difficult time we have just been through we may have been hurt by uncaring professionals, tactless friends and relatives or unsupportive pastors. We must forgive them or these little grudges will rob us of all the new things God wants to pour into our lives. It was not until Job had prayed for his friends that his restoration began.

Job finished his story with a far deeper relationship with God than ever before (Job 42:5). Satan must have been infuriated! God also gave Job ten more children and twice as much of everything else he had lost. It is most significant that God did not double the number of children; He did not need to, because the original ten were all waiting to be reunited with Job in heaven!

Thank you, Lord, for that 'sure and certain hope'!

Spiritual springtime

YOUNG WOMAN: My lover said to me, 'Rise up, my darling! Come away with me, my fair one! Look, the winter is past, and the rains are over and gone. The flowers are springing up, the season of singing birds has come . . .' YOUNG MAN: 'My dove is hiding behind the rocks, behind an outcrop on the cliff. Let me see your face; let me hear your voice. For your voice is pleasant, and your face is lovely.'

Song of Songs 2:10–12, 14, NLT

Long ago King Solomon wrote a love poem for the peasant girl he loved so passionately. It is a beautiful piece of literature, but why should it form part of our holy Scripture? Simply because God not only sees us as His servants, His children and His friends, but He also sees us as His Beloved. He wants the same kind of deep, intimate relationship with each of us, individually, that Solomon enjoyed with the woman he loved. Isn't that just mind-blowing? God wants to use Solomon's words to show how He feels about me – and you. The words of the girl in the poem can be our response to Him.

Many of us shrink away from that level of intimacy. Perhaps our parents never showed us how to love and be loved, so we back off when anyone, including God, seems to be getting too close. The Love that willingly died in order to draw us close longs to heal that wound inside us, which makes us 'hide our face' from Him in the rocks, preferring to worship Him from a respectful distance. How would you respond if you heard Him say this to you?

'Come away with Me; let Me heal your heart and turn your spiritual life into springtime. Let me show you what love really is.'

The Secret Garden

You have captured my heart . . . Your love delights me . . . You are my private (secret) garden, my treasure, my bride, a secluded spring, a hidden fountain.

Song of Songs 4:9, 10, 12, NLT

When I was a child my favourite book was *The Secret Garden* by Frances Hodgson Burnett. Naturally I identified with the two children who discovered a walled garden that had been locked and forgotten for many years. As an adult, reading the book to my grandchildren, I feel more for the young man and his bride who created that garden in the grounds of their stately home. They wanted a secret place where they could be together and hide from the eyes of servants and a curious world. They filled it with flowers, fragrance and their own happy laughter. Today's verses are God telling us that the private, personal relationship that He has with each of us is like a secret garden where He meets with us and has us all to Himself. When we spend time with Him, He enjoys it as much as He loved walking in the cool of the day with Adam and Eve in the Garden of Eden (Gen. 3:8).

When the young bride in the story died giving birth to their baby the heartbroken husband locked the garden and threw away the key. Soon it became neglected, overgrown and smothered in weeds. Our own spiritual gardens can quickly go the same way if our relationship with God goes sour. We may keep going into the 'garden' out of duty but we only stay a short time because it all feels so boring and lifeless.

Yes, Lord, my relationship with you has felt drab lately. If I'm holding a grudge against you in my heart please show me so I can let it go.

MARCH 21

Come, Lord Jesus!

THE WOMAN: 'Breathe on my garden, fill the air with spice fragrance. Oh, let my lover enter his garden! Yes, let him eat the fine, ripe fruits. THE MAN: 'I went to my garden, dear friend, best lover! I breathed the sweet fragrance. I ate the fruit and honey; I drank the nectar and wine.'

Song of Songs 4:16–17; 5:1, *The Message*

When I'm out in my garden – weeding, snipping, raking – the idea that God sees my spiritual life as a garden fascinates me! Yesterday as I enjoyed a 'sea of golden daffodils' I cried with joy at the thought that my spiritual Bridegroom (Jesus) says He enjoys savouring the flowers and fruit that I grow for Him in my heart. The King of the Universe takes so much pleasure in our relationship that He hurries eagerly to meet me in our 'secret garden' whenever I invite Him in.

As I sniffed my daffodils I began to wonder how my spiritual garden was looking today. I hoped it might resemble a physical garden in summer, blazing with colour, ripening fruits and cascading flowers. I would hate God to be disappointed if He found it looking like a wintry garden – bleak, bare, hardened to iron by frost – and no colour anywhere. He would probably be bored if my 'garden' was as regimented as a park – straight rows of stiff flowers, doing their religious duty – devoid of passion or excitement. Perhaps the 'garden' that would worry Him most, however, would be one that was far too full, over busy with too much crammed into the beds, so that nothing had the space to flourish!

Forgive me, Lord, when I so often keep you outside the high walls of my Secret Garden because I'm too busy to invite you in.

Thwarted plans

The LORD will . . . look with compassion on all her ruins; he will make her deserts like Eden, her wastelands like the garden of the LORD. Joy and gladness will be found in her, thanksgiving and the sound of singing.

Isa. 51:3

How I loved our first garden. We were newly married when we created it out of a heap of clay. One day we heard our village was going onto main drains and the pipe would run slap through our precious garden. I'll never forget the day the earth-mover came through, destroying our carefully constructed rockery and crazy paving, and every plant and shrub we had nurtured so carefully. At the end of the day we were left with a worse mess than we had started with, and an aching sense of loss.

Sometimes we can feel as if 'earth-movers' have demolished our plans when something we hoped for is suddenly yanked away and our goals and expectations are abruptly thwarted.

For months I could hardly bring myself to look out of the window at the mess. Then one day I noticed how the ugly heap of rubble at the far end of the garden caught the evening sunshine and realised it would be the perfect spot for a patio. The next weekend we discovered our rockery stones in the hedge; kind neighbours offered us cuttings and seedlings and, with a lot of hard work, a new garden began to take shape. Eventually it looked even better than the first!

If you are having to rethink your life in midstream, tap into the many promises God gives to broken people; with His help you may even enjoy the challenge of creating something beautiful out of a rubbish tip.

Lord, I feel raw and exposed like bare clay; everything that I valued is lost. So please come and landscape my life all over again.

My Father is the gardener

I am the true vine, and my Father is the gardener. He cuts off every branch in me that bears no fruit, while every branch that does bear fruit he prunes so that it will be even more fruitful.

John 15:1–2

All gardeners know that if you don't prune regularly you soon have weak, straggly plants. Sometimes God needs to prune away good things in our lives to allow better things to become the best. But *no one* realises how painful pruning feels until they experience it!

Gardeners also have to move plants in order to promote growth. When we first came to live here I realised the magnificent oak tree I had admired was actually taking all the light and moisture from half the plants in the garden. I had to dig up the spindly little things and replant them on the sunny side of the lawn. For a while they wilted pathetically, and then they all began growing dramatically.

Our spiritual lives can be overshadowed too, by someone whose faith and knowledge of God we admire greatly. We begin to lose our confidence and start depending on them for wisdom and guidance rather than looking to God Himself. Sometimes He has to remove us from under their shadow so that our relationship with Him can begin to grow again.

When He 'prunes' away someone important from our lives, or trans-plants us somewhere else, we 'wilt' for a while like my poor plants. We miss the situations or people we relied on, yet God knows that the stress that change produces often helps us cling more tightly to His hand.

Lord, please help me to move out of the safe shadow of the familiar, so I can gain a clearer view of you.

The God of springtime

God's loyal love couldn't have run out, his merciful love couldn't have dried up. They're created new every morning. How great is your faithfulness!

Lam. 3:22–23, *The Message*

My granddaughter loves me to read the story of Sleeping Beauty, the princess who pricked her finger and slept for 100 years. This morning as I opened my curtains I thought how shocked I'd be if I'd gone to sleep like that princess, back in the dark, dismal, colourless days of January, and then suddenly woken up this morning and seen my garden. The sight of all those vivid yellow daffodils, swathes of polyanthus, multi-coloured tulips and green shoots *everywhere* would have made me shout, 'A miracle has happened!' But because it has all happened so gradually it is easy to take it for granted and lose the sense of wonder. What God causes to happen every new spring really *is* a miracle!

He uses the world He created as a visual aid to demonstrate His character, using the vast, awe-inspiring mountains to help us taste His magnificence, the intricate patterns on a butterfly's wings to show us His love for detail and order, waddling ducks to let us know He has a sense of humour, and hens with their chicks to show us his soft, warm, protective care. Everything He created tells us something about Him, and through the spring He seems to say, 'I am a God of new beginnings and fresh hope, and I am able to cover all the brown, shrivelled deadness of your lives with new vibrant beauty.'

The joy of a new spring intoxicates me; thank you that you are the God of renewal. Please come and refresh and invigorate my spirit. Spring-clean me all through!

Give me a drink

A woman, a Samaritan, came to draw water. Jesus said, 'Would you give me a drink of water?' ... The Samaritan woman, taken aback, asked, 'How come you, a Jew, are asking me, a Samaritan woman, for a drink?'

John 4:8–9, *The Message*

She ignored the man who sat by the well. He was probably one of those supercilious, judgemental rabbis who felt they were 'unclean' if even the shadow of a woman like her were to touch them. He was likely to start preaching at any minute – the quicker she got away, the better! When he looked up and simply asked her for help, she was astonished!

We love it when Jesus says things like, 'If anyone is thirsty, let him come to me and drink' (John 7:37), but how do we react when He says to us, 'Give *me* a drink'? When our six children were young I often used to feel sorry for my husband when he arrived home, tired, from work. The clamouring demands engulfed him.

'Dad, I *urgently* need help with my maths homework.'

'The deposit for the school trip is due *tomorrow*!'

'My best car is all broke up.'

'I need a lift to swimming *right now,* Dad.' I probably did not help by telling him the washing machine was leaking!

I wonder if Jesus ever yearns for one of us to say, 'How was it for *you* today, Lord?' and then to listen quietly while He tells us? Violet, my prayer partner, sometimes used to imagine herself silently washing His feet, and massaging them with the perfume of her love.

He wants us to see Him as the source of everything we could ever need, but He is thirsty for our love, our time, our company.

Jesus never had to grow old!

I want to know Christ . . . and the fellowship of sharing in his sufferings, becoming like him in his death.

Phil. 3:10

Getting older is not much fun for anyone! And it is very easy to think, 'Jesus died in the prime of life, at the peak of His fitness and vigour; He never had to endure all the miseries that are hitting me at this end of my life: sickness, injuries, failing sight and hearing, painful back, feet and hands, the loss of friends, rejection and failure at work, loneliness, slowing down of the mind, lapses of memory, aching joints, the sense of being ignored by others, or being an irritation to them.'

Although He may not have suffered these things through growing old, He experienced most of them suddenly, during a short, twenty-four-hour period, from Thursday evening to Friday afternoon. To us they happen slowly, with more time for us to accept them well – or perhaps badly. They are, in fact, our crucifixion, and if we can share all the 'nasty bits' of growing old with Jesus as part of the fellowship of His suffering, they can become a creative way of getting to know Him better.

Lord, I hate growing old: it hurts, it's frustrating, and it's lonely! Rather than fighting it – and resenting you for letting it happen – help me to use all these pains and irritations as a way of drawing closer to you than ever before.

Protective love

Love . . . always protects.

1 Cor. 13:6–7

When Madeleine first moved to our village, I secretly christened her 'the Mystery Lady'. She joined our church but didn't seem keen to make friends with anyone. Gradually, as she began to let down her barriers, she told me she had been a lay minister in her last church but had left, and had also moved house, because there had been so much unkind gossip going around about her.

'It all began because I shared something about myself with a person I trusted. When I later clashed with her over something I felt she was doing wrong, she spread my secret all round the whole community – with embellishments she'd created herself.'

Then Madeleine added, 'Before moving house I had to renew my insurance policy and itemise anything of value. I always thought my diamond brooch was my most precious possession, but now I realise it is my reputation!'

What other people think of us matters a lot more to some than to others, but most normal people prefer to be liked and respected rather than loathed or ignored. After talking to Madeleine, I think that one of the most vital things 'love should always protect' is someone else's good name. When we talk to 'A' about 'B' in a negative or critical way, the way 'A' thinks about 'B' changes. They may refuse to believe what we say, but a little doubt is usually sown. Jesus tells us we must love one another (John 13:34): that doesn't mean *feeling* loving but just acting towards them in a loving way. If 'love always protects' then gossip is out, and so is sharing a confidence under the guise of a 'prayer need'!

Lord, if I can't build up someone's good name with positive words, help me to keep quiet!

Rockets in the dark

*For our struggle is not against flesh and blood, but against . . . the
spiritual forces of evil in the heavenly realms . . . With this in mind,
be alert and always keep on praying . . .*

Eph. 6:12, 18

Prayer has never been easy for me; I even prayed once, 'Lord, show
me if it makes any difference at all!' God answered by using my crazy
imagination! It was like watching an internal video; I could see myself
sitting in my chair, launching prayers like missiles through the dark
night sky and out towards the blazing light of heaven. As they zoomed
away I realised they were under heavy enemy attack. Swarms of demons
surrounded each rocket, hell-bent on destroying it before it reached its
destination. Some of my more selfishly motivated prayers soon flopped
back to earth, defeated, but others managed to twist and dodge through
their attackers – heading straight on towards their target. Angels
reached down to collect the requests they carried, and hurried off with
them to the throne room (Rev. 5:8, 8:3, 4).

Imagination? Perhaps, but Satan is still Earth's ruler (John 12:31) and
dominates the airspace above (Eph. 2:2). My private video show helped
me to realise that, if my prayers were important enough to warrant so
much enemy attention, then launching these missiles was not a boring
waste of time but the most vital thing I could possibly do!

The 'spiritual forces of evil' know that prayer is the one weapon
that can defeat them. They are not concerned when they see us working
to help others, but they are terrified once we begin to pray for them!

If we once realised how much good we could bring to others by
praying for them, we would treat prayer as the most important activity
in the day.

Horizontal rockets

But when you pray, go into your room, close the door and pray to your Father, who is unseen. Then your Father, who sees what is done in secret, will reward you.

Matt. 6:6

One memorable Guy Fawkes Night my son-in-law was letting off fireworks in my garden. As he lit the fuse of the biggest rocket of all, the bottle that supported it fell over. The rocket shot horizontally across the lawn and hit Grandpa in the foot. He was not badly hurt but he was very cross, and all the beautiful sparks and stars the rocket contained were never seen.

Not everyone finds it difficult to pray. Have you ever been in a small group or church meeting and felt you could never compete with all those magnificent prayer rockets that others are launching? Their words flow so effortlessly – but are their sizzling missiles actually any more successful than our jerky, breathless efforts?

If the enemy can't stop us from praying he tempts us to think we are really rather good at it. We begin to use praying as a way of impressing others, and positively bask in their respect for our spiritual power or special relationship with God.

The enemy also feels quite safe if we use prayer as an alternative to preaching. I once belonged to a house group in which the leader encouraged us to share our 'prayer needs' and then prayed at length for each of us, saying, in embarrassing detail, where she thought we had gone wrong and what we ought to do about it! We couldn't discuss or challenge her opinions because she appeared to be addressing the Almighty – but was she really? Perhaps, if we were all honest, we might admit quite a few of our prayer missiles are fired horizontally rather than vertically!

Lord, teach me to pray!

Boring babbling

And when you pray, do not keep on babbling like pagans, for they think they will be heard because of their many words.

Matt. 6:7

Do our prayers ever bore God? For years I dutifully worked through a list of people every day, repeating the same set of words for each person: 'Lord bless . . . Be with . . . Help . . .', but my mind was already on the day ahead; I was bored even if God was not! My personality type needs prayer to be creative and spontaneous, not a mindless chore like cleaning my teeth.

To be effective we must *mean* our 'missile-prayers', and sometimes a drastic change in our 'launching' methods helps considerably. Once I realised I was rut-bound I began writing my prayers down. Banning my old clichés 'Bless . . . Help . . . Be with . . .' I made myself put down a few words beside each person's name asking for one specific thing, which had to be different every day. Now I read back through my prayer file several times each year, and it is so faith-building to see how many of those short requests God has answered.

Because I love bursting out of my routine, sometimes I switch to launching my missiles without using any words at all. I find pebbles or buttons to represent the people I want to pray for, and one by one I silently hold them up to God. I picture His healing light beaming down on them as they lie in my hand, bringing them health and hope.

Jesus says the Father knows what we need before we ask but it is the action of praying that releases the blessing – how we actually pray is not important.

Please help me to keep on releasing you, Jesus, and your grace and power, into the lives of those I love.

Anger-powered rockets

Love your enemies. Let them bring out the best in you, not the worst. When someone gives you a hard time, respond with the energies of prayer for that person.

Luke 6:27–28, *The Message*

We all know that Jesus commands us to pray for the people who hurt us and make our lives miserable. We quite enjoy muttering, 'Lord, discipline him . . . make her see my point of view . . . may their new life together be horrible!' However, that kind praying was not what Jesus meant. He wanted us to pray blessings (good things) for the people who ruin our lives. Satanists stick pins in effigies that represent their 'difficult people' and attempt to curse them with bad things; Jesus wants us to do the exact opposite.

He gives forgiveness the highest possible status because by refusing to forgive we lay ourselves, and our prayer missiles, wide open to enemy attack.

When we've been badly hurt, Christian friends always urge, 'Forgive; let all your anger go,' but it isn't as easy as that! Forgiving is something we have to keep on doing, over and over again – but it starts the moment we *choose* to forgive. We feel we've failed when those angry feelings return but we just have to choose to forgive yet again.

Most of us feel we could be such good Christians if only God would remove one particular person! So we *pray* them out: 'Make him find another job . . . move house . . . go to a different church . . .'

Unfortunately, loving our enemies means accepting and encouraging them, not trying to manipulate God into making life more comfortable for us by removing them!

'Every time you forgive, the universe changes . . . with every kindness and service, seen or unseen, my purposes are accomplished and nothing will ever be the same again.'

Words spoken by the Holy Spirit in *The Shack* by William P. Young *(Hodder & Stoughton Ltd, 2008), p. 235.*

APRIL 1

Anti-rocket weapons

And blessed is he, whosoever shall not be offended in me.

Luke 7:23, KJV

When my baby granddaughter died – after I had prayed long and hard for her healing – I began wondering, 'Were all those prayer missiles I kept on launching just a waste of time? Perhaps I didn't have enough faith, or I must have sinned.' Doubts buzzed in my head until I remembered that the enemy can stop our missiles before they are even launched when he uses a weapon called Discouragement. He often uses Condemnation too!

When our prayers are not answered in the way we expect, he tells us it was 'all our fault'. Once I realised what he was up to, I faced him, and told him roundly that I agreed with him! My faith *is* weak and I *do* sin, but no one has to be perfect to pray – just forgiven!

Yet I was still left with the pain of having my agonised prayers apparently disregarded. When the dungeon door first slammed on John the Baptist he probably felt confident that Jesus would miraculously release him. It had been foretold that the Messiah would set captives free (Isa. 61:1), and surely His own cousin would be first on His list? But Jesus never came, and John's last recorded words are full of doubt (Luke 7:20).

When God doesn't answer our prayers with a 'yes', we're left with a choice. We can feel 'offended' and not bother to pray for God's healing on future occasions, or we can release all the good things He wants to bring into painful situations by continuing to pray anyway.

Thousands follow Christ when He gives them what they want;
few follow Him when he confronts them with what He wants.

From *Every Day With Jesus* by Selwyn Hughes (1928–2006)

Just a look

So Moses made a bronze snake and put it up on a pole. Then when anyone was bitten by a snake and looked at the bronze snake, he lived.

Num. 21:9

This story gives us a wonderful insight into prayer. As the Israelites travelled across the desert to the Promised Land, they were attacked by snakes. When anyone was bitten they did not have to crawl to God and make long speeches or costly promises – just a look of faith was enough to save their lives. For years I struggled with a terrible sense of guilt over prayer, and books on the subject only made me feel worse! Then I heard Joyce Huggett say, 'Pray as you can and not as you can't,' and I was totally released.

For some mysterious reason God seems to limit himself to working through the prayers of humans like us, but it is not our words or the time we spend praying that matters; He just needs that look of faith. I love the story of King Jehoshaphat who, when faced by an invading army, prayed, 'O our God . . . we do not know what to do, but our eyes are upon you' (2 Chr. 20:12).

I was about four when my parents took me to a large wedding reception. Suddenly I discovered I was lost in a forest of grown-ups' legs. Terrified, I scrambled up onto a table and scanned the room for my father's face. The moment our eyes met over all those heads, I knew I was totally safe. It is amazing how many messages can be conveyed by one glance across a crowded room.

Turn your eyes upon Jesus,
Look full in His wonderful face,
And the things of earth will grow strangely dim,
In the light of His glory and grace.

Helen H. Lemmel (1922)

APRIL 3

Praying without words

Hannah was praying in her heart, silently. Her lips moved, but no
sound was heard. Eli jumped to the conclusion that she was drunk.

1 Sam. 1:12–13, The Message

The little Christian retreat house felt like the perfect place to be alone
with God and seek Him in silence. Well, that's what I thought when
I arrived, but I soon found the rest of the house was occupied by a
large group of Korean Christians, who were also on a prayer retreat.
The chapel where they met was right next to my room, and they prayed
in teams continuously round the clock, all praying together, out loud
– each man at the top of his voice. Fortunately for me, the weather
allowed me to find peace in the garden where God could hear my
silent prayer just as easily as their shouts.

As we saw yesterday, prayer does not always have to involve words.
I was once on my way to speak in Wales when I was caught in a
motorway 'logjam'. I arrived hopelessly late – steaming with stress.
The organiser took me into the vestry, closing the door on the waiting
congregation. 'Sit down,' she said gently, 'and let me impart to you
the peace of Jesus.' She put one hand on my shoulder and lifted the
other towards heaven. As we waited in complete silence, I began to
feel the peace pouring into me, just as if she had been a drainpipe
conveying the refreshing water of life right into my spirit!

To be an effective prayer drainpipe we merely have to be open at
the top (towards Jesus) and at the bottom (towards other people), and
not blocked by rubbish (sin) in between!

Lord, use me as a silent drainpipe today; flow through me into the
people you long to touch and comfort.

APRIL 4

Joy-seeds

Light-seeds are planted in the souls of God's people, Joy-seeds are planted in good heart-soil.

Ps. 97:11, *The Message*

I was on my knees in my flower border yesterday, planting seeds in the bare brown earth. I was also praying for my granddaughter, who has been in pain and feeling low for many months. She told me she feels so 'dark' inside that she's given up hope of ever feeling well again. When I finally went indoors for a 'cuppa' today's verse really made me think.

I'd been praying for months that God would bring the light and joy back into her life, but I was feeling discouraged because nothing ever seemed to change. As I sipped my tea I was thinking about the tiny, dead-looking seeds I'd just covered with soil. For a long time no one else will know they are there, and then slowly they will develop into glorious clumps of vivid colour that everyone will enjoy later in the summer. I realised that my prayers are the seeds God will use to grow light and joy, as well as faith and hope, in my granddaughter's heart. I may feel my 'seed prayers' are making no difference but, like those flower seeds hidden in the dark soil, they are waiting to spring up into vibrant life. Later when I was out shopping, every time I saw a person looking sad or worried in the supermarket I pictured myself sprinkling joy-seeds into their hearts. Who knows what wonderful things God will grow from them?

Thank you, Lord, that although you could manage to run this universe perfectly well without any help from us, you do actually want us to work with you as we plant our mustard-seed prayers.

Abide with me

'Praise, My Soul, the King of Heaven' must have been our head teacher's favourite hymn – we sang it so often in assembly. I hated school so I hated the hymn! Later I discovered that it had been written by a young curate to encourage a dying friend who was not sure he was going to make it to heaven. In spite of being a clergyman, Henry wasn't sure if he would either! So together they searched the Scriptures until they found the secret of salvation.

Many years later, when Henry himself was dying of tuberculosis, he wrote an even more famous hymn, 'Abide with Me'. It is sung at football matches and royal weddings alike. As he watched the sun go down over Torbay in Devon, where he was the curate of the little fishing village of Lower Brixham, he managed to put into words all he felt about life and death. Next day, after preaching his last sermon, he handed a copy of his hymn to the churchwarden as he walked out of church. He died two weeks later but what a heritage he left to the rest of us! Is this the way I would feel if I knew I had only days to live?

Abide with me; fast falls the eventide;
The darkness deepens; Lord with me abide.
When other helpers fail and comforts flee,
Help of the helpless, O abide with me.

Swift to its close ebbs out life's little day;
Earth's joys grow dim; its glories pass away;
Change and decay in all around I see;
O Thou who changest not, abide with me.

Hold Thou Thy cross before my closing eyes;
Shine through the gloom and point me to the skies.
Heaven's morning breaks, and earth's vain shadows flee;
In life, in death, O Lord, abide with me.

Henry Francis Lyte (1793–1847)

Songs in the night

But let all who take refuge in you be glad; let them ever sing for joy.
Spread your protection over them that those who love your name may
rejoice in you.

Ps. 5:11

I woke this morning groaning, as I thought of the busy day ahead. As
I opened my curtains I noticed a thrush on a branch near my window.
His beak was wide open, breast puffed out, and music was just pouring
from his entire being.

The Bible talks a lot about singing, not only songs of praise and
triumph when everything is going wonderfully, but also 'songs in the
night' like the ones Paul and Silas sang in a Roman prison after being
flogged. The power of their singing freed them dramatically (Acts
16:25–26). One Old Testament king sent a choir ahead of his army
'singing to the LORD and praising him for his holy splendour'. As they
sang, the Lord caused the invading armies to start killing each other
(2 Chr. 20:21–23).

In their little book *God Calling* (published by Arthur James Ltd in
1953), the Two Listeners record beautiful things they heard God say.
Here is one I've tried to remember today as I rushed through my job
list: 'Sing unto the Lord . . . Go on until you can take the most crowded
day with a song. Sing unto the Lord. The finest accompaniment to a
song of praise is a very crowded day.'

The Psalms are full of 'I wills': I will praise . . . I will be glad . . .
I will trust . . . I will sing . . . They usually come just after the psalmist
has poured out all his woes to God, but then *chooses* instead to start
singing by willpower rather than inclination. Perhaps our singing has
to be an 'I WILL' sometimes?

Because you are my help, I sing in the shadow of your wings.

(Ps. 63:7)

APRIL 7

What a difference

Rejoice greatly . . . Daughter of Jerusalem! See, your king comes to you . . . gentle and riding on a donkey, on a colt, the foal of a donkey.

Zech. 9:9

For four hundred years, since those words had been written, the Jews had waited to see their Messiah ride into Jerusalem on a donkey. How excited they must have been to see it happen at last! A very large crowd spread their cloaks on the road, while others cut branches from the trees and spread them on the road. The crowds . . . shouted . . . 'Blessed is he who comes in the name of the LORD!' 'Hosanna in the highest!' (Matt. 21:8)

Yet, within days of that tumultuous welcome, the same excited crowds turned on Jesus, screaming for His crucifixion. Rather than turning furiously on those rejecting crowds, Jesus went through the terrible experience of the cross. He was willing to do that because He could already taste the joy of having us all with Him in His home in heaven for all of eternity (Heb. 12:2).

The next time He comes, however, no one will dare reject Him! 'And then they'll see the Son of Man enter in grand style, his Arrival filling the sky – no one will miss it! He'll dispatch the angels; they will pull in the chosen from the four winds, from pole to pole.' (Matt. 13:27, *The Message*)

> *I looked again. I saw a huge crowd, too huge to count. Everyone was there – all nations and tribes, all races and languages. And they were standing, dressed in white robes and waving palm branches, standing before the Throne and the Lamb and heartily singing . . .*
>
> (Rev. 7:9–11, *The Message*)

What a prospect, Lord! One day I'll be in that crowd to see your glory!

APRIL 8

Why didn't He run away?

The chief priests and the teachers of the law were looking for some sly way to arrest Jesus and kill him.

Mark 14:1

Jerusalem was swarming with thousands of Jews from all over the world – all arriving for the feast. Flocks of sacrificial lambs were herded through the city gates and traders prepared for a business boom. Security was on red alert, and extra troops were being marched in because rumours were rife that this might be the moment when the notorious Nazarene would lead an uprising against Rome. The religious leaders, seriously alarmed, met often to discuss endless plans for His secret arrest, while on every street corner people wondered whether Jesus would dare to come this year.

When He rode into that crowded city, in what appeared to be 'His finest hour', Jesus knew in horrendous detail all that was about to happen to Him (Matt. 26:2). So why didn't He run away? We know He *wanted* to (Mark 14:36): crucifixion was a ghastly prospect, but He knew the reason He had come to Earth was to die in our place, as our sacrificial lamb (John 1:29). So it was nothing but love that kept Him in Jerusalem.

Are there things in your life that you long to avoid? Health problems, difficult relationships, work stress? These things can feel even worse because we know Jesus could change situations and people – instantly – but He has not! Sometimes He asks us to walk with Him right through to the far side of our Calvary – just as he walked through His own.

For the joy set before Him, He [endured the cross] (Heb. 12:2). Jesus, that joy was the prospect of my company throughout eternity. I don't feel I was worth such a high price, but you obviously did. Thank you!

Lonely in a crowd?

While he was in Bethany, reclining at the table in the home of a man known as Simon the Leper . . .

Mark 14:2

If you knew you were going to die in a few days, how would you spend the time? Jesus went to a party but, as He looked round the loaded table at the people He loved so much, I wonder if He actually felt like partying?

He had spent all day among the noisy crowds in Jerusalem but at dusk He escaped to the peaceful village of Bethany. When He arrived, was it to discover His friends had thrown a surprise party in His honour?

The apostles were there, Peter cracking jokes, Thomas looking worried, Judas firmly clutching their kitty. Simon, the host, was beaming with gratitude because, before Jesus had healed his leprosy, he had been an outcast, separated from family and community. Tradition has it that he was Martha's husband, and, in John's version of that evening, he tells us that she was bustling around in the kitchen while her brother Lazarus was among the guests (John 12:2). He was also grateful to Jesus, who had recently raised him from the dead. They were all laughing and talking but how did Jesus feel? It is possible to be lonely, even among friends. Jesus had told them specifically that He would die at this Passover but they were still sure He would found an earthly kingdom. Was Jesus hurt by their misunderstanding?

It is so easy to forget Jesus *still* has feelings! When we are lonely, He understands, and He minds – and if only we realised how angry He is with the people who hurt us, we wouldn't need to be so angry with them ourselves!

Lord, help me sense how you feel about the people I meet today, and help me feel the same way.

At His feet

A woman came with an alabaster jar of very expensive perfume, made of pure nard.

Mark 14:3

There was one person at that party who understood Jesus perfectly – and John tells us it was Mary (John 12:3). We meet her three times in the Gospels and each time she is at Jesus' feet. Once to listen raptly to every word He said (Luke 10:39), while her sister Martha clattered about in the kitchen. Then to kneel while she poured out her pain, anger and grief because she felt He had failed to come when she needed Him (John 11:32). Finally, she is there at His feet again to give Him the most valuable treasure she possessed. It was a stone flask containing the rare aromatic oil used for anointing the dead. It was worth a year's wages and was probably an investment for her future marriage.

Because Mary had always spent so much time listening attentively to Jesus she was the only person who realised He was about to die. Executed prisoners seldom received a proper burial, so she wanted to honour His body while she had the chance.

Jesus said, 'Those who love me will keep my word' (John 14:23), and simply because Mary loved Him so much she not only listened, but believed what He said – and acted on it (Matt. 7:24)! How different we can be! We read our daily Bible passage because we feel we 'ought', but skim through so quickly we've forgotten it in five minutes. We can also ignore the bits that don't quite fit our personal agendas, telling ourselves, 'Jesus didn't mean that *literally*,' or 'This doesn't apply *nowadays*.'

In every person lies a zone of solitude that no human intimacy can fill, and there God encounters us.

Brother Roger of Taizé (1915–2005)

Lavish love

She broke the jar and poured the perfume on his head.

Mark 14:3

If Mary had simply removed the stopper from her jar and poured a few drops of oil onto Jesus' head, everyone would have smiled and nodded their approval because it would have been an appropriate way to treat a guest of honour. She did not have to cause a sensation by smashing it wide open so she could scoop out all the precious oil that clung to the inside of the jar. Yet that is exactly what she did, while everyone looked on, shocked by such extravagance. John tells us she not only covered His head but His feet too, and wiped up the excess with her hair. She wanted Jesus to have everything she had, with nothing kept back for anyone else! Perhaps we should all ask ourselves if Jesus has to make do with just a small part of our love, time and possessions.

Alabaster is tough, so Mary must have had a difficult, and very noisy, job smashing it. Some of us feel our love for God needs to be encased in a hard outer shell of respectability: we shouldn't get too enthusiastic, emotional or 'carried away', and we've all heard sermons that stress the Christian life is not about feelings – but faith. Of course we can't rely on feelings alone, because they can go up or down with circumstances or hormones, but knowing Jesus is a love affair, not a code of ethics! There are two kinds of Christian, those who confine God to carefully scheduled daily or weekly slots and others who want to love Him with all they have and all they are!

God spilt the life of His Son that the world might be saved; are we prepared to spill out our lives for Him?

Oswald Chambers

APRIL 12

God loves variety

Some of those present were saying indignantly to one another, 'Why this waste of perfume? It could have been sold for more than a year's wages and the money given to the poor.' And they rebuked her harshly.

Mark 14:4

Just as the whole house was filled with the beautiful fragrance of the ointment, the indignant snorts began – led by Judas Iscariot (John 12:3). Disapproval often follows when someone worships God lavishly. When King David danced 'before the LORD' his wife 'snorted' with contempt (2 Sam. 6:16). Mary certainly worshipped Jesus in a very unconventional way – but Simon the Leper was also expressing his gratitude to Jesus by organising the party, and Martha did so by serving the food, while Lazarus just wanted to sit close to Him (John 12:2). They were all trying to please Jesus in their own way but, because Mary's way was so costly, it was considered 'over the top'.

Someone once said, 'The favourite hobby of Christians is criticising other Christians!' We dismiss people as 'happy-clappies' or 'traditional stick-in-the-muds' without realising that God adores variety! Worship is not just singing or saying nice things to God in a religious voice; it is allowing our innermost being to connect with His Spirit in total abandonment – just as a small child stretches out to take the hand of someone he loves and trusts. This 'reaching out' can be expressed through hymns and words, but just as easily through art or dance or simply by a silent smile in heaven's direction. *How* we worship is not important, but it does matter that we respect each other's individuality and remember it is the Lord we are trying to please!

Lord, please refresh and revive the way I worship you.

A beautiful thing

'Leave her alone,' said Jesus . . . 'She has done a beautiful thing to me
. . . wherever the gospel is preached throughout the world, what she
has done will also be told, in memory of her.'

Mark 14:6–9

Obviously, Jesus wanted every one of us to know what an enormous
amount of pleasure Mary gave Him by her act of love and understanding.
Perhaps most of us wish we could have had Mary's chance to do something like that for Jesus ourselves, but now that He doesn't have a human
body we can't – or can we? I remember being fascinated once by a TV
programme about Mother Teresa. A dying vagrant was brought to her
from the Calcutta streets; he was filthy, emaciated and covered in open
sores, yet she gently washed him, tended his wounds, dressed him and
fed him from a spoon. The interviewer finally asked why she took so
much time over a dying man. She simply replied, 'To me, his body is the
body of my Lord.'

Sometimes we are tempted to think that people who do the major,
'up-front' things for Jesus give Him the most pleasure, but we can't
all be Billy Grahams or Mother Teresas. Jesus said, 'She did what she
could' (v. 8) because He wants us to know that we all have equal opportunities of doing 'what we can' for Him. He is delighted by those little
secret acts of kindness that we do for people who never notice or
bother to say thank you. When these are offered to Him as worship
they give off a beautiful spiritual fragrance, which He deeply enjoys.

Please, Lord, show me how I can do a 'beautiful thing' for you today.

An ugly thing

Then Judas Iscariot, one of the Twelve, went to the chief priests to betray Jesus to them. They were delighted to hear this and promised to give him money. So he watched for an opportunity to hand him over.

Mark 14:10–11

Judas was not always a black-hearted thief (John 12:6). Three years before, he had been just as willing to give up home, career and comfort as the other Eleven. Yet it may not have been pure love for Jesus that motivated him to do all that, but love for The Cause – getting rid of Rome. Perhaps Judas looked forward to the wealth, power and status he would have when Jesus 'seized power'.

Many of us serve Jesus because it gives us a sense of importance or power over people; for others, it fulfils a need because helping others makes us feel good about ourselves.

It was Judas' responsibility to share the group's money with the poor (John 13:29b), but handling it had become a temptation which eventually defeated him.

However much we may identify with Mary, and want to give Jesus everything, we all have the potential to become a Judas. We do not fall away suddenly; each day we are all given the choice of moving one step nearer to Jesus or one step further away. Judas made the wrong choice too many times. When Mary's action finally shocked him into realising that Jesus really was going to die he had already become so self-centred that all he could think about was a way of salving something for himself out of the approaching chaos. So he sold Jesus for half what Mary's ointment had been worth (Matt. 26:15).

Please, Lord, purify my motives and show me where I am trying to meet my own needs through serving you.

X-ray eyes

The LORD does not look at the things man looks at. Man looks at the outward appearance, but the LORD looks at the heart.

1 Sam. 16:7

As a child, visiting Scotland's Sweetheart Abbey, I was fascinated by the ancient story of the Crusader who died fighting for Jerusalem. Friends placed his heart in a golden casket and brought it home to his wife, who built the abbey around it.

'Why didn't they bring all his body?' I asked ghoulishly.

'His heart represented all that he was on the inside,' was my grandmother's reply. She was using the word 'heart' as the Bible does – not the pump behind our ribs but the part of us that thinks, feels, makes decisions and reaches out for God.

Actually we all use the word 'heart' quite often in everyday conversation. We describe someone as 'kind-hearted' or 'soft-hearted', or we say they 'have a heart of gold'. On the other hand we might describe them as 'hard-hearted' or 'faint-hearted'. We can 'lose heart' or want something so much we 'set our hearts' on it and go for it 'wholeheartedly'. Are we simply acknowledging that the invisible part of us is more important than anything else?

When my brother rings me from Canada he doesn't say, 'How are you?' in the way most other people do – expecting the automatic response, 'Fine, thanks.' He always says, 'Tell me how you are *in your heart*.' He is interested in all the little happenings of my life but even more concerned about how these happenings are affecting me inside.

I think the Lord looks at us like that. He sees right through the 'Fine, thanks' masks we wear for everyone else, and understands just how we are really feeling.

Thank you, Lord, for your X-ray eyes!

Wounded heart

Above all else, guard your heart, for it is the wellspring of life.

Prov. 4:23

She was just a very nervous young mum, stumbling through her first talk at our church women's group – but she affected us all profoundly. She made us close our eyes and ask God to show us a picture of our hearts. I saw nothing at all, and felt rather a failure when others shared pictures of 'an exhausted rag doll', 'a little girl jumping with excitement', 'a football, kicked about by family pressures', 'a shrivelled apple', 'one big question mark'. One girl even felt her heart was being squashed flat by a giant boulder. There were lots of tears and prayer ministry but I went home feeling disappointed. My picture came to me suddenly that evening in the bath. I 'saw' my heart, drained of blood because a knife had ripped it open. Startled, I went to pray with someone the following day and had to face the pain I had been suppressing after a friend's betrayal. I also realised my lack of forgiveness was draining my spiritual life dry. The 'picture', although disturbing, ultimately brought healing.

When our bodies are injured everyone can see the bandage and later the scars, but we often hide our internal injuries even though they can be far more painful. As Christians we feel we shouldn't let things wind us up so we ignore the internal grazes and bruises and even pretend to ourselves that our hearts are not crushed by disapproval and unkindness or ripped open by betrayal. When Jesus said he had come to 'mend the broken-hearted', surely He was promising to heal these wounds, but I honestly think He can't do that without our willingness to forgive the person who has hurt us.

Would you dare to ask God to show you your heart?

❀

Pure in heart

Who may ascend the hill of the LORD? Who may stand in his holy place? He who has clean hands and a pure heart.

Ps. 24:3–4

'I'm always longing to get closer to God,' said Sue one evening at house group, 'but I never feel I'm quite good enough.' Probably we would all love to have a pure heart, but life on Earth contaminates us!

'I'd be such a good person if I lived on my own on a desert island,' finished Sue.

The Bible uses the word 'pure' most often in connection with gold, which has to be heated in a crucible until impurities rise to the surface, and can be skimmed away. The gold itself can do nothing to make itself pure – that is the job of the goldsmith. God knows consistent purity is impossible for us – it is repentance that makes us fit for His presence. Yet so often we feel we must clean up our own inner impurities before coming close to God. We fail to realise that all He wants is for us to open our hearts to Him, mess and all. When He is in the centre He can draw off all our dross and scum and throw it away at the foot of His cross. Then, and only then, can we confidently 'stand in his holy place'. 'For this is what the high and lofty One says – "I live in a high and holy place, but also with him who is contrite and lowly in spirit, to revive . . . the heart of the contrite"' (Isa. 57:15).

Search me, O God, and know my heart. . . Create in me a pure heart, O God.

(Ps. 139:23 and Ps. 51:10)

Ambitious heart

To man belong the plans of the heart ... All a man's ways seem innocent to him, but motives are weighed by the LORD. In his heart a man plans his course, but the LORD determines his steps.

Prov. 16:1–2, 9

Imagine you had reached the end of your life. What would you most like to have achieved and why would that be important to you? The Bible sees our heart as the engine that drives and motivates our plans. We all need goals, but the reason why we make them is all-important. Hidden motives lie behind all our major life decisions. We often make these major plans because we want to feel good about ourselves. We think:

- 'I'll be a worthwhile person when I succeed.'
- 'I'll be safe if I find someone to love me.'
- 'Caring for others will win me respect and approval.'
- 'I'll be secure if I have plenty of money.'

We forget that God longs for us to find our worth and security in Him. He says He 'detests all the proud of heart' (Prov. 16:5); this is because pride is a declaration of independence, the 'I'll do it my way' syndrome. Our self-confidence grows when we achieve our goals, but self-confidence smacks of pride. It is *God*-confidence we need; His approval is all that counts.

Probably a lot of us are not feeling at all proud right now; instead, we feel discouraged or frustrated. Could this be because we are aiming at impossible goals that we, or someone else, have set for our lives – rather than following God's agenda? Unconsciously we may be trying to meet some deep need in our own heart – or fulfil another person's hopes.

Lord, help me to make my life's goal just to do my best to please you. How simple and enjoyable life would be then!

Heart transplant

I will give you a new heart and put a new spirit in you; I will remove from you your heart of stone and give you a heart of flesh.

Ezek. 36:26

Alf was a Jack-of-all-trades: builder, gardener, handyman, and a good friend to me throughout my childhood.

'Alf, why are your hands hard, like leather gloves?' I asked him once.

'Years of blisters, cuts and bruises,' he replied. 'My skin's grown so thick nothing hurts any more.' Hearts can grow hard like Alf's hands. The Bible calls them 'calloused hearts' (Isa. 6:10). When people or events hurt us badly, we can grow new, tough skin over the wound. The more knocks life gives us, the thicker our protective layers become. These 'calluses' may well keep us safe from further pain but they also separate us from others (and God). A calloused heart is no longer soft and warm enough to love and receive love in return.

When I first met Ann she was definitely 'The cat who walked by herself', as Kipling put it in his 'Just So Stories'. Years of abuse, rejection and victimisation had made her heart very hard indeed.

'No one's ever going to get close enough to hurt me again,' she would say – but then she met Jesus. 'How does He expect me to forgive all the stuff people did to me?' she demanded whenever I raised the subject of forgiveness. 'It's humanly impossible!' One day I showed her today's verse.

'You're right, Ann; "humanly speaking" forgiveness is impossible for you,' I explained, 'so you have walled up your heart in stone. Let's ask God to give you a total heart transplant – a new forgiving heart just like His own.'

Please, Lord, melt the hard shell encasing my heart so your love can escape from it, and flow out into my world.

Praying heart

Rise during the night and cry out. Pour out your hearts like water to the LORD. Lift up your hands to him in prayer, pleading for your children.

Lam. 2:19, NLT

When my grandmother died, aged ninety-six, my uncle showed me her well-worn Bible. The pages fell open at today's verse, which must have been important to her because she had marked it several times over in various coloured pens. I knew that she had always prayed for her seven children and twenty-one grandchildren by name, particularly in the night when she couldn't sleep. She must have been a very poor sleeper indeed because an unusually high proportion of her descendants are now active Christians!

When God's people were first urged to 'cry out in the night for their children', they were facing a national disaster. They had turned away from the Lord and their land had been left in ruins by enemy invaders. So often it is innocent children who suffer most for the stupidity and selfishness of adults. We see their faces on our TV screens or read their horror stories in the paper and we think, 'That's dreadful; how could anyone *do* that to a little child?' We forget that we can connect that child to the comforting, healing power of heaven simply by stopping for a moment to pray for them. Perhaps we think, 'What difference will my prayer make?' but we all underestimate the power of prayer, which is the greatest weapon against evil in the universe. Most of us believe that – in our heads – but do you believe it in your heart by regularly *acting* on your convictions?

I am only one, but I am one. I cannot do everything, but I can do something. And I will not let what I cannot do interfere with what I can do.

Edward Everett Hale (1822–1909)

God's heart

I reached out day after day to a people who turned their backs on me, people who make wrong turns, who insist on doing things their own way.

Isa. 65:2, The Message

Recently, while I was visiting a retirement home, an old man proudly showed me numerous photos of a little boy – the son he adored.

'He was the joy of my life, but I haven't seen him for years,' he told me finally, tears filling his eyes. 'He got upset with me, and I can't seem to put it right.' The anguish in his voice reminded me of the picture of God's heart that Hosea gives us: 'When Israel was a child, I loved him . . . But the more I called to him, the more he turned away from me . . . Yet I . . . taught Israel to walk . . . but they did not acknowledge that I took care of them. I drew them to me with affection and love. I picked them up and held them to my cheek; I bent down to them and fed them . . . How can I give you up, Israel? How can I abandon you? My heart will not let me do it! My love for you is too strong' (Hos. 11:1–8, GNB). What a remarkably forgiving, loving heart God has!

Because love is at the centre of God's being, our failure to open our hearts to others in love, acceptance and forgiveness breaks His heart.

Lord, forgive me for excluding so many people from my heart simply because they have irritated or upset me. Give me a wide-open heart like yours. Please show me if there are people I have been ignoring or old friends who may feel sad because I have forgotten them.

After God's own heart

God removed Saul and replaced him with David, a man about whom God said, 'I have found David son of Jesse, a man after my own heart. He will do everything I want him to do.'

Acts 13:22, NLT

What was it about David that made God describe him like this?

Well, he was certainly a remarkably gifted man – creative, intelligent, a brilliant statesman and soldier, with a huge capacity to love, and such enormous personal charisma that he made everyone he met feel loved and valued – unless they happened to be a Philistine!

But God saw something more in him than human gifts.

Was it because he was perfect? No! His enormous heart often got him into terrible trouble – but, unlike many other kings, he always repented the moment he realised he had done wrong. I think the answer to our question lies in the words 'He will do everything I want him to do'. David never did anything without consulting God first, except on two disastrous occasions! His greatest desire was to please God, so if God said, 'Go, kill that impossibly big giant,' David promptly did it, and when God said, 'Don't kill your enemy,' David did not – even though his friends said he was crazy! (1 Sam 26:11)

Having a heart after God's heart means being the kind of person whose innermost being strains with all its energy to connect with God's innermost being. Because a person like that trusts God so implicitly, they are willing to do absolutely anything that He commands. What a marvellous legacy David left us all by recording all his feelings towards God in the worship songs (psalms) that still bless us today.

O Lord, I badly want to have a heart that runs after your heart as devotedly as David's did.

Stunted by an unhappy childhood?

The LORD Himself is my inheritance, my prize. He is my food and drink, my highest joy.

Ps. 16:5, LB

Farmer Jesse must have been most gratified when the great prophet Samuel arrived to pick one of his sons to be the next king, but mystified when, one by one, Samuel rejected them. Their muscles and good looks dazzled Samuel, but God looked right into their hearts and saw the selfishness and pride behind the suntanned smiles (1 Sam. 16:1–13). God wanted a king for His people who would think, feel and act as He would. He could see David sitting out on the hillside, with the sheep – even if his earthly father had forgotten him.

David's childhood really ought to have screwed him up emotionally. His mother is never given a name, probably because she was a servant girl and not a proper wife. This might account for his father's apparent total disregard for David. He allowed his older sons to bully and ridicule him and seems to have considered him only fit to watch sheep, the lowest job of all.

It would have been lonely for a teenage boy out there on the hills, ignored by his family; he could have been full of resentment. Instead he wrote, 'When my father and my mother forsake me, then the LORD will take care of me' (Ps. 27:10, NKJV). He must have deliberately turned to God to provide the love, protection and affirmation he ought to have received from his parents. Today's verse shows us how totally satisfying David proved God to be.

Some of us may have had parents who failed us badly, but God longs to provide the love they failed to give and to heal all our emotional scars.

Starlight and wild flowers

Consider how the lilies grow. They do not labour or spin. Yet I tell you, not even Solomon in all his splendour was dressed like one of these.

Luke 12:27

The woods at the bottom of my garden are carpeted with bluebells now, and I love sitting on a tree stump just bathing my spirit in their beauty and fragrance. During his lonely boyhood David the shepherd boy didn't have a Bible, but he learnt about God's character through the things that God created. Instead of being afraid during a thunderstorm he told himself, 'This must be what God's voice sounds like!' During the calm that followed the storm he thought, 'This is like the peace the Lord gives His people' (Ps. 29). To David, the natural world was God's see-able, feel-able body: 'The heavens declare the glory of God; the skies proclaim the work of his hands' (Ps. 19:1).

With so many older brothers David must often have felt small and insignificant, but one night, stretched out beside his campfire, the sheer number of stars made him feel even smaller than usual. 'When I look at the night sky and see the work of your fingers – the moon and the stars you set in place – what are . . . human beings that you should care for them?' Then he realised just how important people are to God: 'Yet you made them only a little lower than God and crowned them with glory and honour' (Ps. 8:3–5, NLT).

How tragic it is that most of us don't have time to enjoy our natural world. Beauty exists, unnoticed, as we dash to our next appointment, but, to David, sharing the enjoyment of nature with God was a way of worshipping Him.

Please help me to hear you speaking right into my heart today through the beautiful things you have made.

Destructive words

When Eliab, David's oldest brother, heard him speaking . . . he burned with anger at him and asked, 'Why have you come . . .? I know how conceited you are and how wicked your heart is . . .'

1 Sam. 17:28

Siblings can be very cruel! Eliab called David an irresponsible, stuck-up, evil-hearted rubberneck, which makes me suspect he had lashed David with cruel words all his life.

As a counsellor, I spent time with Denise.

'My sister's girl is getting married,' she explained, 'but I can't face the wedding. My sister ruined my life; she was so jealous she was always calling me stupid, clumsy, ugly! I've never had any confidence because I grew up believing her!' Gently I pointed out that no one has the power to ruin our lives unless we let them. Unkind words hit like darts but they lose their power when we decide to pull out the dart and ask Jesus to heal the wound it left. Denise decided that when she 'heard' her sister's words echoing in her memory, she would say 'Yes you hurt me, but I choose to forgive.' She not only went to the wedding, but enjoyed it!

David also suffered from friends who verbally abused him: 'It is not my foes who so arrogantly insult me . . . Instead, it is you – my equal, my companion and close friend . . . His words are as soothing as lotion, but underneath are daggers!' (Ps. 55:12, 13, 21, NLT). If someone is bad-mouthing you, David's tip for survival comes later in this psalm: 'Give your burdens to the LORD, and He will take care of you' (v. 22, NLT).

If you are carrying a burden of distress because of painful words, shift it over onto the Lord to carry for you.

Who is your Goliath?

David said to the Philistine, 'You come against me with sword and spear and javelin, but I come against you in the name of the LORD Almighty.'

1 Sam. 17:45

We all have our Goliaths – a difficult boss, a critical colleague, an awkward teenager, a possessive mother-in-law, a tempestuous two-year-old or a selfish neighbour. How easy life would be if God removed, or drastically changed, these giants! He doesn't often; instead He faces us with a choice: we can allow them to either grow us or shrink us.

Galatians 5 lists the supernatural qualities God wants to produce in our lives, i.e. 'love, joy, peace, patience . . . self-control'. Human love grows effortlessly when the people around us are lovable: we feel peaceful with mellow friends; patience is easy when everyone agrees with us. However, supernatural love grows only when our own love runs out; God's type of peace develops best during conflict, and spiritual patience when someone is winding us up! It is when we face our Goliaths, as David did, in the power and protection of the Lord that our supernatural qualities blossom.

Everyone else thought Goliath was far too big to fight against, but David dared to take him on because he saw the giant in a different way. When we compare our 'giants' with ourselves, they look so enormous that we feel small. We know we don't have enough wisdom, patience or experience to cope, but David did not compare Goliath with himself; he compared him with God. When we see our giants dwarfed by our enormous God we stop trying to 'kill' them in our own strength, and realise He puts all the resources of heaven at our disposal.

When you're next confronted by that angry, or disapproving, face, imagine the cross of Jesus between you. Let it absorb their anger and your pain while you hide in its shadow.

Control freaks

Saul dressed David in his own tunic. He put a coat of armour on him and a bronze helmet on his head . . . 'I cannot go in these,' [David] said to Saul . . .

1 Sam. 17:38–39

Many painful relationships start well and then go sour. Saul and David shared a love for music; David's harp helped calm Saul's stress and catapulted David out of the sheep pen and into the limelight. Things began to go wrong when Saul tried to force David to do things *his* way, wear *his* armour and become *his* look-alike, rather than encouraging David to use the skills and experience that were unique to him.

Have you ever worked with someone, or had a friend, who did that to you? At first you respected them highly, wanting to please them, but gradually you realised they were trying to live their lives through you or use you in order to achieve their own goals – a disillusioning discovery.

David knew he could never fight Goliath dressed up as Saul. He did not yet have the strength, skill or experience that Saul had acquired through many years of soldiering. His only hope was to trust God rather than copying someone else.

Shaking off someone else's control takes courage. I've met too many people who spend their lives trying to be what someone else wanted them to be. Anthony's mother never had the chance to become a doctor, so she transferred her ambition onto her only son. He would have preferred farming but became a bad GP who covered his pain by drinking too much. God likes you as you are, so don't try to dress up as someone else.

Lord, I don't want anyone else to control me but you. Give me wisdom to know when I'm being driven through life by anyone else's goals or desires.

Detecting difficulties

*The women came out from all the towns of Israel . . . singing . . .
'Saul has slain his thousands, and David his tens of thousands.' Saul
was very angry . . . from that time on Saul kept a jealous eye on
David.*

1 Sam. 18:7–9

It is often hard to pinpoint the moment when a relationship begins to
crumble. One minute Saul adored David; the next he hated him. Most
of us want others to like us and feel bewildered when a boss, colleague
or church leader shows unmerited disapproval or dislike. Emma was
thrilled when she was promoted to assistant manager of her company's
largest hotel but she soon realised her manager detested her. She tried
hard to build bridges but nothing worked and every day was a nightmare. Finally, she asked for prayer at church. Her vicar sensed that the
name 'Pippa' was important, so, after more prayer, Emma asked her
manager if the name meant anything to her.

'She's my stepsister,' was the reply, 'and you're just like her!' 'Do
you get on well?' ventured Emma. 'I hate her! She turned my father
against me.' Bravely Emma mentioned the animosity she had sensed
between them.

'I've tried so hard to improve our relationship because it matters
to me – but I wonder if it's really Pippa you resent and not me?' That
was the turning point in what became a successful working relationship. The way we get on with each other matters intensely to Jesus,
and He longs to help us put difficult relationships right.

If things are going wrong between you and someone else, could you
be slightly envious of their gifts, appearance or possessions? Or could
they remind you of someone unpleasant?

Where have you gone, God?

My God, my God, why have you forsaken me? Why are you so far from saving me, so far from the words of my groaning? O my God, I cry out . . . but you do not answer.

Ps. 22:1–2

David knew that God had chosen him to be the future king, so he must have felt everything was fitting into place after he killed Goliath, married the king's daughter, was appointed court musician and was made a five-star general! When his success abruptly disintegrated, did he wonder what God was doing? Here he was, holed up in the desert, with Saul and his soldiers hunting him relentlessly; he'd lost his bride, home, job and reputation and suddenly he felt he'd lost God too!

Have you ever had your hopes and dreams suddenly smashed like that? Perhaps you had been so sure God had placed you where you were, so why did He let this happen?

A string of traumas, all close together, sometimes cause us temporarily to lose the sense of God's presence, and maybe you have cried out to God as David did, 'Why have you abandoned me?' If so, you are in good company: Jesus quoted this psalm on the cross (Matt. 27:46).

Perhaps the seeds of Psalm 22 were sown in David's desert, but by v. 19 he has stopped complaining and started praying again – through gritted teeth! When he reaches v. 24 he seems to be telling himself, 'You've known God long enough to be *certain* He keeps His promises,' and by v. 25 he's praising God again. He is soon feeling so much better he can even see himself worshipping again back home, so he plans the party he'll throw on that occasion (v. 26).

It's not the horrible things that happen to us that damage us, but the way we think about them – and it is these thoughts that control our feelings.

❀

Keep watch

Show me your ways, O LORD, teach me your paths; guide me in your truth and teach me, for you are God my Saviour, and my hope is in you all day long.

Ps. 25:4–5

When we are in a tight corner, the first thing we want to do is work out a solution. Questions like, 'Shall I do this . . . or try that?' follow us round like swarming bees. David was sure God wanted him to be king so he must have wondered whether he should be proactive and raise an army against Saul.

This kind of uncertainty is very tough for most of us because we like to be in control of our lives; we feel better if we know where we are heading and what we should be doing. Sitting still and leaving God to sort out the mess feels like weakness! Actually it is the opposite, and David, one of the strongest people ever, realised he could never solve this problem himself, so in today's verses he asks God for wisdom. In v. 9 he tells us that it is pride that makes us want to control our lives, but God promises to guide those who are humble enough to let Him be in charge.

David had successfully led Saul's armies into many battles; he knew a good soldier always keeps his eyes on his commander – watching for his signals. So, even though waiting about must have been extremely difficult, in v. 15 he says, 'My eyes are ever on the LORD,' believing that God would tell him what to do at exactly the right time. If you are in turmoil, David's example is a good one to follow.

Relieve me of my worries and save me from all my troubles. Protect me . . . keep me from defeat. I come to you for safety.

(Ps. 25:16–17, 20, GNB)

May Day

*O LORD my God, I cried to you for help . . . You kept me from falling
into the pit . . . Sing to the LORD, all you godly ones! Praise his holy
name.*

Ps. 30:2, 4, NLT

My grandmother grew up in rural Buckinghamshire and loved telling
me how young girls, long ago, celebrated May Day. 'We were up at
dawn to wash our faces in dew,' she told me. 'Then we ate an egg
shell full of salt because we all wanted to be chosen as May Queen!'

Maypoles and Morris dancing probably date back to pagan festi-
vals, but to me this time of year feels like an explosion of joy; England
looks as if God has painted it with a whole palette full of glorious
colour!

In today's verses David is thanking God for keeping him safe during
all the hard years behind him, but mustn't it break the Lord's heart
when we forget to thank Him for the amazing things He does? Yesterday
I bumped into Jill. I hadn't seen her since she was so ill with cancer
ten years ago. How our church had prayed for her healing.

'I've been totally well ever since you all prayed,' she told me, and
then added, 'but I don't go to church any more. I don't have time.'

David was often positively ecstatic with gratitude as he worshipped,
but last Sunday, as we all sang, 'Praise, My Soul, the King of Heaven',
I looked round at the rest of the congregation. I wondered why their
faces looked so wooden and expressionless – until I realised my face
did too! If I could see the God I am worshipping, surely my face, and
body, would express the meaning of the words I was singing?

Lord, please teach me to worship you as David did – abandoning
myself to you utterly.

A great leader

David . . . escaped to the cave of Adullam . . . All those who were in distress or in debt or discontented gathered around him, and he became their leader.

The LORD is close to the broken-hearted and saves those who are crushed in spirit.

1 Sam. 22:1, 2, Ps. 34:18

While David was waiting in the wilderness for a sign from God, did he sit about doing nothing? The phrase 'wait for the Lord', which David often uses in his psalms, doesn't mean being stuck in a vacuum. It wasn't long before a whole rabble of other outcasts, debtors, escaped slaves and criminals had found David, and settled down to live with him in caves and rock shelters. Rather than throwing a massive pity-party, David began to teach these drop-outs about God's love; Psalm 34 was composed at that time. I guess they spent many a night grouped round the campfire while David told them about God's love and forgiveness. He was a brilliant leader, and over the following years he gave this bunch of 'no-hopers' back their self-respect and transformed them into a highly disciplined army.

Has God asked you to be a leader in your family, or to organise activities in your church or in your job? If so, do you think you mirror God's accepting, unconditional love to those for whom you are responsible? Or, looking at you, might they think your God is hard to please, and more interested in getting the job done than in their personal welfare? Do you build people up with encouragement, appreciation and affirmation or stunt their confidence with petty criticism and disapproval? Edward Hale's tip for managing people was: 'Make it your habit not to be critical about small things.'

Lord, make me the kind of leader who believes in the potential greatness of others until they believe it themselves.

Loving against the odds

Michal, Saul's daughter, looked out of the window and saw King David dancing and jumping around in the sacred dance, and she was disgusted with him.

2 Sam. 6:16, GNB

In fairy stories the hero always wins the hand of the princess, but David and King Saul's daughter did not live happily ever after. We are told twice that she was in love with David, and she risked her life to save him when her father sent soldiers to arrest him. Saul punished her by marrying her off to someone else after David's banishment. But was she broken-hearted?

Years later, when David returned from exile, he demanded her return, but what should have been the climax of a glorious romance seems to have been more of a tragedy. Perhaps by then she had settled happily with her new husband. We are told that he was distraught at losing her and she may have felt the same; she certainly seems to have become bitter and critical.

Perhaps the problem was that Michal did not share David's faith; she had a heathen image in her house and despised her husband's passionate love for God. Was it this fundamental difference that divided a marriage that had started off so well?

Living close to someone who is not yet a Christian, or not as committed as you are, can be lonely. Although David had many wives, Michal was his first and therefore the most important, yet there was no intimacy between them (2 Sam. 6:23). For such an affectionate man it must have been hard to be mocked and despised in his own home.

Lord, I ask you to strengthen anyone who is the only Christian in their family; please satisfy their loneliness and anoint them with an extra share of your love to give their families.

Love at first sight

Don't hit back . . . Don't insist on getting even; that's not for you to do. 'I'll do the judging,' says God. 'I'll take care of it.'

Rom. 12:17–19, *The Message*

My neighbour's husband left her with two tiny children, and moved in with her best friend. She was so angry she set off with a chisel to scratch the paint off his new car, and a carving knife to slash his tyres. She obviously knew how to hurt him most! On the way she met a friend. 'Your husband's in the wrong; don't join him!' was the friend's advice, so they went off together for a good laugh in the pub instead.

David was once on his way to wreak vengeance on a man who had treated him appallingly. On the way he met the man's beautiful young wife, Abigail, who persuaded David not to make a terrible mistake he might regret all his life (1 Sam. 25:31). As in a Hollywood film Abigail's mean old husband conveniently died and she and David were married!

When someone treats us unfairly, and insults us or damages our reputation with catty gossip, it is natural to want to get our own back, but Abigail not only prevented a massacre, she taught David the importance of leaving justice to God. Forgiving also means forgoing our right to put the record straight by telling our side of the story.

Patsy was wrongly accused by a colleague of malpractice in the care home she ran. Even when the authorities dropped the case and reinstated her she still kept all the records, documents and letters, hoping for a chance to clear her name publicly. When she asked for prayer for arthritis she realised she needed to let go of her grudge by burning these papers, and after doing that her pain level rapidly dropped.

Lord, make me a willing cheek-turner!

Coping with conflict

David was greatly distressed because the men were talking of stoning him; each one was bitter in spirit . . . But David found strength in the LORD his God.

1 Sam. 30:6

How do you usually react when you sense there's a row brewing? Some people thrive on conflict; it provides such an adrenaline rush they become addicted to arguments! Others go for 'peace at any price' even if that means becoming a doormat. Whatever our temperament, healthy relationships depend on handling confrontation well. David and his men came back to their desert hideout one evening and found it desolate. Raiders had stolen their wives and children, and burned everything they could not carry. The men wanted someone to blame, so they turned on David, who was reeling from his own grief. Instead of choosing either of the options most of us prefer during conflict – running away or fighting it out – he simply withdrew to be comforted and strengthened by the Lord.

It was the arguments I found hardest about bringing up six children, but an older friend gave me some excellent advice. When her four children were teenagers she also had to care for a disabled husband and his manipulative mother.

'They used to wind the children up with their bitter little comments until meals became battles and everyone got hurt. So, as soon as I could see tempers were rising, I would run to the loo for a few minutes, to ask God to bring His peace. By the time I emerged either I had the strength to take control or the whole thing had miraculously blown over!' Following her advice probably saved me from murder on a number of occasions!

Lord, I don't think I handle conflict very well. When I'm in the thick of the next one, please help me follow David's example.

Live dancingly!

There are many who pray: 'Give us more blessings, O LORD *. . .' But the joy that you have given me is more than they will ever have with all their corn and wine.*

Ps. 4:6–7, GNB

Food would have been in short supply for fugitives in the desert and wine non-existent, yet the psalms David wrote during those bleak years are full of joy. He had found the secret that so few of the rest of us ever discover: God Himself is the source of our happiness, not His blessings, gifts or the material possessions He provides. Perhaps we only fully learn that secret when life forces us into the desert and we lose all the earthly props we once looked to for pleasure and satisfaction.

During a particularly tough time in my life I remember snorting crossly when my devotional book suggested I should 'live dancingly as David did'! 'Fat chance with all my problems,' I thought, but the phrase hung in my mind. We know David danced exuberantly in worship when he became king (2 Sam. 6:14), but this writer suggested that his heart was dancing for joy all the time whatever was going on in his external world.

It is God's greatest desire that we should depend on Him for *everything*, and make Him the source of our happiness. I think today's verse shows us how this quality of dependence was developing in David. In Psalm 4 he whinges at first but talks himself round until he reaches vv. 6–7, where he realises that the greatest blessing God can ever give us is not comfort or success or even spiritual power – but God Himself!

Lord, I realise I've mislaid my joy under the heaps of dull little jobs, disappointments and worries that keep piling up on me. Show me how to 'live dancingly' underneath the mess . . .

MAY 7

Worship through tears

O God, you are my God, earnestly I seek you; my soul thirsts for you, my body longs for you, in a dry and weary land where there is no water. I have seen you in the sanctuary and beheld your power and your glory. Because your love is better than life, my lips will glorify you. I will praise you as long as I live, and in your name I will lift up my hands.

Ps. 63:1–4

'Living dancingly' must sometimes have been a major faith struggle for David. We know he adored worshipping in God's house (Ps. 27:4) but he was banned from public worship for years. Not being able to worship with others soon causes the kind of spiritual dryness David expresses in today's verses, but he goes on to remind himself that when we don't feel like praising God we just have to do it by willpower (v. 4).

Have you ever thought, 'It's no good going to church today; I'm too upset (or angry) to worship'? So you either stay at home or force yourself to go but feel as if your soul is being rubbed with sandpaper! David not only worshipped God with music and singing, he worshipped by offering all his emotions to God – not just his joy but also his grief. He asked God to 'put my tears into your bottle' (Ps. 56:8, NKJV). There is something desolate about crying alone with no one else there to comfort us, but David assures us that God see our tears and they are so precious to Him that He carefully preserves every one.

Lord, I don't seem to have much to offer you at the moment, but please take all these painful emotions as my act of worship today.

Who is your Mephibosheth?

Mephibosheth bowed down and said, 'What is your servant, that you should notice a dead dog like me?'

2 Sam. 9:8

The way David treated Saul's disabled grandson is my favourite David story, but modern culture and values make it hard for us to appreciate its poignancy and depth. When David finally gained the crown God had promised, everyone would have expected him to kill every member of the previous royal family. Saul's last remaining grandson had been left crippled after a childhood accident and was living rough in the hills, terrified the new king would find him. David went to a lot of trouble to trace him and when Mephibosheth was finally brought to Jerusalem he must have thought he was about to die.

Shock waves would have echoed round the country when the news broke that David had not only spared his life but invited him to share his home like an honoured son. In those days disabled people were despised and never allowed to appear in public, so the sight of Mephibosheth banqueting at the King's table would have been astonishing! Everyone also expected David to seize all Saul's wealth but instead he gave it to the rightful heir, making Mephibosheth a very rich young man.

What a glorious picture of the way the Lord hunts us out, disabled by sin, poor of spirit, cringing away in shame, and gives us the right to be his beloved child, lavishing us with everything we need and inviting us to sit close to him for eternity. This story shows us how like Jesus David was – in many ways. In which ways are you like Jesus?

Who is your 'Mephibosheth'? Do you know anyone who is unattractive, unpopular or unnoticed who might need your help, time and friendship?

Who is your Uriah?

Put Uriah in the front line where the fighting is fiercest. Then withdraw from him so he will be struck down and die.

2 Sam. 11:15

How could a man like David do something like that? Uriah was his neighbour and loyal employee, a man of integrity and faith, yet David stole his wife for a one-night stand, and when she found she was pregnant he had him murdered so he could marry her himself!

Probably none of us has wronged anyone to that extent, but we all have our own Uriahs. Perhaps, as adults, we realise how much we hurt our parents during our obnoxious teenage years. Or, after they have died, we wish we had cared for them better during old age. Maybe 'Uriah' was one of our children whose soul we scarred by unwise words, and we writhe with remorse when we remember the things we did when stress made us lose our cool. It might be the boyfriend or husband we 'dumped', the boss we let down for a better job, the colleague we treated unfairly, the friend we betrayed by gossip. I guess none of us can 'cast the first stone' at David.

Some people deny, even to themselves, their part in any failed relationship, fiercely maintaining they were in the right. Others spend the rest of their lives in regrets and 'if-onlys'. Replaying the 'videos' endlessly, they allow shame to destroy their confidence and warp their souls. Both of these extremes insult Jesus! He died on the cross to take the blame for all our thoughtlessness and deliberate cruelty – but He died for nothing if we insist on carrying our load of shame or refuse to admit we need His forgiveness.

Lord, my regrets would break my heart if I couldn't find forgiveness at your cross.

Christians, beware!

But the thing David had done displeased the LORD.

2 Sam. 11:27

For centuries David's relationship with Bathsheba has given smug satisfaction to the untempted and comfort to the tempted who fell! Actually it should also warn us that, even when we are as close to God as David was, we are only a hair's breadth away from a devastating fall. You might think, 'I'm not about to commit adultery!' but Jesus told us that we do not have to sleep with someone else's spouse to commit adultery; sexual fantasies are just as wrong (Matt. 5:27–28), but we conveniently ignore that.

A few years ago I was speaking at the first night of a large Christian conference. At the end of my talk I said, rather nervously, 'I feel the Lord wants to warn someone who is married and deeply involved in your church's ministry team, music group or youth work. You have become very close to someone you work with and spend a lot of time praying, planning and preparing together. You feel understood, appreciated and spiritually stimulated by this person. Although this friendship is platonic it makes you resent your spouse who, you feel, holds you back spiritually by their negative attitude and lack of faith. The Lord is asking you to give up this friendship now before it causes pain to others and dishonours Him.' During the following days dozens of people slipped up to me and whispered, 'That word was for me,' while others sought help in the counselling tent. I was stunned by the response. Christians in loving churches are in danger of forming deep emotional ties that leave their spouses out in the cold. The spiritual stimulation they feel actually masks sexual excitement, and even innocent friendship can destroy marriages.

Please be Lord of my daydreams.

Who is your Nathan?

Then David said to Nathan, 'I have sinned against the LORD.' Nathan replied, 'The LORD has taken away your sin.'

2 Sam. 12:13

How do you react when another Christian you respect pulls you up over your behaviour? Do you give them a piece of your mind, find a new church or prayerfully consider what they said?

For months David pushed his guilt down so firmly he couldn't feel it! Kings in those days could help themselves to any woman they fancied, and murder was also their right. Perhaps David thought, 'It's alright because all the other guys do this, and anyway God loves me so much, He'll understand.'

God *is* loving, but He is also holy; He can't come near sin of any kind – but David didn't even realise God had withdrawn! He became so spiritually deaf that after a few months God had to find someone brave enough to go and confront David with the horror of his sin. Nathan risked his life; angry kings were dangerous! But David listened, and the realisation of what he had done drove him instantly to his knees in repentance. Our spiritual growth is in jeopardy when we refuse to listen to the Nathans in our lives.

Many biblical kings started really well but wealth and power corrupted them and they not only sinned but pulled the whole nation down after them. The difference between David and other kings was simply repentance. David poured out his agony in Psalm 51 and God forgave and restored him, as God always does – when we are sorry.

Remove my sin, and I will be clean; wash me, and I will be whiter than snow. Let me hear the sounds of joy and gladness; and though you have crushed me and broken me, I will be happy once again.

(Ps. 51:7–8, GNB)

Forgiveness needs to be accepted

As high as the sky is above the earth, so great is his love for those who honour him. As far as the east is from the west, so far does he remove our sins from us.

Ps. 103:11–12, GNB

How was it that someone who had fallen as badly as David could still be so full of joy? Perhaps it was not only because he was forgiven, but because he *knew* he was forgiven! God holds out forgiveness to all of us but we have to reach out and receive it. I meet so many regular churchgoers who simply do not understand the full extent of what Jesus did for them on the cross. When they sin they carry their regrets around like an armful of smelly garbage, rather than instantly throwing it all in the dustbin at the foot of the cross.

Many struggle through life feeling worthless; they can't pinpoint a specific sin; they just feel they always get everything wrong. The enemy loves smothering their joy with shame.

Or maybe this feeling is linked with something they *did* do once, which was so bad they feel they don't deserve to be forgiven. Their sins are certainly no worse than David's, so if he could be forgiven, so can they! There is no sin that God cannot forgive if we ask Him!

In today's verses David tells us that God removes our forgiven sins as far as the east is from the west, which, as any scientist will tell you, is an infinite distance. When God forgives our sins He deletes them from existence!

Jesus, help me never to stop revelling in the fact that you, the creator of the world, loved me enough to die for me – personally.

Acceptance

While the child was still alive, I fasted and wept . . . But now that he is dead, why should I fast? Can I bring him back again? I will go to him, but he will not return to me.

2 Sam. 12:22–23

Watching his baby die must have been agonising for David, particularly as he felt responsible (2 Sam. 12:14). Their relationship was tragically brief but David was sure it was not finished (v. 23).

Although we can enjoy all the benefits of complete forgiveness, we need to remember that we are often left with the inevitable consequences of our sins and mistakes – which may cause the innocent to suffer.

The story of David and his dying child helped me during the worst faith crisis of my life. When my husband left after thirty, apparently happy, years, I was convinced God would bring him home because He says He hates divorce! So I prayed, fasted, waged spiritual warfare and claimed all the Bible promises. Then, when five years were up, my husband filed for divorce so he could marry again. I was devastated. Perhaps all my praying had been a waste of time. After a few weeks of black despair David's example of acceptance steadied me. Sometimes, in spite of our pleading, God allows the very thing we dread. He always has His reasons but doesn't always explain them! Like David, we are then faced with a choice: we can go on lying on the floor in misery or get up, wash, eat and worship a God who is able to bring good out of everything – if we are willing to let Him (Rom. 8:28).

In acceptance lieth peace.

Amy Carmichael (1867–1951)

Not there for me!

She sprinkled ashes on her head, tore her robe, and with her face buried in her hands, she went away crying.

2 Sam. 13:19, GNB

As a counsellor I meet people who were sexually abused as children and seem angrier with their mother than with the abuser: 'She must have known! She should have stopped him!' Is that how Tamar felt about her father, David, when his weakness laid her open to rape? David, in spite of all his gifts and achievements, was a rotten father! He overindulged his sons until they ran wild. When his eldest son, Amnon, fancied his half-sister he only had to pretend to be ill and ask for Tamar to nurse him for David to do something as unheard-of as allowing an unmarried princess to leave the shelter of the harem to spend time with Amnon alone.

Did your parents put the needs and demands of a brother or sister before yours, leaving you always feeling 'second best' or vulnerable to their bullying?

David's careless lack of protection destroyed Tamar's hope of happiness and sentenced her to lifelong desolation (2 Sam. 13:20). Was she excluded from the palace because they all decided to keep quiet and not disgrace the family (v. 20)? 'Anything for a quiet life' is the motto of a weak parent and, because David failed to discipline Amnon, Tamar's full brother, Absalom, was so frustrated that he punished him himself – by murdering him. David appeared to love his children but real love has to be tough enough to stand up for the rights of the weak and to stop the strong from damaging themselves.

It is often easier to forgive people for the bad things they do to us than for the good things they fail to do.

Toxic guilt

So now there is no condemnation for those who belong to Christ Jesus.

Rom. 8:1, NLT

Ginny's teenage sons were obnoxious. She was a forceful woman, who ran her own successful business, but she let her sons treat her like dirt, spoilt them rotten with too much money and never seemed able to say 'no!' One day she told me why. When the boys were small she had an affair that finished her marriage.

'It is my fault they lost their dad, so I keep trying to make it up to them.' She loved her boys but her relationship with them was ruined by guilt. Perhaps David had the same problem with his children. Did his affair with Bathsheba and treatment of Uriah undermine his self-respect, so he failed to discipline his children?

When Ginny became a Christian she realised she could be free of her guilt by leaving it at the cross. 'Suddenly the boys had nothing to "hook" me with – and I felt confident enough to be much firmer with them. Also, they had a new dad to help me to control them – Jesus!'

When we feel we have hurt someone, instead of trusting God to heal their scars, we sometimes try to overcompensate by giving in to their every demand. It is one thing to receive God's forgiveness but quite another to forgive ourselves. Even though we know that Jesus said if we are not willing to forgive someone else, we put ourselves outside God's blessing (Matt. 6:15), we forget that forgiving ourselves is just as vital. Is guilt altering the way you relate to anyone?

Suppose someone close to you once did something that hurt you: a mistake, a bad decision, an affair? Forgiving means deciding never again to use their guilt to manipulate them into giving you your own way.

Communication failure!

'I don't want to see him,' the king said, *so Absalom lived in his own house and did not appear before the king.*

2 Sam. 14:24 GNB

Honest communication is a vital part of good relationships, and David seems to have been rather bad at it. He banished his son Absalom for murdering his brother, and then weakly let him return, but he never attempted to mend the relationship by talking their problems through. If only he had, Absalom's smouldering resentment might not have flared into a rebellion that split the nation. General Joab also upset David, who said nothing at the time but carried the resentment to his deathbed (1 Kgs 2:5–6). Silence can be just as divisive as saying too much! Were you brought up in a family where everyone hid their true feelings behind a wall of silence?

Obviously, saying too much is just as hurtful. During a row Kelly told her husband he was 'rubbish in bed'! It wasn't true, but he needed to make sure, so he had an affair – which led to their divorce. Controlling our anger is vital, but Paul says, 'In your anger do not sin' (Eph. 4:26a). In other words, it is OK to be angry so long as you express it appropriately.

Perhaps the secret of good relationships is to be assertive without being aggressive. There is a world of difference between shouting, 'You're a filthy slob, littering the place with all your junk!' and quietly remarking, 'Sorry, but tidiness matters to me; living in a mess makes me feel stressed.' The former is a personal attack; the latter expresses your feelings about their behaviour but not your disapproval of them personally.

Lord, you know how afraid I am of hurting other people by saying too much or too little, so please 'keep watch over the door of my lips'. (Ps. 141:3)

Agony of rejection

A messenger came and told David, 'The hearts of the men of Israel are with Absalom.'

2 Sam. 15:13

David adored Absalom, who looked very like him. Absalom also inherited David's attractive personality and many of his gifts, but he did not have a heart that pursued God – he was a dishonest schemer. Yet David's love for his son blinded him to all Absalom's faults. Even though Absalom turned half the kingdom against him, drove him out of his home and did his best to kill him and steal everything he had, still David went on loving him. Just before their opposing armies met, David told his generals, 'Be gentle with the young man Absalom.' He would rather have handed Absalom his crown than see him hurt, and when he heard he was dead, 'He went up to the room . . . and wept . . . "O my son Absalom! If only I had died instead of you!"' (2 Sam. 18:33)

Have you loved someone – only to have them fling it back in your face? A child who was once the centre of your world, who never makes contact now, the husband who preferred someone else, or a close friend who abandoned you? Nothing hurts more than rejection, and the only way David coped was by sharing the agony with God: 'If an enemy were insulting me, I could endure it . . . But it is you, a man like myself, my companion . . . But I call to God, and the LORD saves me' (Ps. 55:12–16). God knows all about rejection! The people He loves turn against Him constantly – and because He understands, we can safely share our pain with Him.

David's love for Absalom was like God's love for us; He never 'switches it off', however much we fail or reject Him. Are you excluding anyone from your heart because they hurt you?

The king's friend

Hushai the Arkite was the king's friend.

1 Chr. 27:33

I thought we were in for a dull sermon as the preacher proceeded to read out a list of David's court officials – but when he reached verse 33 tears were pouring down his cheeks. What moved him was that right in the middle of all these important, dynamic, useful men with their vast responsibilities was Hushai the Arkite. David did not value him for his achievements, skills or resources; Hushai was listed in the roll of honour simply because he was the king's friend.

Humans tend to gauge a person's worth by what they do and how successful they are at it, or by their appearance or how much they own. God simply looks to see if we return His love. He says, 'I no longer call you servants . . . I have called you friends' (John 15:15). He doesn't just want to use us; He wants to enjoy our company!

The preacher had recently been devastated by the loss of his high-profile job in the civil service. He felt insignificant and useless until he discovered Hushai and realised that friendship is God's priority.

Have you ever looked round your church and 'graded' the other members of the congregation? 'She's a first-class Christian, right at the centre of everything'; 'Our minister must be a great man of God; he speaks at conferences all over the country.' You probably don't even notice the disabled lady, parked in her wheelchair in the back row. It's the hours she spends with the Lord that make her a spiritual lightning conductor to the entire church – but no one on Earth knows that!

Lord, the dictionary says a friend is 'a person whom one knows, likes and trusts'. You certainly know me, but like me and trust me? The wonder of that boggles my mind!

Old photos

You give me your shield of victory; you stoop down to make me great. You broaden the path beneath me, so that my ankles do not turn over.

2 Sam. 22:36–37

Successful politicians and generals often spend their old age writing memoirs to dazzle posterity with their achievements. David probably had more to boast about than any of them, yet all he could see as he looked back was how God had enabled him in spite of his inadequacy. I like to imagine him reliving all his memories at the end of his life; right to the end David wanted God to have all the glory! 'It is God who arms me with strength and makes my way perfect' (v. 33).

We are only deluding ourselves if we think we can control our own lives; the truth is, we are all weak and inadequate – in comparison to God. We are only as successful as He allows us to be. David realised that (v. 35).

Many people start out well in their Christian lives, burning with passion for God, but it gets lost under the busyness of careers and family life. Some, however, stay close enough to God to become 'hub people' in their churches or go into full-time ministry, but the pressures of leadership easily crush their private relationship with God. Just a few survive to the end, moving progressively deeper and deeper into God until He becomes more real to them than the earthly life around them. David finished well because he discovered the secret of success: 'You are my lamp, O LORD; the LORD turns my darkness into light (v. 29).

Please, Lord, keep pouring into me the oil of your Holy Spirit because I want to stay burning brightly for you to the very end.

A royal favourite

Peace I leave with you; my [own] peace I now give and bequeath to you. Not as the world gives do I give to you. Do not let your hearts be troubled, neither let them be afraid. [Stop allowing yourselves to be ... fearful and intimidated and cowardly and unsettled.]

John 14:27, AMP

I sometimes love to sing to myself the old-fashioned hymns we hardly ever hear in church these days. The following one is said to have been the favourite of King George V. For such an anxious man with a highly developed sense of duty, it must have been very hard to rule the nation during the horrors of the First World War and the Russian Revolution. He also grappled with sorrows and stresses in his own family; his youngest son was handicapped and, tragically, died young. The wild behaviour of his eldest son, the Prince of Wales, must have caused such a conscientious man some sleepless nights. These lovely old words often bathed his soul; sit back and let them do the same for you.

Peace, perfect peace, in this dark world of sin?
The blood of Jesus whispers peace within.
Peace, perfect peace, by thronging duties pressed?
To do the will of Jesus, this is rest.
Peace, perfect peace, with sorrows surging round?
On Jesus' bosom nought but calm is found.
Peace, perfect peace, with loved ones far away?
In Jesus' keeping we are safe – and they.
Peace, perfect peace, our future all unknown?
Jesus we know, and He is on the throne.
Peace, perfect peace, death shadowing us and ours?
Jesus has vanquished death and all its powers.

Bishop E. H. Bickersteth (1825–1906)

Rabbits can't make me angry

Bridle your anger, trash your wrath, cool your pipes – it only makes things worse.

Ps. 37:8, *The Message*

My garden is totally overrun by rabbits, and every new tender little plant I bed out is soon nibbled to a mere stalk. My dog Phoebe used to see it as her life's work to keep them off our property, but the cunning rabbits know her eyes and ears are failing with old age, so arrive in marauding hoards – even in broad daylight. I realised my blood pressure was rising as I constantly peered out of the window watching for these destroyers, waiting to bang on the glass or dash out screaming like a banshee!

I prayed, I blocked holes in the hedge, I invested in high-pitched sonar deterrents and sprayed the new plants with rotten eggs and distilled lions' poo – but nothing worked. I couldn't afford to wire in the whole garden, nor could I bring myself to shoot them. So I boiled with frustration and rage!

'You're becoming obsessive,' a friend told me. 'The rabbits appear to be here to stay, so you have a choice: you can go on being paranoid or relax and enjoy the new hobby of "Rabbit Watching". There are a few varieties of plants rabbits don't like, so just grow them!'

'But the rabbits make me so angry,' I fumed. 'No they don't,' retorted my infuriating friend, 'it's *you* who are *letting* the rabbits make you angry.'

Then the baby rabbits began to appear – and I realised they are rather sweet!

Lord, there are some people and some situations in my life that I can't change; I've tried, but without success. Help me to accept them and find something in them somewhere that I can enjoy!

'Solomon in all his glory'

Then David comforted his wife Bathsheba . . . and she bore a son, whom David named Solomon. The LORD loved the boy.

2 Sam. 12:24, GNB

I so enjoyed the series we did recently on David that I thought we could also look at his illustrious son! David and Bathsheba's first baby had been conceived in adultery, which led to lies, murder and disgrace – and the baby's death: but God's forgiveness is as amazing as His grace! Far from ignoring their second son, He sent Nathan the prophet to say the baby should be nicknamed Jedidiah – 'Loved by God'! David had already been promised that he would have a son, a man of peace, who would build a magnificent temple and, as he held their baby, David made Bathsheba a solemn promise: 'One day this child will wear my crown.'

Solomon became one of the most dazzling superstars of all time: a multi-gifted genius; billionaire businessman; architect and naturalist. He was a brilliant statesman, who pulled his kingdom out of obscurity and, for a brief time, made his court the cultural and academic centre of the world. He was also an accomplished teacher and a poet and prolific songwriter, and, to cap all that, women found him irresistible! With all that going for him it seems strange that, at eighteen, Solomon seemed remarkably lacking in self-confidence. Perhaps it was hard for an academically gifted child to grow up in a family with so many older brothers, all possessing the kind of qualities their world respected most – physical strength, good looks, military expertise and daring horsemanship. David, however, saw something in Solomon that none of his other sons possessed – a longing to serve God wholeheartedly.

Lord, I'd love to be as rich, wise and talented as Solomon! I never will be, but deep down I recognise it is far better to know that you love me and value my love in return.

Daunted by responsibility

When the time drew near for David to die, he gave a charge to Solomon his son . . . 'be strong, show yourself a man, and observe what the LORD your God requires: Walk in his ways . . . so that you may prosper in all you do and wherever you go.'

1 Kgs 2:1–2

David's courtiers could not believe he wanted Solomon to succeed him. Surely one of his other sons would do a far better job? David also had his doubts about Solomon's abilities (1 Chr. 29:1), so he gave him this deathbed pep talk. In spite of that Solomon still seemed daunted by the prospect of kingship, so God Himself appeared to him in a dream (1 Kgs 3:5).

'What do you want me to do for you?' God asked, and Solomon's reply pleased Him enormously.

'I am only a little child and do not know how to carry out my duties . . . So give your servant a discerning heart to govern your people.' Solomon realised the task ahead was not only to shepherd God's special nation but also to create a centre of worship for the whole world. Beyond his phenomenal natural intelligence he was going to need supernatural wisdom.

Are you struggling at the moment with the job God has given you? Perhaps you feel so ill-equipped you want 'out' – *now*! Could it be time to stop using your own strength and ask God for His supernatural gifting? Just as Solomon asked for wisdom, James 1:5 tells us we can do the same because God loves performing miracles through people who are humble enough to ask for help!

Lord, sometimes I feel daunted by my many responsibilities, but help me to remember that you want me to change and become like a little trusting child (Matt. 18:3).

What do you need most?

'What do you want me to do for you?' Jesus asked him. The blind man said, 'Rabbi, I want to see.'

Mark 10:51

Suppose one night you had a 'Solomon dream'. Or, like the blind beggar, Jesus asked you, 'What do you want me to do for you?' What would you say?

'Lord, my family's in turmoil; my parents (or children) row continuously and treat me like dirt. I need a happy home.'

Or would you reply, 'My finances are a mess; I need more money!' 'My marriage is in trouble; I need my wife (husband) to love me again.' 'My job is getting me down; I need a change.' 'I'm lonely; I need a friend.' 'I need more *time* every day!'

Some of us have so many needs that our lists would be tragically long, but Solomon asked for only one thing – wisdom. God-given wisdom allows us to see people, problems, events and situations through God's eyes, with His perspective; then He helps us act and react to them as He would. So, rather than asking for a happy home, God's wisdom would help us manage family members so well that peace would be restored and we would gain their respect. Wisdom helps us handle our existing money efficiently. Rather than asking for the love of a spouse, wisdom shows us how to be a better spouse ourselves. Instead of asking for a change, wisdom gives us the ability to cope where we are. Wisdom would bring friends because it shows us how to relate, and be a good friend to others. Most of us need wisdom to manage time and juggle priorities rather than have more hours in each day!

Stop for a while in God's presence and 'walk with Him', by imagination, through the various areas of your life, asking yourself where you most need His wisdom.

Don't forget Solomon's baby!

Fear of the LORD is the foundation of wisdom. Knowledge of the Holy One results in good judgment.

Prov. 3:13–14, ESV

Not only did God give Solomon wisdom, He also blessed him in everything he did! 1 Kings 4 tells us about his enormous flair for administrative government, his expanding territories, his shrewd trade agreements with foreign powers, and his formidable military strength, which enabled his people to live in peace. Yet history probably remembers him best as the king who *didn't* cut a prostitute's baby in half! Two women came to him for justice, each saying the baby was hers; Solomon knew a true mother would rather give away her baby than see him killed, so he called for a sword and applied his famous test (1 Kgs 3:16–28).

Once, while speaking at a conference, I became aware of massive tension building between leading members of the Christian organisation that was responsible for this large annual event. There seemed to be two sides, each with strong opinions on how the conference should be led. One night the organisers had a violent row! Very embarrassed, I hurriedly slipped out of the room, after scrawling on a large piece of paper, 'Don't forget Solomon's baby.' One side or the other would have to back down or there would be no future conferences!

Churches are ruined when Christians take sides over small issues and refuse to give way. If only God's glory and kingdom mattered to us more than our own personal agenda and desire for power! Are you involved in confrontation of any kind, at home, church or at work?

Remember that God-given wisdom enables us not only to resolve conflict satisfactorily, but also to perceive what is really going on in a given situation – and then to enable God's will to be done.

'One greater than Solomon is here'

A thick cloud filled the Temple of the LORD. The priests could not continue their service because of the cloud, for the glorious presence of the LORD filled the Temple.

1 Kgs 8:10–11, NLT

For years, Solomon's chief goal had been to build God the most glorious temple imaginable. Now it was finished at last, and its sheer magnificence made it one of the wonders of the ancient world.

He took huge care over every detail of the service of dedication, which had to be *perfect*! Can you picture all that gold glinting in the sun; cheering crowds; hundreds of priests in flowing robes; massed choirs; farmers herding innumerable animals; craftsmen admiring their handiwork; and above them, on a great bronze platform, sat Solomon, dressed sumptuously, enjoying his great achievement.

Then suddenly all the activity stopped – frozen into silence! Everyone, including the King, bowed in awe. God Himself turned up! When we encounter God in His power our human goals and achievements seem very small. Solomon was left saying, 'Even the highest heaven cannot contain you. How much less this Temple I have built!' (1 Kgs 8:27).

Sometimes we can become so focused on our traditions, church programmes and activities that if God suddenly descended visibly, to mess up our plans with His own, we would be thoroughly upset!

Have you ever been so conscious of the presence of the Lord that you hardly dared to move in case you touched Him? Perhaps many of us could experience God's tangible presence more often if only we dared to say 'Come, Holy Spirit', and then sat quietly to wait for Him.

Could you take time today just to rest back in God's presence and let Him enfold you?

Glimpsing glory

Unless the LORD builds a house, the work of the builders is wasted. Unless the LORD protects a city, guarding it with sentries will do no good. It is useless for you to work so hard from early morning until late at night, anxiously working for food to eat; for God gives rest to his loved ones.

Ps. 127:1–2, NLT

What an amazing statement to be made by one of the most competent, efficient and hard-working people who ever lived. Solomon did not write nearly as many psalms as his father, David, but this one is a gem. He had concentrated all his considerable genius on building a 'house' for God and when it was done he prayed, 'I have indeed built a magnificent temple for you, a place for you to dwell for ever' (1 Kgs 8:13), but as he sat on his bronze platform surveying his achievements he suddenly glimpsed the full glory of God – and it changed him. Perhaps he wrote this psalm soon afterwards?

Just occasionally during a lifetime we are allowed a brief realisation of just how great, vast and all-powerful God actually is! The curtains of heaven are parted for a moment, allowing us to see the splendour of the God we so often take for granted. Then the workaholic-proficient-organised side of us kicks in and we start being busy again, thinking we can do anything, provided we work hard enough!

I hesitated about including these verses because they seemed to be saying things we have already explored recently, but I sense that someone reading them needs to take in what Solomon is saying. Could there be areas in your life where you are striving to work things out in your own strength? Sometimes we ask for God's help in a particular situation but actually we stay in control ourselves. It is rather like inviting a friend to drive your car but continually grabbing the steering wheel or applying the handbrake.

Psalm 46:10 tells us to 'Be still and know that I am God'. Is there an area of your life where God needs to be God right now?

The Midas touch

No-one can serve two masters . . . You cannot serve both God and Money.

Matt. 6:24

We say, 'Money is the root of all evil,' as we look down on rich Christians whose possessions we secretly envy, but it is the *love* of money that is the root of evil, not money itself (Heb. 13:5)!

Recently a friend told me how, as a young man, he had gone to his minister for advice because he longed to devote his life to serving God.

'My dad wants me to follow him into the family business but I want to lead a church or be a missionary.'

After he had prayed, his minister replied, 'I think God wants to give you a Midas gift.' Feeling confused, my friend remembered the mythological king who was given the gift of turning everything he touched into gold. 'God needs men to make money for His kingdom,' explained the minister.

Thirty years later my friend has turned his father's business into a global company with a turnover of billions but he still lives simply, using only a tiny fraction of his income. With the rest he finances poor churches, Christian organisations and evangelistic ventures, and supports young people through Bible college. He wanted to be a missionary or a minister but, instead, God has used him to launch thousands of others into ministry.

God gave Solomon far more than he asked for (1 Kgs 3:5); He made him the richest man in the world. So, if money-making is just as much a gift from God as preaching or healing, why aren't there more rich Christians? Solomon's later life shows us that money brings huge responsibilities and temptations, so perhaps God can't trust many of us with His wallet!

If church leaders need our prayers for protection and success, so do Christian businessmen!

Midlife crisis!

'Praise the LORD . . . May he give us the desire to do his will in everything and to obey all the commands . . . You keep your covenant and show unfailing love to all who walk before you in wholehearted devotion.

1 Kgs 8:56, 58, 23, NLT

Solomon's life reminds me of the Matterhorn – that famous Swiss mountain which rises so abruptly to a magnificent peak and then drops away just as sharply on the far side. Solomon's story begins with him feeling as daunted as any inexperienced climber setting out to climb the Matterhorn! Fortunately he is humble enough to realise he needs help – and asks God for it. The Almighty seems to let down a rope and pulls Solomon rapidly up the sheer cliff face to the summit – which was the glorious day when the temple was dedicated.

On that occasion Solomon burned with love for God and poured out his heart to Him in one of the most remarkable prayers in the Bible. He also preached an impassioned sermon to his people, which is summed up in today's verses. If only he had practised what he preached and continued to rely on God! Instead, his story ends, twenty years later, with him right down at the bottom of the mountain, in despair and disgrace.

Perhaps everyone who sets out to live for God is actually a mountaineer. Many of us start just as well as Solomon, full of the Holy Spirit and zeal for God's kingdom. We're all convinced we'll never fall, but a tragically high proportion of us do. It is the pressures, successes or disappointments of life that cause us to let go of the rope that connects us to our Mountain Guide.

Lord, please give me the desire to do your will in everything.

Pride comes before a fall

When pride comes, then comes disgrace, but with humility comes wisdom.

Prov. 11:2

Probably none of us would *want* to let go of the rope and fall away from God. So why did Solomon tumble? First and foremost it was pride. That diffident boy who pleaded for God's help soon got lost in all those sumptuous palaces. Brian was the 'Spiritual Superstar' who always reminded me of Solomon. When he first started leading the little church that met in the local primary school he felt so inadequate that he spent hours praying over every sermon. As his confidence increased he found he was very good at preaching, so he relied on God less. Years later he had built a countrywide group of churches and travelled the world addressing international conferences. The more successful he became, the less time there was for prayer and, in order to cope with his stressful lifestyle, he felt he 'needed' to bend God's rules 'just occasionally'. After a financial and sexual scandal he disappeared into oblivion. Pride says, 'Now I've gained so much experience I can manage on my own, thanks, God.'

If developing self-confidence means we rely on God less, then self-confidence becomes lethal in ministry – whatever kind of job we do for God. And why ever would we *want* to have confidence in someone who has no idea what is going to happen next, nor the strength to protect us? One of Solomon's proverbs, which he obviously ignored himself, says, 'the LORD will be your confidence and will keep your foot from being snared' (Prov. 3:26).

So, Lord, I don't ask you to 'give me confidence'; I declare that you *are* my confidence!

Bending the rules

Those who accept my commandments and obey them are the ones who love me.

John 14:21, NLT

The second cause of Solomon's downfall was disobedience. Our grandparents saw God as austere and vengeful; we rightly revel in His tender, accepting love, but if we go too far in this direction we begin to paint Him as an overindulgent 'sugar daddy'. God will not tolerate His rules being broken because He knows that our happiness, and that of others, depends on our keeping them.

Philip lived an apparently blameless life, deeply involved in his church and community, but when work was being particularly stressful he allowed himself a small secret sin. 'God will understand,' he thought, but as the years went by and pressures mounted, the little sin grew bigger until it could no longer be hidden. Finally it blew his life apart, damaging everyone he loved.

God actually appeared *twice* to Solomon, first to grant his wish but the second time to warn him of the terrible consequences of disobedience (1 Kgs 9:6–9). Hundreds of years before, Gad had given Israel's kings six specific rules of conduct (Deut. 17:16–20). Kings must not: be proud; accumulate enormous wealth; have many wives; make military or trade pacts with Egypt; or gain military strength by quantities of horses. Above all, kings must keep God's laws to the letter and one of them forbade marrying foreign wives. In his forty-year reign Solomon broke every one of those rules! He even married 1,000 women, 700 of whom were foreign princesses. These women were idol-worshippers and 'as Solomon grew old, his wives turned his heart after other gods' (1 Kgs 11:1–4).

Search me, O God, and know my heart . . . Point out anything in me that offends you.

(Ps. 139:23–24, NLT)

Faulty sights

One thing only do I want: to live in the LORD's house all my life, to marvel there at his goodness, and to ask for his guidance.

Ps. 27:4, GNB

Could another reason for Solomon's 'slippage' be that his life goal pointed him in slightly the wrong direction? Above everything in life Solomon wanted to be a great king, so he asked God for wisdom in order to achieve that goal. His father, David, expressed his goal in today's verse. It was God himself David wanted, not gifts with which to serve Him. To Solomon, God was remote: 'God is in heaven and you are on earth; therefore let your words be few' (Eccles. 5:2, AMP), but David's God was involved in every detail of his life. When Solomon achieved his goal and became a great king he discarded God. He had served His purpose by providing the wisdom that had made Solomon's goal obtainable, but He was no longer necessary.

David could never have done that – God was his life! 'My soul finds rest in God alone' (Ps. 62:1). In contrast we are told that, 'as Solomon grew old . . . his heart was not fully devoted to the LORD his God, as the heart of David his father had been' (1 Kgs 11:4).

What would you say was your life goal? Do your prayers indicate that you see God as a way of achieving that goal? Is He merely a quick fix for your problems, your personal genie of the lamp? If so, your heart is not 'fully devoted to Him' – but it could be. He would give you David's kind of passionate love if you asked Him for it.

JUNE 2

The hazard of ease

There is wonderful joy ahead, even though you have to endure many trials for a little while. These trials will show that your faith is genuine.

1 Pet. 1:6–7, NLT

This might sound odd to you, but I wonder if another of Solomon's problems was his *lack* of problems! We hate to see the people we love groping their way through terrible experiences – and I am sure God does too – but it is during those bad times that we learn to cling to Him like baby monkeys gripping their mother's fur as she leaps impossible-looking gaps. It is the good times that are dangerous, because there are no gaps to leap!

Solomon's father, David, experienced terrible times of suffering but in his 'valley of the shadow' he learnt to be sure of God's continuous presence (Ps. 23:4). Few things ever went wrong for Solomon. He never knew military defeat, personal failure or family disaster – and if he quarrelled with his wife he had 999 others to comfort him! When David's closest friends rejected him, he 'found strength in the LORD' (1 Sam. 30:6), but his son's popularity was dazzling. 'The whole world sought audience with Solomon to hear the wisdom God had put in his heart. Year after year, everyone who came brought a gift – articles of silver and gold, robes, weapons and spices, and horses and mules' (1 Kgs 10:25). Even the famous Queen of Sheba travelled all the way from Ethiopia and was stunned by the wonders of his court. Jesus knew what He was saying when He remarked, 'Woe to you when all men speak well of you' (Luke 6:26).

God whispers to us in our pleasures, speaks in our conscience, but shouts in our pains: it is His megaphone to rouse a deaf world.

C. S. Lewis (from *The Problem of Pain*)

When wisdom becomes foolishness

I even found great pleasure in hard work ... But as I looked at everything I had worked so hard to accomplish, it was all so meaningless – like chasing the wind.

Eccles. 2:10–11, NLT

Solomon, the once kind and popular king, ended up as a hated tyrant whose craving for magnificence was fed by crippling taxation and slave labour (1 Kgs 12:4). Depressed, he looked back over his life and admitted it had all been worthless vanity.

How could Solomon's famous wisdom have let him down so badly? I guess God withdraws His supernatural gifts when they become more important to us than He is. We long for gifts so we can live for Him more effectively, but we must realise that these gifts have to be handled carefully. We can take God's gift of music, teaching, leading, organising or healing and, instead of using it for God's glory, use it to fill our own inner yearning to be important, needed, accepted, popular and admired. Solomon stands as a terrible warning to those of us who ask God for ministry gifts, because God will not share His glory with anyone else. His gifts must always be held lightly on an open hand.

Solomon started his life by being told he was 'Loved by God' (2 Sam. 12:25); by the end of his life had God's feelings changed? No! Even when we no longer love God he still loves us, and even if we lose our faith in Him He continues to believe in us!

Imagine you were a fly on the wall during a committee meeting in hell. A group of demons are discussing which of your weaknesses they could use to destroy your Christian witness and relationship with God. Help them by drawing up a list and then ask God for protection!

For this I have Jesus

*I am most happy, then, to be proud of my weaknesses, in order to feel
the protection of Christ's power over me . . . For when I am weak,
then I am strong.*

2 Cor. 12:9–10, GNB

When I first heard the song written below it was sung by Sandra from
her wheelchair. She looked so small and frail but the words she was
singing gave us the clue to the strength that had carried her through
her forty-year fight with disability. As you read them, feel yourself
shifting everything that hurts over onto Jesus.

> *For the joys and for the sorrows*
> *The best and worst of times*
> *For this moment, for tomorrow*
> *For all that lies behind*
> *Fears that crowd around me*
> *For the failure of my plans*
> *For the dreams of all I hope to be*
> *The truth of what I am*
>
> *For this I have Jesus*
> *For this I have Jesus*
> *For this I have Jesus, I have Jesus . . .*
>
> *For the weakness of my body*
> *The burdens of each day*
> *For the nights of doubt and worry*
> *When sleep has fled away*
> *Needing reassurance*
> *And the will to start again*
> *A steely-eyed endurance*
> *The strength to fight and win*

Graham Kendrick (Copyright © 1994 Make Way Music)

Praying the Psalms

He who dwells in the secret place of the Most High shall abide under the shadow of the Almighty.

Ps. 91:1, ASV

This week feels like a nightmare! My granddaughter Emilia is dangerously ill and, in spite of prayer from all over the world, seems to be deteriorating. This morning I felt I had totally run out of prayers, so I decided to rewrite Psalm 91 and use that instead.

'Lord, I'm bringing Emilia into your secret place and snuggling her safely under your shadow (v. 1). *You* are her safe place (v. 2).

'You won't let Satan shoot her with his poisonous arrows (v. 3). Wrap her round with the duvet of your comforting love (v. 4) and don't let her be frightened by all the medical procedures and painful tests (v. 5).

'She has given her heart to you, so I claim your promise of protection (vv. 9–10). Surround her bed with your ministering angels; may they prevent any medical errors or dangerous infections (vv. 11–12). She and her parents love you and honour your name so I am trusting you to save them from disaster (v. 14).

'We know you hear us when we pray; I believe you have complete power and authority over this situation (v. 15). So I declare your promise to give Emilia a long and useful life (v. 16).'

I've carried the piece of paper around with me all day and declared it out loud everywhere I've gone! If the neighbours think I've gone mad that will be the least of my worries. Lots of the psalms can be adapted and personalised like this, so why not pick one and use it yourself?

Are you painfully disturbed just now? Then look up and receive the undisturbedness of the Lord Jesus . . . Lay it all out before Him and in the face of difficulty, bereavement and sorrow, hear Him say – 'Let not your heart be troubled.'

Oswald Chambers, *My Utmost for His Highest*

Ticking time bomb

Jesus left the temple and was walking away when his disciples came up to him to call his attention to its buildings . . . 'I tell you the truth, not one stone here will be left on another; every one will be thrown down . . .'

Matt. 24:1–2

They must have been horrified! They had been feeling so proud as they looked back at the magnificent temple Herod had just finished rebuilding. It looked so solid and permanent in the evening sunshine. To them it had seemed like a symbol of the new kingdom they thought Jesus the Messiah was about to establish.

They had been enjoying their evening walk over the Mount of Olives with the prospect of one of Martha's lavish suppers waiting in Bethany. As Jesus explained that the temple, and all Jerusalem, would soon be nothing but a flattened ruin, they were soon too stunned to feel remotely hungry. As they struggled to get their breath back, He went on to describe worse horrors that would happen further in the future (Matt. 24:6, 7, 9) and then a final global disaster that is still to take place (24:21, 29). 'Things will be so dreadful then,' He added, 'that unless my Father intervenes, the human race won't survive the catastrophe (v. 22), but it's right then, at the worst moment in history, that I'll come back and everyone in the whole world will see me' (v. 30).

Years later Peter recalled what Jesus said that evening and used it to pose a question to us all: 'The heavens will disappear with a roar; the elements will be destroyed by fire . . . Since everything will be destroyed in this way, what kind of people ought you to be?' (2 Pet. 3:10–12, NLT)

> *Oh! Teach us to live well! Teach us to live wisely and well!*
> *Come back, God – how long do we have to wait?*
> (Ps. 90:12–13, *The Message*)

Fact or fiction?

People were eating and drinking, marrying and giving in marriage, up to the day Noah entered the ark.

Matt. 24:38

It must have been hilarious watching someone labouring away for years to build a gigantic boat – miles from the sea! People simply ignored Noah's warnings of impending disaster and went back to their selfish little lives – until the rain began, and then it was too late!

Perhaps we all know, deep down, that our world can't survive much longer. TV experts constantly warn of catastrophic global pandemics, nuclear wars escalating out of control, widespread flooding caused by global warming, worldwide financial collapse, fatal food shortages and increasing natural disasters. Yet most of us just do the same as the people in Noah's day – shrug, and tell ourselves, 'The doom and gloom merchants have always loved telling us the world's about to end, but they've always been wrong!'

But they won't always be wrong! God has already placed in many different passages throughout the Bible detailed descriptions of the horrendous events that will finally destroy the world as we know it: 'blood and fire and billows of smoke. The sun will be turned to darkness and the moon to blood before the coming of the great and glorious day of the Lord' (Acts 2:19–20). He told us these things because He wanted us to realise that life down here on Earth is only a brief prelude to the real, lasting and gloriously happy life He has planned for us to enjoy with Him. For the vast majority of us, nothing is fair down here on earth, but God has promised to put everything right when we begin our real life in eternity.

Dear Brothers, you are only visitors here. Since your real home is in Heaven . . .

(1 Pet. 2:11, LB)

If contentment were here, Heaven were not Heaven.

Samuel Rutherford (c.1600–61)

One thing is certain!

They knew nothing about what would happen until the flood came and took them all away. That is how it will be at the coming of the Son of Man. Two men will be in the field; one will be taken and the other left.

Matt. 24:39b–40

How unnerving to be out shopping or working in your office when people begin vanishing all around you! Jesus says that's how it will be when He returns. Paul goes further: 'The Lord Himself will come down from heaven . . . and the dead in Christ will rise first. After that, we who are still alive . . . will be caught up together with them in the clouds to meet the Lord in the air. And so we will be with the Lord for ever' (1 Thess. 4:16–17). What a prospect, but will we 'be taken' before all the terrible events Jesus predicts (Matt. 24:29–30), or will He return *after* all these earth-shaking catastrophes? Theologians can't agree, but one thing is certain: our destiny is to live 'with the Lord for ever'!

Jesus says something else that is not so pleasant: 'One will be taken and the other left.' In passages such as Matthew 25:41–46 He makes it plain that not everyone will choose to spend eternity with Him. He said, 'Men loved darkness instead of light because their deeds were evil' (John 3:19). It isn't fashionable to talk about hell and judgement but it is Jesus Himself who tells us more about these things than the rest of the Bible put together.

Jesus, there are people close to me who have not yet chosen to follow you. I accept them the way they are because I love them, but please keep reminding me to pray that they will meet you and respond to your love – before it is too late.

Live as if . . .

So you also must be ready, because the Son of Man will come at an hour when you do not expect him.

Matt. 24:44

'Why doesn't God DO something?' Have you ever thought that as you watched reports of wars, tyranny or injustice? One day He is going to! John tells us: 'Look, He is coming with the clouds, and every eye will see Him, even those who pierced Him; and all the peoples of the earth will mourn because of Him' (Rev. 1:7). It really *is* going to happen! At long last, Jesus will give our universe a brand-new start, and rule it with love and justice! And you and I will be part of it, whether we have died or are still alive when He arrives.

Living in the light of that glorious prospect needs to change the way we live our lives now, altering our values and putting our grumbles and resentments into proportion (1 Pet. 1:13).

John, one of the men who heard Jesus talking about His return that evening on the Mount of Olives, later wrote, 'Everyone who has this hope in him purifies himself . . .' (1 John 3:3) and '. . . continue in Him, so that when He appears we may be confident and unashamed before Him at his coming' (1 John 2:28). I'll never forget an old lady in our church, called Mary. She cheered everyone up as she hurried about serving God in all kinds of little ways. She often told me to live each day as if I knew Jesus was coming back before bedtime!

Nothing done for Christ is lost. The smallest acts, the quietest words, the gentlest inspirations that touch human souls leave their impress for eternity.

J. R. Miller, In His Steps (1885; 1897)

Living on red alert

So then, have your minds ready for action. Keep alert and set your hope completely on the blessing which will be given you when Jesus Christ is revealed.

1 Pet. 1:13, GNB

'And what will *you* be doing when the trumpets announce that the Lord has returned?' boomed the preacher as he brought his sermon on the second coming to a dramatic crescendo. As we bowed our heads in prayer we all hoped we wouldn't be caught gossiping or indulging in our favourite besetting sin – cleaning the church loo would be far more appropriate! But does Jesus expect us to live on red alert?

We hear stories about fanatics who stopped work and gave away their possessions because they were so sure the second coming was imminent. Jesus tells us in Acts 1:7: 'It is not for you to know the times or dates the Father has set by His own authority.' So I think Jesus just wants us to go on faithfully doing the job He has given to each of us, and that is simply influencing others around us – neighbours, colleagues, family. He wants us to show them His reality because, as the evangelist Gipsy Smith (1860–1947) said, 'People don't read the Bible nowadays; they read us.' If they see that knowing Jesus actually makes us kinder, happier and more peaceful, they will want to know Him too. This is what Jesus wants each one of us to be doing for Him until He returns.

> *God has a place for you to fill, but it will take all of you to fill it.*
>
> Hugh Redwood (From *God in the Slums*,
> Hodder & Stoughton, 1932)

> *Lord, I long to hear you say, 'Well done, good and faithful servant! You have been faithful . . .'*
>
> (Matt. 25:21)

The battered foxglove

*Here is my servant, whom I uphold, my chosen one in whom I delight
... A bruised reed he will not break, and a smouldering wick he will
not snuff out.*

Isa. 42:1, 3

Last year I grew a very rare variety of foxglove from seed. My favourite
specimen was a subtle shade of salmon pink. One night in June we
had a terrible storm; heavy rain and violent wind battered my poor
foxglove to the ground and spattered it with mud. Then, in the morning,
the postman trod on it! Because it was so special to me I carefully
stood it up, and attached it to a strong stake with several pieces of
wire. Finally I carefully sprayed away all the ugly mud.

Later a friend arrived who is a GP in a large group practice. She
had been going through a horrendous time at work since a patient
had spread malicious lies about her. As we walked round the garden
she told me she felt on the edge of a breakdown and had decided to
leave the practice. Then she caught sight of my poor foxglove.

'That's how I've been feeling,' she said, 'battered and mud-splattered!'
Then, suddenly, she felt God say, 'I care about "bruised reeds". I will
stand beside you at work and "uphold" you like that strong stake. Let
me wash all that filthy mud away with the purity of my Holy Spirit.'

Those words gave her confidence to go back to work and face the
whole situation – which actually improved soon afterwards.

Lord, you tell us to 'consider the lilies', because they grow effortlessly
for your pleasure. Sorry that I often try too hard and then land in
the mud. Thank you for not giving up on me and for always being the
strong stake that 'upholds' me.

Separation anxiety

If I settle on the far side of the sea, even there your hand will guide me, your right hand will hold me fast. If I say, 'Surely the darkness will hide me and the light become night around me,' even the darkness will not be dark to you.

Ps. 139:9–12

My dog Stella suffers from separation anxiety! She is so devoted to me that her only goal in life is to stay as close to me as she possibly can. So she follows me constantly, like a shadow. If she discovers a door has closed between us she sits outside, crying plaintively; and when I go out without her, she lies by the front door, paralysed with fear that I have abandoned her. She is also blind, which makes her far more dependent than most dogs.

I wish I loved the Lord as 'doggedly' as Stella loves me! I know He is everywhere around me all the time, but I long to be more constantly conscious of His company – and more miserable when some 'door' separates us – such as the endless business of each day. Brother Lawrence, in his book *The Practice of the Presence of God*, tells us how he overcame that problem. He spent his life cooking in a busy monastery kitchen yet he realised that God was right there beside Him, enjoying every little thing he did. So he began to turn every activity of the day into an act of worship.

I turn the cake that is frying on the pan for love of Him . . . It is enough for me to pick up but a straw from the ground for the love of God . . . There is not in the world a kind of life more sweet and delightful, than that of a continual conversation with God.

Brother Lawrence (c. 1605–91)

The old rocking chair

Desperate, I throw myself on you; you are my God! Hour by hour I place my days in your hand, safe from the hands out to get me. Warm me, your servant, with a smile; save me because you love me. Don't embarrass me by not showing up.

Ps. 31:14–17a, *The Message*

When my three-year-old granddaughter, Molly, comes to my house she loves sharing my big soft rocking chair while we read all her favourite stories. One day I was out when my son brought her over to see me; she was very upset at first and searched the house for me, but when she finally flung herself down in my rocking chair she seemed comforted.

That old chair means a lot to me; for years it has been the place where I have met with God in the mornings. During the worst time of my life, a few years back, I was so grief-stricken that I couldn't even pray – but I used to sit there holding my Bible, not reading it, just holding it, as I rocked. 'If only God had big soft arms to hold and comfort me,' I used to think, but sometimes, when I was safely in that chair, I felt that was what He was doing. Nowadays, when something worries or upsets me during the day or when I just need to connect with Him, I throw myself down in that chair, imagining myself as a little girl running into the arms of her daddy. As I rock I repeat, 'Desperate I throw myself on you; you are my God!'

Do you have a special place where you can go and be when you need to be extra close to God?

Resting 'neath His smile

My beloved is mine, and I am his.

Song of Songs 2:16, KJV

Yesterday I spent the day with friends who waited ten years for a baby. Finally, three years ago, Gemma was born, and she is obviously the apple of their eye. Not only is she surrounded with everything and anything a child could want, but she is loved devotedly by both parents. All day they seemed unable to take their eyes off her and their besotted smiles followed her everywhere she went. As I drove back alone to my empty home, I thought, rather wistfully, 'I wonder what it would feel like to be as completely loved as that?' Then I remembered that I am. And so are you! Here is my favourite hymn, which actually says it all.

> *Jesus! I am resting, resting*
> *In the joy of what* Thou *art;*
> *I am finding out the greatness*
> *Of Thy loving heart.*
>
> *Oh how great Thy loving kindness,*
> *Vaster, broader than the sea!*
> *Oh how marvellous Thy goodness,*
> *Lavished all on me!*
>
> *Simply trusting Thee, Lord Jesus,*
> *I behold Thee as Thou art,*
> *And Thy love, so pure, so changeless,*
> *satisfies my heart.*
>
> *Ever lift Thy face upon me,*
> *As I work and wait for Thee,*
> *Resting 'neath Thy smile, Lord Jesus,*
> *Earth's dark shadows flee.*

Jean S. Pigott (1845–82)

Dog rose

Now when Jesus looked at him, He said, 'You are Simon the son of Jonah. You shall be called Cephas' (which is translated, [Peter] A Stone).

John 1:42, NKJV

This morning I was enjoying all my various rose bushes, which are just coming into their glorious 'first flush'. All their differing shades, shapes, sizes and scents were blending together so gloriously that I couldn't help whispering, 'O Lord, you were so clever to make roses!' Then I suddenly thought about the wild dog roses that are covering the hedges in the lanes round my home – very poor affairs in comparison to my cultivated blooms. They only have five petals and are either white or insipid pink!

'I suppose you didn't really make my roses at all, Lord,' I added. 'They are hybrids, created by the patient work of rose breeders over the last 250 years.' I wonder if it was the Lord replying when I suddenly realised that He had created those wild roses with the potential to be changed, over time and with expert help, into something infinitely more intricate and delightful. I guess He put that kind of potential into every human being born into this world. We are all entrusted with a life, which we can make ugly by selfishness or which, over our span of years – and with God's help – we can make into something infinitely beautiful.

When Jesus first looked at the rough, loud-mouthed, self-opinionated and tactless fisherman standing awkwardly before him the day he first met Simon, He saw the amazing man He could make him into during the years ahead. He promptly changed his name from Simon, which means 'wobbly reed blown by the wind', to Peter – a big solid standing stone. It was many years before that name fitted him well, but eventually Peter grew into the person Jesus knew he could be.

Please, Lord, help me to grow into the person you know I can be.

Poisoned well

*Elisha . . . was staying in Jericho. The men of the city said to Elisha,
'. . . the water is bad. . .' 'Bring me a new bowl,' he said, 'and put salt
in it.' Then he went out to the spring and threw the salt into it, saying,
'This is what the LORD says: "I have healed this water."'*

2 Kgs 2:19–21

I was running late, dashing round trying to get myself off by seven to
speak at a conference, and my frustration boiled over when my son
raced me to the bathroom. We yelled at each other through the locked
bathroom door, until I finally drove off unwashed and furious!

In the fast lane of the motorway I saw a picture in my head of
water bubbling up from deep inside me. I was handing out cups of it
to the thirsty women who would be at the conference that day, but as
they tried to drink they found the water was full of sharp slivers of
glass. As I thought about it I felt God say, 'Jen, your well is polluted.'
I'd read the story about Elisha just the day before, so I knew what He
meant! Jesus said, 'Whoever believes in me . . . streams of living water
will flow from within him' (John 7:38). His Spirit flows out of our
spirits to everyone we encounter, but my spring was contaminated by
anger. So, before I stood up to speak, I had to ask God's forgiveness,
then forgive my son and phone him to say I was sorry! I believe that
is the way to get a handful of His healing salt!

Lord, please keep my inner spring pure and fresh today.

The old teddy bear

The people who walked in darkness have seen a great light. They lived in a land of shadows, but now light is shining on them. You have given them great joy, LORD; you have made them happy.

Isa. 9:2–3a, GNB

Several of us had been helping to clear an old lady's attic when I found him. Squashed in a box full of rubbish, he looked so lonely and forlorn. All the love he had received eighty years before had worn away his fur and during his years of banishment the mice and moths had wrecked him. He leaked sawdust, his ears hung by threads and one glass eye was missing.

'Help yourself to anything you want, my dears,' the old lady told us, and while the others picked plates and vases I chose the teddy. 'These antique bears can be quite valuable,' I told them defensively. 'Not that one!' they replied.

On many evenings that winter I worked away at him, darning, patching, restoring and finally knitting him a colourful new suit and hat. He spent so long on my lap that we grew far too close to each other ever to be parted again. When I look at him now I often remember the promise Jesus makes to mend us when life messes us up (Isa. 61:1). He definitely does just that, but He does seem to take a very long time to do it sometimes! Perhaps it is while He does the mending that we grow 'too close to Him ever to be parted again'?

When we have been loved once but then forgotten, like my bear, loneliness hurts! But Jesus promises to be the sort of friend who never walks away (Heb. 13:5).

He is our clothing; out of love for us He wraps us around, fastens the clasp, and enfolds us in His love, so that He will never leave us.

Julian of Norwich

Door-keeper

How lovely is your dwelling-place, O Lord Almighty! My soul yearns, even faints, for the courts of the Lord . . . Better is one day in your courts than a thousand elsewhere; I would rather be a doorkeeper in the house of my God than dwell in the tents of the wicked.

Ps. 84:1–2, 10

As a child, I loved hearing Fred's story. He was in prison when, one night in his cell, he 'felt something'. He could never explain what it was, but, 'It was so lovely I hoped it would never stop.' The feeling remained throughout Fred's sentence and he cried when he was finally released. Because he thought his 'feeling' had something to do with God, he started visiting different churches, hoping to find it again; and it was while my father was preaching that Fred suddenly shouted in the middle of the sermon, 'It's here! I've found it!'

After his conversion Fred had to learn the lesson we all find hard: while God promises us His presence with us always, He never promises that we will always *feel* it. However, when Fred came to dinner he told me, 'You just has to know it in your knower!'

At the end of a special time at church, do you ever wish you could stay permanently in His presence? That is obviously how the psalmist felt when he wrote, 'I don't have to be one of those important priests in fine robes; I'd be happy to be the lowest servant in the temple so long as I could stay here – always.' Reaching such a depth of devotion is very rare. Most of us want God *and* a useful role plus the respect of others.

Could you honestly pray, 'Lord, I just want you; I don't need all the human perks and "emotional strokes" that come through serving you'?

When His power is greatest

My grace is all you need, for my power is greatest when you are weak.

2 Cor. 12:9a, GNB

In 1822 Charlotte Elliot would have described herself as a very religious young woman – until she had a chance encounter with a man who infuriated her by asking if she was a Christian. She quickly snubbed him, but for three weeks she thought of nothing else. Fortunately she 'chanced' to meet the man again and told him how she had been trying to find Jesus. 'You have nothing of merit to bring to God. You must come just as you are,' he replied. Charlotte later wrote the hymn which has brought thousands to Jesus all over the world:

> *Just as I am, without one plea*
> *but that Thy blood was shed for me*
> *and that Thou bid'st me come to Thee*
> *O Lamb of God, I come! I come!*

All her life Charlotte suffered from illness and crippling fatigue. Confined to her home feeling useless, she often wished she could do wonderful things for the Lord like her brother, Henry, who was a clergyman with a highly successful ministry. She did not live to hear him say one day, when his work was being highly praised, 'I feel far more has been done by a single hymn of my sister's – "Just As I Am".'

O Lamb of God, I come.

A swallow's heart

*We . . . will be caught up together with them in the clouds to meet the
LORD in the air. And so we will be with the LORD forever.*

1 Thess. 4:17

This is an extract from my journal, written during a retreat in Wales
when an illness made walking impossible.

> Lord I'd love to walk off all the cares and responsibilities of my
> life on those hills but I'm tethered here in this chair, imprisoned
> by pain.
>
> But, Lord, look at those swallows! Diving, darting, soaring,
> circling. Let my spirit dance with you like that. I want to share
> your joy as we wheel round and round above the valley together,
> plunging down, rising up, free of this pain which restricts me,
> and the burden of my work which distracts and drains me. I
> want to fly free with you, rising into the blue sky above the
> morning mists, higher and higher, and see the world below as
> you see it, looking like a map laid out for our pleasure.
>
> Oh, Lord, give me that kind of zest for life; help me appreciate
> the glorious fun of being 'caught up . . . in the air' with you.
> Please give me the heart of a swallow!
>
> *I wish I had wings, like a dove. I would fly away and find rest.
> I would fly far away and live in the wilderness. I would quickly
> find myself a shelter from the raging wind and the storm.*
>
> (Ps. 55:6–8, GNB)

A swift's heart

*My heart and my flesh cry out for the living God. Even the sparrow
has found a home, and the swallow a nest for herself, where she may
have her young – a place near your altar, O LORD Almighty, my King
and my God.*

Ps. 84:2–3

Another extract from my journey, during a retreat in Wales:

Yes, Lord, I'd love the heart of a swallow, but I don't want the
heart of a swift! They never land, but keep up in the sky, flying
continuously, even sleeping on the wing – sometimes for as long
two years at a stretch! They keep themselves safe from predators
by their perpetual motion, and I am beginning to realise that I
protect myself from my fears and pain by perpetual busyness!
Perhaps I am afraid of the whole aloneness thing? I banish the
silence, when I am at home, by putting on the TV, radio or background music. I keep checking my emails or using my mobile
phone because I hate feeling unconnected – I will do anything
to distract myself from the dreaded sense of isolation. Yet I know
that only you can fill my loneliness. Help me to find a home for
my spirit like a swallow in her nest by your altar so that you
and you alone can fill my solitude and still my restlessness. As
Pascal once said, 'The sole cause of man's unhappiness is that
he does not know how to stay quietly in his room.'

*Leave me here freely all alone,
In cell where never sunlight shone,
should no one ever speak to me,
This golden silence makes me free.*

Titus Brandsma (1881–1942), who died
as a prisoner in Dachau concentration camp

Under His wings

I will hide beneath the shadow of your wings until the danger passes by.

He will cover you with his feathers, and under his wings you will find refuge.

Ps. 57:1, NLT, Ps. 91:4

As a shepherd, out on the hills, David must often have watched mother birds fluffing out their feathers over their nests, because he talks about hiding under the Lord's outstretched wings in several of his psalms. As a child I loved our hens, particularly when one had a clutch of chicks. If a cat appeared in the yard, the hen would fluff herself up to three times her size while she called her chicks with urgent clucks. They would race from all directions and completely disappear under her widespread wings. One terrible day one of the chicks decided to be independent, and fluttered up onto a hay bale instead of running to his mum when a dog appeared in the yard. The consequences were gruesome!

Once a weasel got into the henhouse at night. Most of the chickens escaped by flying up onto the high perches, but one stayed in the nest box, protecting her nine chicks, while the weasel latched onto her neck and sucked the blood from her body. We found her dead in the morning, still sitting on her chicks – who were all alive and well. Jesus said, 'How often I have longed to gather your children together, as a hen gathers her chicks under her wings, but you were not willing' (Matt. 23:37). I'm still so prone to run to my own 'hay bales' rather than to Jesus, who gave His lifeblood for my protection.

> *Other refuge have I none,*
> *hangs my helpless soul on Thee;*
> *cover my defenceless head*
> *with the shadow of Thy wing.*
> *Thou, O Christ, art all I want;*
> *more than all in Thee I find.*

Charles Wesley (1707–88)

Fragile life

A bruised reed he will not break, and a smouldering wick he will not snuff out.

He won't brush aside the bruised and the hurt and he won't disregard the small and insignificant.

Isa. 42:3, NIV, *The Message*

During painful or confusing times, so many of us feel, 'I just don't seem able to hear God any more.' Try reading this poem and think of God saying these words to you. A friend of mine, Dean, wrote it while he was going through a tough time himself.

Fragile Life

Fragile Life, I will protect you
Tender shoot you will grow strong
And in my hands you'll show my splendour
And in your heart I'll place my song

Fragile Life, I will not break you
Heart so bruised I'll make you whole
Flickering flame you will burn brightly
Your faith in trials refined like gold

Fragile life, my Spirit in you
Will bring you safe to heaven's shore
And here complete you'll stand before me
To share my joy forevermore

Dean Gardner, 7 March 2009

Journey into God's heart

For God so loved the world that he gave his one and only Son, that whoever believes in him shall not perish but have eternal life.

John 3:16

For each of us, our life on this Earth is a journey. It begins when the sperm and the ovum unite and finishes when our spirit finally leaves the body behind. As on all long journeys there are exciting times, boring patches, bewildering changes, and stretches of anxiety and grief, but because life is a journey we have no choice but to keep moving forward. How is your journey going at the moment? Are you trudging through a desert, lazing in green pastures, or clawing your way up a precipice?

For some of us another journey begins at some time during our earthly travels. The moment we open the innermost core of our being and invite God's Spirit to join with our spirit this new journey begins, which will last for ever because it leads us right into God's heart.

The Bible describes many people who made journeys and, although their experiences were physical, they still offer plenty of tips for spiritual travellers. So, at this time of year when many of us are eagerly anticipating journeys to holiday destinations, it might be fun to look at some of those biblical journeys. First, however, let's stop for a moment and focus on the most important journey of all time. It was the journey that God made from heaven to earth.

Thank you, Lord Jesus, for turning your back on heaven and stepping down onto this earth. You came to buy me a ticket, at very great cost, so that I could journey back with you, to live in your home with you for ever. Sometimes the journey feels very hard but thank you that I will never have to travel alone.

Journey into the unknown

By faith Abraham, when called to go to a place he would later receive as his inheritance, obeyed and went, even though he did not know where he was going.

Heb. 11:8

When I set out on a journey I like to have every detail organised, so I feel sorry for Abraham. There he was, living in a luxurious house in a beautiful city, with a loving wife and successful business. At seventy-five he was looking forward to a peaceful old age when God told him to sell up and set off on a journey – but neglected to give him a destination! If he had been like me he would have said, 'I'm not leaving here until you tell me where you want me to go and what you want me to do.' The Bible does not tell us if Abraham argued, only that he obeyed, but it does make it clear that he found the next twenty years very difficult until God made His plans a little more clear.

Sometimes our faith journey takes us along a smooth, level path; we are jogging along happily when suddenly a wide chasm opens up right in front of us. God seems to be expecting us to take a 'leap of faith' even though we can't see the path continuing on the far side of the terrifying gap. God presented Abraham with this 'faith gap' because faith is God's priority for us all (Heb. 11:6). God knows that it grows best when we have to launch ourselves off into the unknown without having a clue where we are going to land!

Lord, you are propelling me out of all my safe routines, familiar structures and safe networks, and all I know for sure is that you are there to catch me if I fall. (Deut. 33:27)

Journey into exile

If God will be with me and will watch over me on this journey I am taking . . . then the LORD will be my God.

Gen. 28:20–21

Jacob was running away from his brother's murder threats. All his life he had been scared of Esau, who was big, strong and definitely their father's favourite. Jacob was the quiet one who never seemed able to win his father's approval.

Like many people who grow up feeling second best, and a disappointment to their parents, Jacob thought that God also disapproved of him. His mother had always told him that, before her twins were born, God told her that the younger one would inherit the family wealth, but, rather than rest back and trust God to fulfil His promise, Jacob decided to help God out – with disastrous consequences!

As he lay down on the first night of his journey the loneliness must have been unbearable. Would he ever see his family again? God must be so angry with him. Then it happened! In the night God spoke to him: 'I'm here, I'll take care of you. I'll never leave you.'

Trusting God fully is impossible until we have grasped the fact that He really loves us and wants only the best for us. Knowing that for sure can be a real struggle if we were never certain of our parents' love, but God is able to make it a reality in our hearts – if we ask Him. After years of not feeling sure of God's approval I asked Him for a 'Bethel experience'. It was not dramatic like Jacob's, just a deep-down knowing that I was loved. When we make the fact of God's love for us the bedrock of our lives, we face the world quite differently.

Have you asked for a 'Bethel' yet?

Journey of pilgrimage

Then come, let us go up to Bethel, where I will build an altar to God,
who answered me in the day of my distress and who has been with
me wherever I have gone.

Gen. 35:3

Last summer I was standing on the edge of a towering cliff overlooking
a blue Devonshire sea. The spot is called Jenny's Leap but I wasn't
planning to jump! I was at Lee Abbey, a Christian conference centre,
and I had climbed the path to find some space! Suddenly I realised a
man was sitting on the seat behind me and seemed anxious to talk.

'I came to this very spot thirty years ago and gave my life to God,
unreservedly,' He told me. 'I've worked abroad ever since but often
thought of Jenny's Leap and what happened to me here. So I decided
to come back and remake that commitment to God.'

He reminded me of Jacob, who had *his* life-changing experience at
Bethel. Both men had wanted to go back to the place where they had
encountered God, perhaps because the pressures and hassles of work
and family life had dimmed their vision of Him. They also wanted to
thank God for His protection and care.

Do you ever feel homesick for God? Of course, we can return to
Him in our hearts any time, anywhere, however far away we have
drifted, or however bad the mess surrounding us. Yet it can sometimes
be deeply helpful to go back to a place that was important in the past.
As we stand there again, looking back at the years in between, we can
measure our progress along our spiritual journey.

In returning and rest shall ye be saved; in quietness and in
confidence shall be your strength.

(Isa. 30:15, KJV)

Journeying away from God

But Jonah ran away from the LORD.

Jon. 1:3

Sometimes I used to share my dog walks with Anne and her Jack Russell, Scruff. While my Phoebe seemed to like walking as close to me as possible, Scruff's passion for rabbits sent him deep into the woods, where he would disappear for hours. We would search endlessly, shouting ourselves hoarse and telling each other stories about Jack Russells that get stuck down rabbit holes, too deep for anyone to hear their frantic cries. Finally he would reappear to enjoy a rapturous welcome; but one day he didn't come back – ever.

I envy people who trot close to the Lord's heels throughout their spiritual journey, but some of us come and go, like Scruff. Often the reason we leave God's side is that something, or someone, else temporarily becomes more important or attractive to us; but, like Scruff's rabbits, we are in danger of being permanently trapped by them.

Jonah left God because he was cross! God told him to go to the enemy city of Nineveh and tell them He would destroy them completely unless they repented. Jonah loathed these cruel people; he was furious with God for offering mercy, so off Jonah went in the opposite direction. Our journeys away from God often begin when we feel disappointed by Him or resent the hard things He allows to touch our lives – or the lives of people we love.

Lord, my heart does feel a bit cold towards you right now. I'm going through the motions of being a 'good Christian' on the outside, but I know I've secretly turned my back on you. I feel lost and alone without you; nothing ever replaces the joy of walking close to you. I know you will welcome me if I return, but please help me not to be too proud to come.

The 'make or break' journeys

His brothers pulled Joseph up out of the cistern and sold him for twenty shekels of silver.

Gen. 37:28

What a terrible start to one of the saddest journeys in the Bible. What must Joseph have felt as he stumbled towards Egypt, hands bound, neck clamped in an iron collar, dragged like a dog into slavery? Each faltering step took him further from the father who loved him, his comfortable home and the person he had always been, and nearer to a new and humiliating identity among strangers.

Disaster can strike any of us at any time, and when life kicks us out of safe familiarity we are forced to begin a journey – the journey of adjustment to change and loss. It can either break us, or make us. Some people 'never get over' their tragedies or seem able to begin to live again, while others grow enormously through them. Joseph's journey to Egypt changed him from a spoilt brat into a man of strength. Jewish rabbis translate the description of his journey in Psalm 105:18 as the time when 'iron entered into his soul'.

Why didn't his terrible experience damage him? Because 'the LORD was with Joseph' (Gen. 39:2). He may often have felt abandoned, as we all do when change undermines our security, but he came to recognise God's presence was with him and, even when he had lost everything, God's hand was still there – guiding him all the way. Years later when he met his brothers again he was able to say, 'You intended to harm me, but God intended it for good' (Gen. 50:20).

People sometimes do rob us of all that matters to us most, and permanently alter our lives, but they can only destroy us if we let them.

Journey of discovery

The Queen of Sheba said to Solomon: 'The report I heard in my own country about your achievements and your wisdom is true. But I did not believe these things until I came and saw with my own eyes.'

1 Kgs 10:6–7

As a child I was fascinated by a Victorian painting of the moment when the Queen of Sheba arrived at Solomon's magnificent palace. The king sits enthroned in his sumptuous robes surrounded by life-sized golden lions, marble pillars and embroidered hangings. Sheba looks like a glamorous girl about to perform the dance of the seven veils! Actually she was a highly intelligent woman driven to make the massive journey from the far side of Arabia by her desire to know if this famous king held the key to the wisdom she craved.

Hundreds of years later three wise men took the same route for their long journey to Jerusalem. Like the Queen of Sheba they rode camels, carried gifts of gold and spices and were searching for a king who was wisdom personified. They found Him at last but in vastly different circumstances! No marble palace for Him, just a borrowed stable; no golden furniture but an animal feeding stall; no grand robes, He was wrapped in rags – and His courtiers were a few surprised farm animals.

Jesus did not need to impress human beings with His limitless wealth, power and wisdom, He came to demonstrate His limitless love – love that wanted to be identified with the homeless and the rejected, and love that longed to share all His wisdom and wealth with anyone who wanted them (Phil. 4:19).

Please, Jesus, give me the same kind of urgent need to know you that inspired those wise people to make that costly journey. Please increase my thirst for you and forgive my apathy.

The summer garden

I planted, Apollos watered, but God [all the while] was making it grow . . . For we are fellow workmen – labourers together with God; you are God's garden and vineyard . . . under cultivation.

1 Cor. 3:6, 9, AMP

I never get over the miracle of July! All the tiny seeds I planted in the greenhouse during the winter are now filling my garden with vivid colour. 'Isn't God clever,' remarked my three-year-old granddaughter. She is right, but not yet old enough to realise how much human hard work is involved in making a garden beautiful! I had certainly played my part in the miracle!

If we are God's garden, I suppose keeping our spiritual lives beautiful is also a partnership and often hard work on our part. I remember once helping my son move into a 'student house'. It was clean enough inside, but the garden had not been touched in years. As I fought my way through the jungle of weeds I realised someone had once filled that garden with roses but bindweed had wound itself round the bushes, strangling their beauty, while giant nettles stole their light. I shuddered as I realised how easily my own garden could look like this. I pounce on weeds as soon as they show their ugly heads because they are so easy to pull when they're small. Surely it's the same with 'spiritual weeds'? Those resentful thoughts, discontented grumbles and negative self-pity can be removed comparatively easily if we 'yank them out' quick! If we ignore them or even 'water them' with encouragement they soon 'take over' and start spoiling everything that is beautiful and valuable in the rest of our lives.

Thank you, Lord, that I don't have to clear all these weeds from my life on my own. I pull them out but you burn them at your cross.

'All creatures great and small . . .'

Do you know when the mountain goats give birth? . . . Do you give the horse his strength or clothe his neck with a flowing mane? . . . Does the eagle soar at your command and build his nest on high?

Job 39:1,19, 27

My brother and I once explored a remote area of Canada's coastline in his little old boat. We saw creatures that would probably never be seen by another human but, according to Job 39, God was deeply interested in every individual eagle, mountain goat, seal, otter and beaver. We only caught fleeting glimpses, but He is continuously absorbed by every detail of their lives.

Job had gone through a terrible experience of multiple loss; he reacted wonderfully at first, gaining his reputation for patience, but then his faith dipped badly. He began wondering why a God who had always cared for him could allow so many bad things to happen (a normal reaction to grief, but Job didn't know that!). He spent chapters of his book arguing and questioning until finally God cut in, reminding Job of His awesome power, and adding: 'If I care so much for all these creatures that no one else will ever enjoy, then surely you must believe how much more I care for you?' That was the gist of what God said, and it reminds me how Jesus assures us that we are infinitely more valuable than the millions of dusty little city sparrows, yet God knows and cares about every one of them too!

For every animal of the forest is mine, and the cattle on a thousand hills. I know every bird in the mountains, and the creatures of the field are mine . . . for the world is mine, and all that is in it.

(Ps. 50:10–12)

Consider the ravens

'I have ordered the ravens to feed you.'

'Consider the ravens: They do not sow or reap, they have no storeroom or barn; yet God feeds them. And how much more valuable you are than birds!'

1 Kgs. 17:4, Luke 12:24

'Ravens are horrid birds,' I decided as I watched these scavengers raiding our Canadian campsite larder. 'No wonder God pronounced them unclean' (Deut. 14:4). Then I remembered what they did for Elijah. He was in terrible danger: King Ahab and his wicked wife, Jezebel, were furious with the prophet and were scouring the country in their desire to kill him. Nowhere was safe from their spies except this mountain hideout, but Elijah could not have survived so far from any source of food without the scavenging instincts of those ravens. Where they stole that daily cache of bread and meat from is a mystery, but the *miracle* is that they shared it with Elijah! I realised that as I tried to retrieve our precious sausages from these sharp-beaked thieves!

Surely it would have been easier for God to conjure up food from thin air, as He did later in Elijah's story (1 Kgs 19)? Why involve the ravens at all? Perhaps He just wanted to show us that He is in control. Paul says of Jesus, 'Everything was created through him and for him. He existed before anything else, and He holds all creation together' (Col. 1:16–17). He can command the weather and prevent rain for three years just as easily as He can order the wild, untamed ravens to do His bidding.

Lord, please forgive me for categorising people too fast – for writing them off as 'unspiritual' before I have time to see that you are using them in some unusual way that is unique to them alone.

Eagle love

He [God] shielded him and cared for him; he guarded him as the apple of his eye, like an eagle that stirs up its nest and hovers over its young, that spreads its wings to catch them and carries them on its pinions.

Deut. 32:10–11

My brother and I saw a lot of eagles during that holiday in Canada. Once we stood under a gigantic nest perched high in an immensely tall tree; the mother sat looking down at us threateningly, while the father circled overhead. They were both guarding the 'apple of their eye' with sharp beaks and claws; we would touch that nest at our peril! As we walked away I thought, 'God feels just as protective about me. If only I could grasp just how valuable I am to him, I would never be afraid of anything ever again!' But have you noticed what a strange way God sometimes has of showing His love? Not always comfortable, is it?

The eagle's love for its chicks is 'tough' too. Because their nests are so often built high up, leaving it must feel terrifying for the chicks. They would probably sit there comfortably for ever if the mother eagle did not begin to demolish the nest and nudge them out, forcing them to try their wings or plummet. They often can't manage more than a few feeble flaps before their little wings tire, but father eagle is already in place, underneath, ready to catch them on his wings and carry them down to a safer practice ground.

Have you even been brutally moved out of your comfort zone, and thrust into a situation where you could no longer lean on your own skills or resources? When we have no option but to trust God completely, that is when we discover that we actually CAN!

Ram on cue

Abraham looked up and there in a thicket he saw a ram caught by its horns. He went over and took the ram and sacrificed it as a burnt offering instead of his son.

Gen. 22:13

As I watched the exhausting efforts of a farmer trying to get three rams out of a field and down the lane to his yard, I suddenly realised how remarkable it was that God provided that ram at the precise moment it was needed most. Had it wandered up the mountain a few hours earlier it would have died from exposure to the blistering sun; if it had been later the consequences would have been tragic, but it arrived right on cue in order to give its life for a young boy called Isaac. An insignificant old sheep died so that a precious son might live. Years later, on the same spot, a precious son died so a worthless old nobody like me could have everlasting life! God certainly is a wonderful provider.

In the Old Testament, if someone sinned and broke one of God's commandments, they could take a lamb to God's house. There the priest would symbolically lay on that lamb the sins they had committed and then it would be killed. The lamb took the death sentence so its owner could be free of punishment. Three years before Jesus died, when he came to the River Jordan to be baptised, John the Baptist said, 'Look, the Lamb of God, who takes away the sin of the world!' (John 1:29b). John was the first person to realise that Jesus had come to this Earth to die in our place and to 'take the rap' that we deserved.

Lord, like that ram, help me to serve you effectively by always being in the right place at the right time.

The fish and the worm

But the LORD provided a great fish to swallow Jonah, and Jonah was inside the fish three days and three nights . . . And the LORD commanded the fish, and it vomited Jonah onto dry land.

Jon. 1:17; 2:10

One day my brother was driving down a lonely forest road in Canada. He was late for a preaching engagement so he didn't bother to slow down as he approached the ungated railway crossing – so few trains ever used that stretch of track. Suddenly a dog ran into the road, right in front of his car! Screeching to a halt he just missed it – and then he saw the train! If he had not slowed for the dog he would certainly have been killed. Was that a co-incidence or a God-incidence? And what about the timely arrival of Jonah's fish?

Later in Jonah's story God again demonstrated His control over the natural world; He didn't use a huge fish this time – but a tiny worm. Jonah was hiding under a vine feeling very angry with God for showing mercy to his enemies, the people of Nineveh. He wanted them dead – not forgiven! So he hid in a nice shady spot, nursing his resentments, but God sent a little bug to eat the root of the vine and it died, leaving Jonah exposed to the sun's heat. Sometimes it is a small, insignificant irritation that finally releases the pent-up emotions hidden deep inside us. Jonah vented his fury at length, but expressing it to God obviously did him so much good that he was finally able to understand God's compassion for the city his preaching had just saved (Jon. 4:11).

Does God need to send a worm to demolish your private hiding hole?

Poisonous snakes

So Moses made a bronze snake and put it up on a pole. Then when anyone was bitten by a snake and looked at the bronze snake, he lived.

Num. 21:9

Jonah was delighted when God used a fish to help him, but mad about the worm He sent later. During their forty-year-long journey through the wilderness, God's people were equally pleased with the flocks of quail He 'blew' in their direction, but infuriated when He spoke to them through snakes!

God is amazingly long-suffering but He really loathes grumbles and complaints, and yet our churches are riddled with them! We feel we have a right to criticise our vicar, moan about the failures of others and generally blame God for everything that goes wrong. Grumbling smothers joy, distances us from others and dulls our faith.

God put up with the endless complaints of His people for a long time but finally His patience snapped. Sending poisonous snakes sounds a bit drastic, but He also provided them with an instant snakebite cure. All the victims had to do was look up at the model snake on the pole, yet some of them probably criticised Moses for that too, complaining that it was too simple, and using their own remedies – with fatal consequences!

When the snakes failed to cure their endless grouching, they were sentenced to wandering in the wilderness for forty years until they had eradicated the habit. If grumbling about the weather, the government, church affairs or aches and pains is one of your habits, remember how much God hates it! Grumbling can become a habitual mindset, but like all habits it can be changed with practice.

Learning to replace negatives with positives can have a wonderfully healing effect on our bodies, minds and emotions, not to mention our spiritual well-being!

Animal rights

A righteous man cares for the needs of his animal . . .

Prov. 12:10

When I was eight my father bought me two guinea pigs, called Punch and Judy.

'No one else is going care for them,' he explained. 'If you don't they'll suffer terribly and it will be your fault.' I looked after those pets (and their numerous offspring) so conscientiously that now, sixty years later, I still dream I've forgotten to feed them!

'You are just as helplessly dependent on God as your guinea pigs are on you,' my father explained, and I think I learned more about God's love through Punch and Judy than I did in Sunday school!

I never realised until recently how many times God urges us to be good to our animals. He wants us to give them a day off each week (Exod. 23:12), and feed them well: 'Do not muzzle an ox while it is treading out the grain' (Deut. 25:4). God's compassion shows when He tells us not to take a mother bird away from her helpless babies (Deut. 22:6) and when He insists we help a lost and bewildered ox or an overloaded donkey collapsing under its burden – even if they happen to belong to our enemy (Exod. 23:4–5).

Recently I heard a doctor lecturing on stress. He said research shows that keeping animals or birds greatly reduces tension and decreases the risk of heart attack, stroke and depression. God built into all human beings the need to be needed!

Lord, thank you for giving us animals to enrich our lives. You entrusted them into our care, and one day we will have to give you an account of the way we have looked after them. Please forgive us for failing them so often and not standing up for their rights.

The talking donkey

Then the LORD opened the donkey's mouth, and she said to Balaam,
'What have I done to you to make you beat me these three times?'

Num. 22:28

This self-important little soothsayer was determined to impress the
king by cursing a national enemy – even when God told him not to!
On his way an angel blocked the path; his donkey saw it immediately
but Balaam was blinded by self-interest. I am sure animals are more
aware of the supernatural than adult humans are, but children often
seem to see angels, or Jesus Himself. 'Imagination,' say adults and, as
the child grows up, he also accepts that explanation. Animals are not
so gullible!

In our arrogance we believe only in things we can detect by our
senses or explain scientifically. Yet we are constantly surrounded by
unseen beings, which God only occasionally allows someone to glimpse
(2 Kgs 6:17). I am sure He lets animals see them far more often.

One night, during a speaking tour, I had to sleep alone in an old
farmhouse. It looked charming when I arrived, but my Labrador,
Brodie, flatly refused to go inside – her hair stood up like a Mohican!
I had to yank her in by force, but how I wish I'd heeded her warning
and made for a hotel! That night her furious barking woke me; an
evil figure was towering over my bed, telling me to 'Go away!' When
I found the light there was no one there – but I spent the rest of the
night settling Brodie (and myself) by repeating the name of Jesus and
playing praise music – loudly. Later, I heard that others had also been
troubled in that house.

Thank you, Lord Jesus, that all things visible and invisible have been
put under your authority. Knowing you means I need fear nothing and
no one!

The first zoologist

God said to Noah, 'I am going to put an end to all people, for the earth is filled with violence . . . make yourself an ark of cypress wood . . . I am going to bring floodwaters on the earth to destroy all life . . . You are to bring into the ark two of all living creatures, male and female, to keep them alive with you.

Gen. 6:12–19

Children love to hear about Noah chasing ostriches, climbing after monkeys, netting bats and holding his nose as he pursued skunks, but all that may have happened many years before the first drops of rain. Noah may have watched and collected wildlife since boyhood and he was 600 when God called him! If you had a passionate interest in nature, were extremely fit and had nothing else to do, you could build up an extensive zoo in that much time! Perhaps he learnt his magnificent carpentry skills making pens for them.

God always prepares and trains his servants years in advance, long before they realise what He is doing. During three months in bed as a child with rheumatic fever I learnt to touch-type – for fun – but years later God used the skill when He called me to become a writer. Mavis loved making interesting soups for her large family; when they all left home she missed the saucepan bubbling on the hob. She felt too old and much too shy to offer help when her church embarked on a town-wide outreach – until she heard they needed someone to make soup for the homeless. She has been doing that for the last ten years and has helped many 'no-hopers' to find new hope in the Lord.

Is your sport, hobby or interest a tool God could use to draw people into His kingdom – if you offered it to Him?

Warhorses

Woe to those who go down to Egypt for help, who rely on horses, who trust in the multitude of their chariots and in the great strength of their horsemen, but do not look to the Holy One of Israel, or seek help from the LORD.

Isa. 31:1

There is no way I would ever put my trust in a horse! After some bad experiences I prefer them safely on the far side of thick hedges! In Bible times they were the equivalent of today's fast cars, military tanks, tractors and even family saloons. They were also the status symbol that cars are today, and the more warhorses a king had, the safer he felt and the more respect he commanded. Recently I visited the ruins of one of the magnificent stables that King Solomon built to house thousands of his Egyptian warhorses. The sight of all those chariots and mounted soldiers plunging over the plains, manes flying, made him feel invincible and may have been one of the reasons why his faith in God began to dwindle.

We sing hymns and songs about trusting God until we convince ourselves that we do, but deep down we could be looking to money in the bank to provide our security, or we feel safe because we have a good job, have found someone to love and affirm us, or have a role that makes us feel good about ourselves. These are all good things, but they are not permanent; eventually they dissolve with age, illness, death, rejection or misfortune. God is the only safe and everlasting source of life.

Lord, I give you permission to show me if I am depending on a 'warhorse' to make me feel secure – rather than on your wisdom, protection and approval.

The dawn chorus

Every morning I will sing aloud of your constant love.

Ps. 59:16, GNB

It is so quiet where I live in the country that the birds always wake me early on a summer morning. The dawn chorus reminds me of the first time I encountered Jesus. I was four and terrified of the dark. One night I woke up, too frightened to call for my mother. She'd told me that Jesus sat on my bed all night and would always help me if I needed Him. I had never believed her, but I was so frightened I said 'Help!' silently inside my head. At that moment a bird began to sing, then another; a cuckoo joined in and soon a whole choir were singing at full throttle. The wartime blackout curtains prevented me from realising it was light outside, but the sheer beauty of the sound delighted and comforted me and I fell asleep, firmly believing Jesus had arranged the concert just for me!

The birds in my garden seem to sing so loudly; they are probably just marking their territory, but I like to think they start their day by praising their creator. I wish I did! Often my first thought on waking is, 'Oh no! Today I've got to . . .' or 'How am I going to cope with . . .' Recently I've been trying to reach out to God instead as I wake, asking Him to refill me with His Spirit and thanking Him for something specific before I start bombarding Him with all my fears, grumbles and requests.

Satisfy us in the morning with your unfailing love, that we may sing for joy and be glad all our days.

(Ps. 90:14)

Lions and lambs

See, the Lion of the tribe of Judah . . . has triumphed . . . Worthy is the Lamb, who was slain, to receive power and wealth and wisdom and strength and honour and glory and praise!

Rev. 5:5, 12

No other animal is as magnificent, bold or ferocious as a lion and, in contrast, a lamb is totally helpless and vulnerable, yet the Bible likens Jesus to both. In the Gospels the two sides of His character existed side by side. Lion-like He demolished an entire market single-handed and fearlessly harangued religious leaders and politicians, calling them hypocrites! Lamb-like He played with children, cared for the elderly and disabled, and allowed Himself to be wrongly accused, tortured and slaughtered without a word of self-defence.

Because God's desire is that we should become Jesus look-a-likes (Rom. 8:29) we need both the lion and the lamb in us too, but it is vital that we hold them in perfect tension. Some people who are naturally gifted and full of enthusiasm view the tasks God gives them with a lion's boldness. Yet when we rely on our own skills and experience we are in danger of doing things in our own strength and forgetting that we are actually as helpless and inadequate as lambs.

On the other hand, many of us feel so much like weak little lambs that we lie down in the buttercups and daisies and never attempt anything for God. It is when we allow His lion-like spirit to fill us that little lambs can change the world!

Lord, I know that it is often the people who secretly feel weak and vulnerable who roar like fierce lions to make others think they are strong! And really strong people are sometimes surprisingly gentle. So please give me genuine strength, which shows itself in gentleness.

Fleas

*Your enemy the devil prowls around like a roaring lion looking for
someone to devour.*

1 Pet. 5:8

The Lord has been speaking to me recently, through fleas! My dogs
have never had the problem before – but suddenly, a month ago, Stella
began to scratch. The pet shop recommended various cures but nothing
worked; the scratching grew worse until it became continuous and
drove us both demented! So we went to the vet.

'It only takes one to jump on board,' he said kindly, 'then, hey-
presto, there'll be thousands!' He parted the hair at the back of Stella's
neck in the shape of a cross and applied some oil. By the next day
peace reigned once again!

Christians pick up fleas just as easily as curly-haired spaniels. These
fleas don't bite; they talk to us instead: 'Poor old you; no one appre-
ciates you . . . they never say thank you.' The kind that hop on me say,
'You'll never cope; you might as well give up now.' I believe these fleas
come straight out of hell to torment us and ruin our peace. Of course
I'm not suggesting that we are demonised or possessed by the devil
when we are plagued by these negative thoughts, but our enemy loves
to bully and discourage us by planting them in our minds. Perhaps we
are more likely to spot him when he prowls around like a 'roaring
lion' than when he disguises himself as a tiny parasite? I'm beginning
to understand that the moment I realise one of his minions has 'jumped
aboard' I need to expel it – fast – in the name of Jesus before it gets
the chance to breed.

Lord, I'm sick of these gloomy, self-pitying, resentful little mutterings
that irritate me constantly like a dog's fleas. I bring them to your cross
and ask you to set me free from these parasites, in your name.

The perfect rainbow arch

Fill us each morning with your constant love, so that we may sing and be glad all our life. Give us now as much happiness as the sadness you gave us during all our years of misery.

Ps. 90:14–15, GNB

It was during a long, disabling illness that my friend gave me a very precious gift. It was a battered, worn old book. I was exhausted from trying to find healing through prayer as well as medical channels, and my faith and hope had almost died.

'Maybe this will help,' said my friend. It was an anthology of prayers, poems, hymns and quotations, which had blessed her throughout her eighty-year-long life. As I turned her well-marked pages it wasn't long before I found this little prayer that felt like the sun coming out after a storm.

Lord, take all my broken purposes and disappointed hopes and use them to make Thy perfect rainbow arch. Take all my clouds of sadness and calamity and from them make Thy sunset glories. Take my night and make it bright with stars. Take my ill health and pain until they accomplish in Thy purpose as much as health achieves. Take me as I am with impulses, strivings, longings so often frustrated and thwarted, and even with what is broken and imperfect make Thy dreams come true. Through Him, who made of human life – a sacrament, of thorns – a crown, of a cross – a throne, even through Jesus Christ my Lord, Amen.

Dr Leslie Weatherhead, *The Private House of Prayer*

Rock of ages

My soul finds rest in God alone; my salvation comes from him. He alone is my rock and my salvation; he is my fortress, I shall never be shaken.

Ps. 62:1–2

When I was six I remember my father taking me to Cheddar Gorge in Somerset and showing me a boulder with a deep crevice running right through it.

'That's the Rock of Ages,' he told me. 'During a terrible thunderstorm in 1776 a clergyman called Augustus Toplady was walking up this very path. He didn't want his black suit and top hat to be ruined by the rain so he crept inside this rock to shelter.

'While thunder rolled all around these hills he began to scribble some words on the back of an envelope. "Rock of ages, cleft for me, let me hide myself in Thee . . ." Soon he had written a whole hymn, which became so famous that it has been sung at the funerals of kings and queens.' My father was such a great storyteller that it is no wonder I have loved Toplady's hymn ever since!

Rock of ages, cleft for me,
Let me hide myself in Thee . . .

Not the labour of my hands
Can fulfil Thy law's demands;
Could my zeal no respite know,
Could my tears for ever flow,
All for sin could not atone;
Thou must save, and Thou alone.

Nothing in my hand I bring,
Simply to Thy cross I cling;

Blocked goals

I've learned by now to be quite content whatever my circumstances. I'm just as happy with little as with much, with much as with little. I've found the recipe for being happy whether full or hungry, hands full or hands empty. Whatever I have, wherever I am, I can make it through anything in the One who makes me who I am.

Phil. 4:11–13, *The Message*

Gerhard Tersteegen is one of the people I'm really looking forward to meeting in heaven. He lived in the 1700s and gave up life as a successful businessman to live completely alone with God in an isolated cottage. He hoped for a life of solitude in which to find peace for prayer and writing hymns and books. Obviously that was *not* God's plan for his life! In 1727 the revival for which Gerhard had earnestly prayed actually broke out, and suddenly people started coming to his hideout in their hundreds, seeking spiritual help. Before long he was giving personal counsel from morning to night and eventually he had to move to larger premises to make room for so many visitors. Life had become the very opposite of what he had hoped for, but something he wrote gives us a clue to how he reacted:

> *Oh take this heart that I would give,*
> *Forever to be all thine own;*
> *I to myself no more would live, –*
> *Come, Lord, be Thou my King alone.*

God tells us that He has wonderful plans for all our lives (Jer. 29:11), but sometimes they are far from the plans we would have chosen! This faces us with a choice: we can either try to manipulate God into changing His ideas, feel resentful and sorry for ourselves, or react as Gerhard did.

Lord, please make me as malleable as soft clay under your expert hands; mould my life into any shape you like and use me in whatever way you want.

Time to sniff the roses

In his hand are the depths of the earth, and the mountain peaks belong to him. The sea is his, for he made it and his hands formed the dry land.

Your hands shaped me and made me.

Ps. 95:4–5, Job 10:8

I am writing this on a secluded beach in Devon. Getting here involved a long hike and a risky climb down the cliffs, so there are no ice-cream kiosks, deckchairs or beach huts. Absolutely everything I can see was made by God himself: the gulls soaring over the towering cliffs, the gigantic cumulus clouds drifting above them, and the sea as it sucks gently around the rocks. I've spent the afternoon enjoying the rock pools, fascinated by all the different colours of the pebbles, the swaying anemones and the tiny darting fish.

So few people ever come here that all this staggering beauty exists almost exclusively for God's pleasure alone. Today's verses tell us that He made it with His own hands, but does God *really* have hands? Did He roll the Earth into a ball in His palms and fling it into orbit? God is so powerful that He can create anything merely by a word of command, but the Bible mentions His hands many times and even says our names are tattooed on them (Isa. 49:16); King David tells us that His fingers made the moon and the stars (Ps. 8:3). These days we all live such hectic lives, except perhaps when we are on holiday. We hurtle through our days, trying to keep to our tight schedules, leaving ourselves no time to look closely at the beautiful things God made for our pleasure – as well as His own.

Forgive me, Lord, for taking your amazing creation for granted.

Expressive hands

It was not by their sword that they won the land, nor did their arm bring them victory; it was your right hand, your arm, and the light of your face, for you loved them.

Ps. 44:2–3

While I sat holding my mother-in-law's hands, as she slept her way into heaven, I kept thinking of all the things those hands had done throughout her eighty-six years. Feeding and changing her three babies (and my six); the many grazed knees and elbows they had tended; the countless birthday cakes they iced, the meals they cooked and the mountains of washing up they had worked through. She was always shy about expressing her love in words, but her hands did it for her.

Hands are an important part of communicating our emotions; we make a fist when we are angry, and shake hands to show friendship or end a quarrel; we clap to show appreciation or hold hands when we fall in love. It is not surprising that people in Bible days connected God's hands with His love and care. Ezra the priest wrote an astonishing account of how he led thousands of Jews back to their homeland over a bandit-infested desert. He comments, 'Because the hand of the LORD my God was on me, I took courage' (Ezra 7:28). And God Himself says, 'Do not fear, for I am with you . . . I am your God. I will strengthen you and help you; I will uphold you with my righteous right hand' (Isa. 41:10). Do you need His hand to guide, protect or comfort you today?

Lord, thank you that I am 'covered with the shadow of your hand' (Isa. 51:16).

Holding hands

For I am the LORD, your God, who takes hold of your right hand and says to you, 'Do not fear; I will help you.'

Isa. 41:13

Some of the children I used to foster had been so badly treated that they found it very hard to trust adults. David had been regularly tied to his bed for sixteen hours at a stretch. His body was covered with bruises and festering sores, and the way he cowered away when I tried to touch him was heartbreaking. I wondered if he could ever learn to trust me.

He had never seen the sea, so when we took all the children for a day at the beach he became rigid with terror at the sight of the waves rolling towards him. Suddenly I felt a cold, clammy hand slip into mine. All day he clutched my hand tenaciously, refusing to let it go. By the afternoon his confidence had grown enough to allow him to run with me through the sandy puddles left by the retreating tide. His little legs had never been given the chance to run and jump before, so he often stumbled.

'You won't let me fall, will you?' he would say anxiously. 'Keep hold of my hand – promise?' That day changed him. Gradually he became a normal, happy child but it was the action of grabbing my hand that began our relationship. God longs for us to grab His hand like that, whenever we feel afraid, lonely or confused.

My soul clings to you; your right hand upholds me.

If the LORD delights in a man's way, he makes his steps firm; though he stumble, he will not fall, for the LORD upholds him with his hand.

(Ps. 63:8, Ps. 37:23)

Warning hands

The LORD's hand has gone out against me!

Ruth 1:13

Suddenly, round the corner, I saw a policeman, holding up his hand. As I jammed on my brakes he shouted, 'There's been an accident. You'll have to go back.'

While we all enjoy the comforting verses about God's hands protecting and guiding us, there are also many that describe His 'hand against' individuals or nations. Sometimes God says, 'If you don't get out of this relationship . . . stop this habit . . . activity . . . you'll be in danger of losing your integrity . . . your spiritual health . . . people you love.' There are also several references to God's hand being heavy, rather as a father's hand might feel heavy to his disobedient offspring!

When we ignore God's hand of warning, and allow some temptation to become a way of life, His punishment does not always fall in this life. God's grace is so enormous He gives us time for repentance, but these days we are dangerously inclined to think that God is *all* love and *only* love. He *is* love, of course, but He is also righteousness. He cannot overlook sin, because it hurts innocent people: justice has to be done, so every sin we ever commit has to be punished, ultimately. When we repent Jesus Himself takes that punishment for us, but there are Christians who find a particular sin so attractive they prefer to continue in it, rather than to repent and change. The sin robs them of God's favour and blessing, which they once enjoyed, but they refuse to recognise consequences, such as loss of joy and peace, as 'God's heavy hand' on them.

The LORD will judge his people. It is a dreadful thing to fall into the hands of the living God.

(Heb. 10:30b–31)

Held in His hands

You will be a crown of splendour in the LORD's hand, a royal diadem in the hand of your God.

Isa. 62:3

Crowns are usually associated with heads rather than hands! But as I turned this verse over in my mind I realised you can't see a crown if you are wearing it; you have to hold it in your hands to enjoy it to the full. You need to feel the smoothness of the gold, and turn the jewels in the light to see them sparkle. Kings and queens of Great Britain hardly ever have the chance to enjoy their magnificent crowns. The jewels are so valuable they have to be locked in a special building at the centre of the Tower of London and guarded round the clock! Yet none of those crowns cost as much as you did! Being that valuable feels bizarre; we think, 'I've never done anything important enough for God to hold me in his hands and *enjoy me*!'

Fortunately, to become this crown we don't have to *do* anything; it is all about how we react to what *other people* do. Pearls are formed when a grain of sand gets into the oyster's shell, irritating its soft body until it wraps it round with the protective layers that later form a valuable jewel. Diamonds are created only after years of pressure deep underground. Gold has to be exposed to intense heat so that all the impurities surface and can be skimmed off (Job 23:10). Accepting, without bitterness, the heat of life's traumas, grinding pressures or endless small irritations is what forms our 'treasures of darkness' (Isa. 45:3).

Thank you, LORD, that you promised me I will 'sparkle like jewels in your crown' (Zech. 9:16).

Jesus' hands

Jesus took him by the hand and lifted him to his feet, and he stood up.

Mark 9:27

Just think! The 'hands that flung stars into space' once became tiny and fragile, curling round Mary's little finger. We can only imagine what Jesus did with His hands during His first thirty years, but what He did in the last three is well documented. Not only did He place them on the sick but he wrote in the dust, washed feet, served meals and even cooked a beach barbeque.

They would have been strong, skilful, suntanned hands, roughened by years of manual work, but they were also incredibly gentle and tender. Mark remembers how Jesus used a child as an illustration for His quarrelling disciples. He didn't just point him out to them from a safe, adult distance: 'He took a little child (by the hand) and had him stand among them. Taking him in his arms, he said to them, "Whoever welcomes one of these little children in my name welcomes me"' (Mark 9:37).

Mark also tells us how Jesus bent down and lifted a child to his feet after an epileptic fit. The child's father was there so Jesus could easily have left him to care for his son, who had been writhing on the filthy ground in his own dribble, urine and, possibly, vomit. Instead, Jesus himself reached down to restore his dignity. Perhaps he wiped the little boy's mouth and smoothed the sweaty hair from his bewildered eyes before taking his hand and lifting him up.

Lord, I long to see your hands; and one day, simply because of those terrible scars, I know I will see them, touch them, hold them and kiss them. Thank you, Lord, for those scars!

Dirty hands

Filled with compassion, Jesus reached out his hand and touched the man. 'I am willing,' he said. 'Be clean!'

Mark 1:41

It amazes me to realise how willing Jesus was to get His hands dirty. In those days people who were considered holy washed their hands repeatedly throughout the day (Mark 7:1–6). They held their cloaks tightly when they walked through a crowd in case they became 'unclean' by brushing past a prostitute, a disabled person, lepers or menstru-ating women. Yet Jesus, who had the power to heal by 'remote control', touched people like that all the time.

He was nearing a village one day when he met a funeral proces-sion. In the middle of the crowd of wailing women one face looked so agonised that 'his heart went out to her' (Luke 7:13). She was the mother of the young man who had just died, and he was all she had left in the world. 'Don't cry,' said Jesus softly. He could have raised the corpse with a word, as He did Lazarus; instead, He put His hand on the coffin and the bearers stopped, amazed, because touching a corpse would have made Him ritually unclean. Jesus is not high above the ugliness of grief; He's right there in the centre of it.

Another time his path was blocked by the grotesque figure of a kneeling leper. This disease eats away the flesh of its victims, leaving them covered with infectious and disfiguring sores.

'You could help me, if you wanted to,' the man said. Because lepers were outcasts, maybe he didn't feel Jesus would bother to help. The hand of Jesus was the first that had touched him in years!

Sorry, Lord, for the way I categorise people, looking up to the 'Spiritual Superstars' at church and ignoring people I think are not quite 'my sort'.

Generous hands

The LORD upholds all those who fall and lifts up all who are bowed down. You open your hand and satisfy the desires of every living thing.

Ps. 145:14, 16

Jesus had no money or possessions to give people, but He loved giving His blessing. When mothers eagerly approached Him, hoping He would pray for their children, the disciples rudely shooed them away. Mark tells us, 'Jesus was indignant'; 'And he took the children in his arms, put his hands on them and blessed them' (Mark 10:16). Don't we all long to see his hands touching our children like that!

On the first Easter Sunday evening a couple asked Him to supper. Because they were traumatised by the crucifixion they did not recognise him until He stretched out His hand to give them a piece of bread during the simple meal. The nails had left that hand so horribly bruised and distorted that they recognised Him instantly.

There is one thing the hands of Jesus did that always reduces me to tears when I read the story. At a Jewish dinner party the host would dip a piece of bread in the sauce and hand it to the guest He honoured most highly. Just minutes after Jesus had used His hands to wash the feet of Judas Iscariot, He also handed him this 'sop'. He already knew what Judas planned to do that night, so was He offering him one last chance to save himself from being labelled as the worst traitor in history?

Could you stop for a moment and picture those wounded hands reaching out to you? Ask Him what they are offering you. A chance to change; the opportunity to know him better; blessings for your family; some new spiritual gift or anointing for service – whatever you need today.

JULY 26

Restoring hands

*So he went to her, took her hand and helped her up. The fever left her
and she began to wait on them.*

Mark 1:31

I can remember lying in bed fuming, during my eight years of illness,
when I often had to listen, helplessly, to my husband and children
creating chaos in the kitchen below. Illness, disability, loss and old age
rapidly sap our confidence, making us feel marginalised. Was this how
Peter's mum-in-law felt the day a very special visitor came for a meal?
One touch of his hand and she was up, dressed, and busy in the kitchen!
Jesus does not always restore health, youth or mobility but His touch
always restores hope and gives us a reason for living. His servants are
never 'off sick' and never retired. Serving Him may not mean doing
the active, practical jobs any more, but the words for 'worship' and
'serve' are the same in Hebrew. So perhaps you need His touch to
restore your ability to enjoy His company and intercede for others?

Jesus' hands restore not only health – but life itself! When He
returned to Capernaum, a few months later, an agitated father flung
himself down on the quayside where Jesus had just stepped out of
Peter's boat. By the time they had fought they way through the crowds
to the man's home, his daughter was dead. Gently, Jesus took her hand
and gave her back her life again (Mark 5:41)!

Is there an area of your life that has died – your faith, hope, creativity;
the love or respect you once had for a spouse, parent, child? Has your
joy died, killed by despair; has your peace been strangled by worry?
Could Jesus be holding out His hand to you, longing to restore life to
that dead place?

Healing hands

People brought to him a man who was deaf and could hardly talk, and they begged him to place his hand on the man. After he took him aside, away from the crowd, Jesus put his fingers into the man's ears. Then he spat and touched the man's tongue. He looked up to heaven and with a deep sigh said to him, 'Ephphatha!' (which means, 'Be opened!').

Mark 7:32–34

Tracy finds crowds very confusing because of her deafness; often she can't understand what is happening. I wonder if that is how the man in today's story felt, when the crowd dragged him to Jesus. They wanted to see a miracle; how cross they must have been when Jesus took him by the hand and walked off with him! Jesus knew what a shock it would be for someone who had never heard anything before suddenly to have their hearing restored in the middle of a noisy, cheering crowd.

Rather than startle him, Jesus used His hands to communicate what He was doing by sign language. He put his fingers in the man's ears, touched his tongue, looked up to indicate that He was praying and then spoke a single word that would have been easy to lip-read.

During eight years of illness I read all the Christian books on healing, desperately trying to discover the secret formula that would make me well. Finally I concluded there isn't a formula at all; Jesus works differently with each one of us.

Thank you, Lord, that you treat us all as individuals. May I never try to put you in a box, tied up neatly with academic ribbons and theological bows. I don't understand why you heal some and not others, but I know you do not require me to understand you, only to trust you.

Helpless hands

*When they came to the place called the Skull, there they crucified him
. . . Jesus said, 'Father, forgive them, for they do not know what they
are doing.'*

Luke 23:33–34

Surely the most incredible thing that Jesus ever did with His hands
was to allow them to become helpless enough for thugs to nail iron
stakes right through them. As their heartless, cruel faces bent over
Him, he could have lashed out and, with just one hand, He could have
destroyed the whole of humanity, but love for those men who were
torturing Him – and love for you and me – held Him stuck fast on
that cross.

It must have been hard for those active, generous hands to be
rendered completely helpless; He must have longed to wipe the tears
from his mother's face and reach out to comfort his friend John. I
guess we can all identify with that sense of helplessness as we watch
someone we love plunging headlong into a destructive situation, when
they are no longer a child that we can grab and pull back to safety.
We also feel helpless as we watch someone dying in pain, or when our
marriage is disintegrating. It is always a comfort to know that Jesus
understands how we feel, but in actual fact He was *not* helpless. He
could have stepped down from that cross, but He chose not to. We
are not helpless either. Praying, which can seem so inactive, actually
brings God's power into any situation.

Lord, I refuse this suffocating sense of helplessness as I watch these
people I love. I choose, instead, to fight for them by prayer.

But if not

Our God . . . is able to deliver us from the burning fiery furnace, and He will deliver us from your hand, O king. But if not, let it be known to you, O king, that we do not serve your gods.

Dan. 3:17–18, NKJV

There they stood, three devout young men, about to be burnt to death unless they bowed down to worship an idol! Their faith in God did not depend on whether He saved them from the flames or not; while they believed implicitly that He was able to rescue them, they were determined to go on worshipping Him whether He did or not. That is high-level faith!

Over the last few days the granddaughter for whom I've been praying throughout her long illness has become a lot worse. As a family we are facing the horror of losing her. As I prayed yet again this morning I was suddenly overwhelmed by rage.

'If you don't give her back to us, don't think I'll bother to finish writing this book or talk to people about you again!' Almost at once I remembered those little words spoken beside the roaring furnace, 'But if not', and I realised I needed to reach out and grab their kind of faith.

I have seen so many people who were convinced God would heal their dying friend, but when the friend died they completely lost their faith. Perhaps God was asking me to prepare myself in advance before the shock and grief distorted my thinking. I needed to decide, by willpower, that nothing God did or didn't do was ever going to make any difference to my trust in His goodness and care.

We declare that you can. We believe that you will. We know you might not. We pray that you do. We'll trust if you don't.

Mark Stibbe

Dragonflies

For I reckon that the sufferings of this present time are not worthy to be compared with the glory which shall be revealed in us.

Rom. 8:18, KJV

'There has to be something more to life than this!' sighed the harassed mother next to me in the checkout queue. Thomas William Parsons (1819–92) was an American dentist who expressed that kind of feeling in a poem he wrote between tooth extractions:

Believ'st thou in eternal things?
Thou knowest, in thy inmost heart,
Thou art not clay; thy soul hath wings.

As I sat by a neighbour's pond, I was captivated by the dragonflies that darted and zigzagged over the surface of the water. Their gossamer wings glittered in the sunshine as they carried those amazingly coloured bodies to and fro. How free they looked; then I remembered that those beautiful creatures had literally spent years in darkness as ugly grubs, wriggling about in the mud at the bottom of the pond. Until at last one day they climbed up the rushes and felt the sun begin to split their ugly skins and expose the 'fairy' wings and vivid colours trapped inside.

We are so earthbound, plodding endlessly through the routines of life, too busy, sad or bored to look up and realise all that God destined us to be. We may feel like dragonfly larvae stuck in stagnant mud, but our wings are there, ready inside, waiting for the day when we will be even more gloriously free than a dragonfly.

Because I know this is my eternal destiny, Lord, help me sometimes to climb that stalk into the sunshine above while I worship or sit quietly with you. Let my soul dance in pure delight far above the dullness of this world.

Serving Her Ladyship

Unto you I lift up my eyes . . . As the eyes of a maid to the hand of her mistress, So our eyes look to the LORD our God. . .

Blessed the man, blessed the woman, who listens to me, awake and ready for me each morning, alert and responsive as I start my day's work.

Ps. 123:1–2, NKJV, Prov. 8:34, The Message

As a child I loved visiting Mrs Walster. She had been in service, and often told me stories about the grand dinner parties her mistress held.

'Her Ladyship had six of us maids waiting at table, but during the evening she never spoke a word to us; she directed everything we did with the first finger of her right hand! If you didn't watch her, you were sacked next morning.'

God needs our help to show His love down here on Earth, but in order to do that effectively we need to be as attentive as Lady Fladgate's maids. So *how* can we watch Him? Just as servant girls were carefully trained to serve their mistress, I believe we have to learn to 'follow the nudge'. If we suddenly feel that God wants us to do something, we should do it at once! Of course we'll get it wrong while we are learning, but God always honours obedience. When I turned up with a bunch of flowers for a neighbour she looked mystified – and cross! I felt such a fool telling her I thought God had asked me to bring them! Years later, when she had become a Christian, she said those flowers started her search for faith.

Because God confines Himself to working through our prayers He has to have a panel of people He can galvanise into prayer-action at a moment's notice. Are you willing to be available to Him like that?

Except you become like little children . . .

But I have stilled and quietened my soul; like a weaned child with its mother, like a weaned child is my soul within me.

Ps. 131:2

As I pulled my carry-on bag through the surging airport crowds I thought how badly I needed this holiday! Life recently had been so confusing, uncertain and painful that I needed to get away from everything to hear God speak to me and show me what to do. When the indicator told me my flight would be delayed for at least four hours I muttered, 'Typical!' To pass the time I watched two families, each with a toddler about the same age. The first child was obviously tired, hungry and frustrated. Nothing her father offered her seemed to help as she squirmed and writhed on his knee, roaring with rage. The other father put his toddler into a backpack. As he carried him about he pointed out interesting things until the child's head lolled forward, fast asleep – resting between his father's shoulders. The details of the journey – which gate, which flight, which seat, what if we are delayed overnight – all these worries that ruffled my peace did not disturb this child at all. He trusted his father to get him where he needed to go and to provide the care he needed on the way. Suddenly I realised God had spoken into my life, before I'd even arrived at my holiday destination. I had been kicking and screaming like the little girl while God just wanted me to trust Him like that little boy on his daddy's back.

Let the beloved of the LORD rest secure in him, for he shields him all day long, and the one the LORD loves rests between his shoulders.

(Deut. 33:12)

Sign of maturity

A farmer planted seed. As he scattered the seed, some of it fell on the road, and birds ate it. Some fell in the gravel; it sprouted quickly but didn't put down roots, so when the sun came up it withered just as quickly . . . Some fell on good earth, and produced a harvest beyond his wildest dreams . . . The seed cast on good earth is the person who hears and takes in the News, and then produces a harvest beyond his wildest dreams.

Matt. 13:3–8, 23, *The Message*

Walking the dogs along the footpath through the wheat fields today felt more like moving through a golden sea, as the breeze rippled the crop into leisurely waves. When we met Roger, the farmer who works all the fields round here, he was smiling broadly.

'Soon be ready for harvest,' he said.

'How can you tell?' I asked curiously.

'The stalks look humble,' he replied simply. 'A few weeks back they were stood up, stiff and proud like soldiers on parade, but once the ears of wheat start to ripen the weight of them pulls the heads down – bows them over, see?' As his tractor rattled away I thought, 'The same applies to us Christians! When we are immature in the faith, most of us have a tendency to think we know it all and we'll never fall or be defeated. Someone whose life is "heavy" with fruit and has lived a long time with Jesus has discovered just how many pits they can fall into and just how good He is at rescuing them out of every one. So it is hardly surprising that they bow in humility like a ripe stalk of wheat.'

I know that self-confidence and pride are the most destructive sins in my life; please Lord, rip them out of me and give me God-confidence instead.

God's biggest problem

God is love.

1 John 4:16

That is God's biggest problem! If He were *only* holy and omnipotent, things would have been so much easier for Him! But love causes vulnerability; it needs someone to love – and craves for that love to be returned. Right from creation God wanted every individual person to know Him, enjoy His love and trust Him for care and protection. Yet the humans He had created couldn't relate to a distant being they couldn't feel or touch. So what could God do to reveal His love to them?

This was God's plan! He decided to choose a man who would know Him so well that he could show the rest of mankind what He is really like – and the advantages of trusting Him. Hopefully this man's family would do the same, and eventually the family would develop into a nation who could demonstrate to the world all the benefits of living under God's protection (Gen. 18:18).

Great plan! But to launch it, why pick a childless old man of seventy-five? God chose Abraham because, while the rest of the world worshipped gods they made themselves, Abraham doggedly held to his belief in Yahweh. Yet Abraham didn't know his God very well at first, so his faith was small. God needed to set about developing more faith in Abraham if He was ever going to be able to use him effectively. Because faith grows best in difficult conditions the first thing God did was to ask him to leave everything that made him comfortable and secure, and take a long, dangerous journey into the unknown (Heb. 11:8).

Abraham is famous for two things: his faith *in* God and his friendship *with* God. Dependence and intimacy are God's priorities for our lives too, so which of the situations in your life has He used to develop them in you?

First faith challenge

The LORD had said to Abram, 'Leave your native country, your relatives, and your father's family' . . . So Abram . . . took his wife, Sarai, his nephew Lot, and all his wealth . . . and headed for the land of Canaan.

Gen. 12:1, 4–5, NLT

Abraham had enough faith to pack up and leave, but not yet enough to obey God fully. He was told to leave his relatives behind, so why drag his nephew along? God had said Abraham would father a great nation but because he had no children he obviously assumed that Lot was heir to his wealth *and* God's promise. Actually Lot caused nothing but trouble, and Abraham disobeyed God by bringing him. So often, when we are not quite sure we can trust God's power we fall back, disastrously, on our own common sense!

The first thing Abraham did when he arrived at his destination was to build an altar to God. A brave action when you are surrounded by pagan strangers – 'blending in' is always easier – but God needed Abraham to be willing to stand out in a crowd. When a relative of mine joined the army, he knelt down by his bed the first night in barracks and said his prayers while boots were hurled at him from all directions! It took a few weeks before the rest of the recruits stopped laughing at him and began to like him instead.

We are told in Galatians 3:7 that we Christians are Abraham's spiritual descendants – as such we are part of God's plan to show His reality to the world. We live in days when few people worship Him, but God has placed each of us in our own corner of the world to persuade the people we network with that He is well worth knowing.

Lord, give me the courage to 'be different'.

The showjumping ring

Now there was a famine in the land, and Abram went down to Egypt to live there for a while because the famine was severe.

Gen. 12:10

Oh dear! Today's verse reveals Abraham continuing to find human solutions to his problems, but isn't it tough when you are sure God has asked you to make some major life change, and when you obey everything starts to go wrong?

'Why drag us away from our comfortable homes to live in draughty tents among uncivilised savages – just so we can starve in a famine?' Can't you hear Abraham's family saying all that? 'Come on,' they probably urged. 'Let's go to Egypt, they have loads of food down there, *and* they live luxuriously!' Abraham didn't ask for God's help or guidance; he just set off for Egypt.

His next challenge was fear. He was sure Pharaoh would steal his exceptionally beautiful wife, Sarah, so, once again, Abraham failed to pray and decided to lie instead, by pretending she was his sister. Actually she *was* his half-sister, so perhaps he thought a half-truth was all right, but the lie made things much worse and they would all have died had God not helped them to escape back to Canaan. God is holy so He requires total truth from His representatives, so perhaps we should all take 'white lies' and exaggerations more seriously and ask God, daily, to guard our tongues?

With God, failure isn't final. He grows our faith by presenting us with a series of graded challenges, like a showjumping course. If we 'refuse' or fail to clear a jump He gives us time and then brings us back to try again.

Can you think of a faith challenge you failed? Are you brave enough to ask the Lord to give you a second chance?

Vital choices

*Lot looked up and saw that the whole plain . . . was well watered . . .
like the land of Egypt . . . So Lot chose for himself the whole plain of
the Jordan and set out towards the east.*

Gen. 13:10–11

Lot hated leaving the pleasures and profits of Egypt. Returning to a
nomad's existence definitely didn't appeal, but the family herds
increased so massively that it became necessary for Abraham and
his nephew to move away from each other to find enough pasture.
'Which way do you want to go?' Abraham asked, even though seniority
entitled him to the first choice. His faith must have been growing
because someone who trusts God's provision doesn't need to grab. Lot
looked at the isolated hill country and then the lush valley – and the
prosperous cities of Sodom and Gomorrah which lay at the far end.
His decision was easy!

If we want to love God we are told we can't also love the things
that motivate the rest of mankind (1 John 2:15). We need a totally
different mindset. When physical pleasures, relationships, possessions
or ambitions subtly creep into God's place in our lives, we are 'loving
the world' more than Him. Lot's desire for worldly pleasures ultimately
lost him everything in this world and the next (Gen. 19:30). He wanted
comfort *now*; Abraham was beginning to trust God's promises for his
future (Gen. 12:7). Perhaps we often need to ask ourselves, 'Are my
eyes more focused on the things that make life pleasant in the here
and now, or on the glories of heaven awaiting me?'

*No eye has seen, no ear has heard, no mind has conceived what
God has prepared for those who love him.*

(1 Cor. 2:9)

*Faith is being sure of what we hope for and certain of what we
do not see.*

(Heb. 11:1)

Beating the vultures!

'Do not be afraid . . . I am your shield your very great reward.' But Abram said, 'O Sovereign LORD, what can you give me since I remain childless?'

Gen. 15:1–2

Abraham's famous vultures were a real help to me today, but, first, here's the story! It had been ten years since God promised Abraham a son – yet nothing had happened and frustration and disappointment were spawning big-time doubts!

There is something so poignant about the way God reassures him: 'Trust me just a little bit longer, Abraham, then I myself will be your reward.' Abraham growled back, 'I don't want you or your rewards; I only want a son!' I've seen so many people reach that point of desperation when their prayers are not answered. By turning their backs on God they lose all the good things He had waiting for them.

Fortunately Abraham did not give up on God – quite! So God decided to reiterate His promise in a tangible way. Bargains, in those days, were sealed when both parties walked together between animals they had killed and cut in half. For Abraham the ceremony was ruined by vultures, which kept swooping down to steal the meat. He had to keep fighting them off until he was exhausted. That's the bit that blessed me today. For weeks I've been battling doubts as I pray over a particular matter. Doubts about God's goodness and power keep attacking me just like those vultures. It feels like a continuous fight to stop them 'landing' to steal my faith – as well as my peace. Faith-growing is not a relaxing pastime; it feels like all-out war!

> *Faith is a poor thing if we cannot trust in the dark, whether we understand or not.*
>
> Canon Guy King (died 1956)

> *It is the darkness which makes faith a reality.*
>
> Bramwell Booth

The surrogate mother

So Sarai, Abram's wife, took Hagar the Egyptian servant and gave her to Abram as a wife. (This happened ten years after Abram had settled in the land of Canaan) . . . when Hagar knew she was pregnant, she began to treat her mistress, Sarai, with contempt.

Gen. 16:3–4, NLT

This was Abraham's worst faith failure of all! He simply got tired of waiting for God to act and decided to 'help Him out'. Yet by the standards of his day it wasn't *wrong* to father an heir through a surrogate mother; it was the custom, but it *was* wrong for Abraham to fall back on his common sense yet again, without consulting God. Complete God-dependence is obviously the vital ingredient of a life of faith.

Many of us think we have a problem over feeling inadequate, but that definitely didn't bother Abraham! His problem was that he didn't feel inadequate *at all*! His greatest enemies were his natural wisdom, experience and self-reliance. It took God twenty years to eradicate them! Perhaps some of us need to write out Proverbs 3:5–6 and stick it up on our fridges! 'Lean not on your own understanding; in all your ways acknowledge him and he shall direct your paths.'

The consequences of Abraham's 'Declaration of Independence' were catastrophic! The descendants of Hagar (the Arabs) have been fighting with the descendants of Abraham's legitimate heir (the Jews) to this very day.

I love the way that Abraham and Sarah are so like the rest of us. Genesis 16:2 tells us the surrogate mother idea was Sarah's. Then, when everything went wrong, she told her husband, 'This is all your fault' (v. 5)!

Some of us are blame-takers, always feeling everything must be our fault. Blame-shifters live much more comfortable lives but are very hard to live with. Which kind of 'Blamer' are you?

Oh no! I hate change!

Abraham said to God, 'If only Ishmael might live under your blessing!' Then God said, '. . . your wife Sarah will bear you a son, and you will call him Isaac . . . I will establish my covenant with him . . . And as for Ishmael, I have heard you: I will surely bless him.'

Gen. 17:18–20

Poor Abraham: he'd given up hope of having a legitimate heir and was making the most of 'second best'. It was thirteen years since Hagar had given Abraham a son, and he had grown to love Ishmael. It must have been a shock when God suddenly told him his long-awaited baby would soon arrive. When you are ninety-nine, perhaps the last thing you want is the stress and hassle that change involves.

Have you ever thought, 'Just leave me in peace, God; I can't face having to grow any more faith!' Few of us enjoy upheavals; they disrupt our comfort zones, and even the changes we plan ourselves involve a certain amount of loss. Yet resisting change usually means choosing a second-rate existence, while God wants us to keep pressing forward to grasp His very best.

Perhaps, like Abraham, it is impending change for someone else that bothers you most. Abraham didn't want Ishmael's life disrupted; he hated the thought of him being hurt by disappointment and rejection. Sometimes, when we pray for the people we love, our own desires get in the way of God's bigger plan. God said 'no' to Abraham's prayer but reassured him by saying how greatly He intended to bless Ishmael – in His own way and at His own time!

> *To live is to grow, to grow is to change, so to live successfully is to change often.*
>
> Cardinal J. H. Newman (1801–90)

God's friend

Abraham believed God . . . and he was called God's friend.

James 2:23

What epitaph would you like to have carved on your tombstone: 'He worked for God until he dropped', or 'God was her best friend'? Although the New Testament holds Abraham up as an example of faith in three different passages, the Bible also tells us three times that he was 'God's friend' (2 Chr. 20:7; Isa. 41:8; Jas 2:23). We've been watching how slowly his faith developed over the years, but I think his intimacy with God grew just as gradually.

When God first called Abraham he believed in the one and only God, worshipped by his ancestor Noah, but his religion was a 'hand-me-down' affair; he did not personally know the God who spoke to him suddenly out of the sky. When he finally arrived in Canaan God did more than speak; he appeared (Gen. 12:7), and in each subsequent 'God-encounter' their recorded conversations grew progressively more intimate until by chapter 18 God came to lunch in Abraham's tent.

Would you say you are a better servant to God than you are a friend? Jesus made it clear that He does not want us to be mere servants, but values our company and friendship far above our service (John 15:15). Abraham did not use up his time on Earth dashing about doing great things, but he obviously spent a lot of time just sitting in God's presence, looking at the stars at night (Gen. 15:5) or enjoying the shade of His oak trees in the heat of the day (18:1). Friendships deepen as two people talk and listen to each other, yet our Bible reading and prayer times can so easily become mechanical – unless we frequently ask God to refresh them.

The greatest enemy of devotion to Christ is service for Christ.

Oswald Chambers

When God came to lunch

'Sirs, please do not pass by my home without stopping; I am here to serve you . . .

Gen. 18:3, GNB

Brother Tom was a monk who loved cooking. One night he dreamed he was preparing a meal for Jesus: fish in a perfect cheese sauce, fluffy potatoes and fresh-picked peas. The following day a hungry tramp came begging at the monastery door – just after Tom had served the community. The only food left was Tom's own plate of dinner. Grudgingly he placed it before the tramp, then realised it was exactly the same food he had served to Jesus in his dream! That tramp later became one of the most enthusiastic Christians I've ever known. Hebrews 13:2 tells us to welcome visitors who might turn out to be angels; two of the dusty travellers who disturbed Abraham's midday nap *were* angels – but one was God Himself. Is your home your well-defended 'castle' or a place where you make others feel safe and comfortable?

By then Abraham's faith had grown so strong that he had no difficulty in believing when God announced that Sarah would bear a child, but this was her first personal encounter with God. Her reaction was hardly surprising considering she was ninety! She laughed in total disbelief! She regretted it the moment one of their visitors turned and looked directly at her, apparently reading her thoughts. It can feel daunting when we first become aware of God's gaze and realise He is asking us to do something that feels totally impossible.

We, like Sarah, could easily be tempted not to take God's instructions seriously instead of making ourselves vulnerable to His will.

Ask yourself the question God put to Abraham and Sarah; 'Is anything too hard for the LORD?' (Gen. 18:14)

AUGUST 12

Knowing God's character

Then the men left and went to a place where they could look down at Sodom, and Abraham went with them to send them on their way

Gen. 18:16, GNB

It wasn't just an evening stroll; it would have been a very long trek from Hebron to the hills overlooking Sodom. Abraham could simply have waved his heavenly visitors goodbye but he wanted to linger in God's presence for as long as possible, because being there was his greatest delight. That idea really spoke to me this morning. I so often watch the clock while I have my 'quiet time', then dash off as soon as I feel I've done my duty! Real friends enjoy being together; they share their thoughts and feelings, desires and plans. This is the kind of intimacy that had developed between God and Abraham, and made it possible for God to share His heart with Abraham as they walked (Gen. 18:17–20) and then for Abraham to speak honestly to God in reply. He knew God's character so well by then that he did not try to persuade God into changing His mind about obliterating Sodom, the city where his nephew Lot lived. Instead he focused on God's justice and compassion, knowing He could never annihilate a city so long as a few good people remained there. Unfortunately there was only one good man left in Sodom – Lot – and God had him and his family smuggled out just in time.

We are told that Lot despised his neighbours' behaviour (2 Pet. 2:8), but he failed to influence any of them for good, or the city would have been spared. Edmund Burke (1729–97) said, 'All that is necessary for the triumph of evil is that good men do nothing.'

The pain of letting go

One day Sarah saw the son that Hagar the Egyptian had borne to Abraham, poking fun at her son Isaac. She told Abraham, 'Get rid of this slave woman and her son' . . . The matter gave great pain to Abraham.

Gen. 21:10, 11, *The Message*

At seventeen Ishmael must have been a nightmare. He had been born with a wild, aggressive personality (Gen. 16:12) and after he had been deposed as Abraham's heir he was probably a volcano waiting to erupt! The 'fun' he was poking at two-year-old Isaac hid the murder lurking in his heart, but Sarah's ultimatum put poor Abraham in a heart-wrenching dilemma. This time, however, he asked God what to do. He was probably surprised by God's reply. Surely the loving God he had grown to know would not ask him to kick his precious boy out into the world?

God, however, knew He must protect Isaac's life *and* save Ishmael from a murderer's execution. He had also already committed Himself to protecting and prospering Ishmael (Gen. 17:20), and the boy was obviously old enough to cope on his own.

It is one thing to trust God for ourselves but so much harder to trust Him to care for those we love! Yet we get in God's way when we won't let them go because He wants to teach them to rely on Him rather than on us.

When Hagar managed to get lost in the desert and they both nearly died of thirst, it was God Himself, not Abraham, who came to their rescue, and led them into a successful new life (Gen. 21:17–21).

Sometimes God's instrument of blessing looks harsh or even cruel when He applies it to the people we love. We need to keep remembering that He loves them a whole lot more than we do!

O Lord, help me to hold out to you on an open hand the people who matter most to me.

Who is your Isaac?

Take your son, your only son, Isaac, whom you love, and go to the region of Moriah. Sacrifice him there as a burnt offering.

Gen. 22:2

For nearly forty years God had been 'growing' Abraham's faith – this was the 'final exam'. Would Abraham trust Him even when his old enemy Common Sense screamed 'Madness'? He passed with an A Plus.

I often wonder whether, during the eighteen years since Isaac had been born, Abraham had come to rely on him to meet all the needs that God Himself had once met. Nowadays, sons can mean muddy washing, empty fridges and a missing car! In Abraham's day, they meant security – someone who would provide for you in your old age, care for you and keep you company. All through the years in which Abraham had waited for Isaac God had come to mean everything to Abraham, providing not only material things but his source of happiness as well. Now he had Isaac, perhaps Abraham did not need God quite so much. Isn't it so easy to build our lives around a person rather than make God the centre of our existence?

When my husband left me, our son Richard supported me emotionally and helped in all kinds of practical ways. Five years later when he told me he was emigrating I realised I had been relying on him instead of turning straight to the Lord for comfort and help. I had to walk up Mount Moriah too, but it was actually the making of us both.

Pure faith always puts God first and relies on Him alone. Of course, we need human relationships, but we are only safe when God comes first in our lives. If we build our security around a human being and they leave, die or become ill, our security crashes.

Do you have an 'Isaac' in your life?

Great in His sight

He will be a joy and delight to you . . . for he will be great in the sight of the LORD.

Luke 1:14–15

My mother found that promise in her Bible reading the day she gave birth to my brother. Five years later we were caught in a sudden storm while on a family boat trip. When the monster waves looked like capsizing our tiny craft we were all terrified, except for Justyn.

'I can't be drowned,' he stated calmly, 'because Mummy always says I'm going to be great in the sight of the Lord, and I haven't done anything important enough yet.' Sixty years later, we were recalling that adventure when Justyn said sadly, 'I still haven't done anything important enough to be great in His sight.'

'Don't be so ridiculous!' I said indignantly. 'You've loved and obeyed Him all your life, and you're full of love and compassion towards everyone! Of all the people I've ever met, *you* are the most like Jesus. Surely being "great in the sight of the Lord" isn't about achievements; it's about faithfulness?'

If we lined Abraham up beside other great Bible characters – such as Noah the ark-builder, David the soldier, Solomon the architect, Paul the church-planter and Peter the preacher – poor old Abraham would look extremely ordinary! All he did for God was live a peaceful life, protecting and providing for his family, tithing anything he earned and being a good witness for God to his neighbours (Gen. 21:22); yet God used him to bless more people than all those other 'big names', not because of what he did but simply because of what he was!

Every Christian is to become a little Christ. The whole purpose of becoming a Christian is simply nothing else.

C. S. Lewis

Amazing Grace

There is no other name under heaven given to men by which we must be saved.

Acts 4:12

> *How sweet the name of Jesus sounds*
> *in a believer's ear!*
> *It soothes his sorrows, heals his wounds,*
> *and drives away his fear.*
>
> *Weak is the effort of my heart,*
> *and cold my warmest thought;*
> *But when I see Thee as thou art,*
> *I'll praise Thee as I ought.*

It is almost unbelievable that those words were written by a man who had once been the captain of a slave ship, notorious for his violence and cruelty. John Newton's mother taught him about Jesus and His 'Amazing Grace' and prayed earnestly for him, but as she lay dying, when John was only seven, she might well have wondered how he could possibly survive spiritually in the care of his godless, sea-captain father. How she would have hated the diabolically evil trade that became his life; yet her prayers were eventually answered during a terrible storm, when John remembered her faith and cried out to her God. Later, in his cabin, he committed the rest of his life to serving Him. I love John Newton's most famous hymn, 'Amazing Grace'; it demonstrates that grace by showing us that God not only saved John for a life of service, but made him His intimate friend.

If you have been praying for one of your grown-up children for years and you are feeling discouraged because they have turned their backs on God, let the story of John Newton and his mother's prayers restore your hope today.

Praising by willpower

The crowd joined in the attack against Paul and Silas, and the magistrates ordered them to be stripped and . . . after they had been severely flogged, they were thrown into prison . . . the jailer put them in the inner cell and fastened their feet in the stocks. About midnight Paul and Silas were praying and singing hymns to God, and the other prisoners were listening to them.

Acts 16:22–25

It has been a wonderfully inspiring week seeing hundreds of Christians, all singing God's praises at the tops of their voices, during the conference I've just been attending. By the last night we practically blew the marquee away! At the end of the evening, as I walked out into the shadows I noticed a woman standing by herself among the guy ropes – she was crying.

'It is so easy to worship in there,' she said, smiling through her tears, 'but tomorrow, when I'm back home facing all the problems again, it's going to be so much harder.' After making good use of the tissue I'd handed her, she suddenly added, 'But I often think, when I'm trying to cope with a husband with MS and a house full of stroppy teens, not to mention a mother-in-law "from hell", that when I can still manage to praise Him, by willpower alone, it means a load more to Him than all the bouncing and waving that's been going on here, during such a happy holiday.' I forgot to ask her name, but I hope I'll never forget what she said.

How God rejoices over a soul, which, surrounded on all sides by suffering and misery, does that upon earth which the angels do in heaven; namely loves, adores, and praises God!

Gerhard Tersteegen (1697–1769)

The Lord is there!

'Am I only a God nearby,' declares the LORD, *'and not a God far away?*
Can anyone hide in secret places so that I cannot see him? . . . Do not
I fill heaven and earth?'

Jer. 23:23–24

Yesterday evening I just didn't fancy going to church. I knew it would
only be a visiting preacher and I was feeling so worried I was sure I
would not be able to worship. I was right! The guitars were too loud
and the violin wasn't in tune, and when the preacher announced he
would speak from Ezekiel I switched him off and turned back to my
worries. Earlier in the day I'd had a phone call telling me that one of
my daughters and her family, who are serving the Lord abroad, are all
trapped in a difficult and dangerous situation.

'Lord, they are so far away!' I prayed silently as the sermon droned
on over my head. 'How are they going to manage without their family
round them for support?' Then suddenly, onto the screen at the front
of the church flashed the last frame of the preacher's PowerPoint pres-
entation. Just one verse – written in huge letters – and it positively
yelled at me.

'THE LORD IS THERE' (Ezek. 48:35). There was no doubt in my
mind that the Lord had spoken, saying, 'I'm there with them, so relax
and leave their care to me.'

I have so often enjoyed knowing that God was here, with me in the
present moment, but knowing that He was also *there*, right on the spot,
able and willing to intervene on their behalf, felt deeply reassuring.

Lord, I'm so sorry that I spend so much of my precious time with you
at church, or at home, in fruitless worry over things that you already
have in hand.

Running free

*You, my brothers, were called to be free. But do not use your freedom
to indulge the sinful nature; rather, serve one another in love.*

Gal. 5:13

When Stella, my cocker spaniel, came to live with me she had already
been blind for over a year, and was always kept on a lead in case she
bumped into things or got lost. I like to give my dogs freedom to run
in the long grass, crunch through autumn leaves or stop to enjoy an
interesting smell. So I tried letting Stella off the lead when we were
out in the open fields. At first she was intoxicated by the freedom,
running around with ears flying, but suddenly she would stop, in panic,
realising she was alone. My voice brought her dashing towards me,
tail wagging with relief.

The freedom that she now enjoys depends entirely on her ability
to respond to my commands. If she is heading for a tree, a deep
stream or a busy road she must respond to my 'Stella, *STOP!*' or
suffer painful consequences. Today she was *bad*! Glorious smells
caused a mysterious attack of deafness, which meant I had to put her
back on the lead.

Jesus said, 'Now a slave has no permanent place in the family . . .
So if the Son sets you free, you will be free indeed' (John 8:35–36);
the freedom He came to buy us is very like the freedom I give Stella.
It depends on our ability to hear His voice and obey His commands.

Lord, some of the things you tell me to do are just so hard! Like loving
others at church, forgiving people who hurt me and sharing my
possessions. Yet I know I'll never be free if I'm trapped by bitterness
or greed.

Message from the past

Jesus, Thou joy of loving hearts,
Thou fount of life, Thou light of men,
From the best bliss that earth imparts,
We turn unfilled to Thee again.

We taste Thee, O Thou living Bread,
And long to feast upon Thee still;
We drink of Thee, the Fountainhead,
And thirst our souls from Thee to fill.

Here is another old hymn we don't often sing these days. It was written by a monk, Bernard of Clairvaux, who died on 20 August 1153. When he was a boy, growing up in his father's castle in Burgundy, he had a dream one Christmas Eve. He was in the stable, with the shepherds, looking at the newborn baby Jesus, wrapped up in the manger. When he woke up he could not stop thinking about the incredible wonder that God Himself should step down into our world and be born as a baby. That dream totally changed his life and, instead of living the comfortable life of a wealthy nobleman like his father, getting married and founding a family, he deliberately chose not to sample 'the best bliss that life imparts' in order to find fulfilment in Jesus alone.

For Bernard, that meant joining a very austere order of monks, but what about those of us whose lives are happy and fulfilled? Are we merely 'second-class Christians' because we haven't sacrificed everything to go and care for inner-city street children? No way! It is actually more faith-stretching to keep Jesus in the centre when our lives are going well than it is during times of hardship. Surely what Bernard is saying is *when* Jesus is the one from whom we derive our joy (happiness, satisfaction, fulfilment), anything else just becomes unimportant in comparison.

Please, Jesus, keep my spirit restlessly yearning for you alone!

The accuser

*Then he showed me Joshua the high priest standing before the angel
of the LORD, and Satan standing at his right side to accuse him . . .
Now Joshua was dressed in filthy clothes . . . The angel said to those
who were standing before him, 'Take off his filthy clothes . . . I will
put rich garments on you.'*

Zech. 3:1–4

How this story encourages me! If God has asked you to work for Him,
either up-front or out-back, you'll know how wobbly poor Joshua was
feeling! Perhaps other people put you on a pedestal too: they admire
your gifts, personality or leadership role – but you don't want to be
there because you know what you're like inside!

Joshua kept telling himself he was totally unworthy of the job of
high priest; but his friend Zechariah the prophet showed him who was
actually behind all these accusations. Satan's objective is to stop us
from serving God, either by telling us we are brilliant until we are
rendered useless through pride or by plaguing us with our past and
present failures until we give up in despair.

Is Satan using his second tactic on you, and covering you with a
stifling grey cloak of condemnation? Remember it is the Holy Spirit's
job to tell you when you have done something wrong, so you can
quickly 'dump it' at the cross and receive instant forgiveness. He's
always clear and specific, but Satan's 'cloak' is just a vague sense of
shame and defectiveness.

Of course it's vital to remember that Jesus said, 'Apart from me
you can do nothing' (John 15:5), but when Satan starts 'having a go'
we need to tell him, 'There is now no condemnation for those who
are in Christ Jesus' (Rom. 8:1).

Please, Lord, replace these grimy robes Satan tells me I'm wearing
with your own 'Robes of Righteousness' (Isa. 61:10).

I'm loved!

I have loved you with an everlasting love; I have drawn you with loving-kindness.

Jer. 31:3

School was a perpetual nightmare for me, so I've always struggled with a fear of teachers! Then, on a Christian holiday, I met Louise. She must have been in her eighties and I loved her on sight. She told me how excited she had been when she was given her first headship in a tough, inner-city junior school.

'I asked God what my goal in school should be. Most of the children came from abusive, criminal, dysfunctional families, so should I aim to teach morality? Would academic excellence boost morale or ought I to concentrate on supporting my beleaguered staff? I felt God answered me through something I heard a retired clergyman say: "All things are at their best when they are loved."

'So I tried to make each child feel loved and appreciated for their unique contribution to the life of the school. Most had never experienced love but they responded amazingly – so did my staff! Somehow, with love coming first, the other things like morality, academic success and a happy staffroom just came automatically. There is a bloom on a child, or an adult, who is loved; they have confidence to grow into their own potential. In contrast, someone who is unloved just seems to shrivel up inside.'

Many people have never been loved unconditionally. So, are such people doomed to 'shrivel up inside'? *No!* God is reaching out to us with the greatest love it is possible to know, and by accepting it we can live covered by that 'bloom' that says 'I am loved, wanted and enjoyed by a dad who thinks I'm wonderful!'

Lord, let me open myself to your love today, as a sea anemone opens itself to the incoming tide.

The mother-hen ministry

In Joppa there was a disciple named . . . Dorcas, who was always doing good and helping the poor. About that time she became sick and died . . . All the widows stood around . . . crying and showing him (Peter) the . . . clothing that Dorcas had made while she was still with them . . .

Acts 9:36–39

One of the things we all have in common is that, for at least six months of our lives, we all had a mother. Some never knew them for any longer than that, others had such bad mothers they wish they'd never known them at all! When people have never been well mothered, or lose a mother they loved, they often grow into adults who long for a mother-substitute. Marjorie was mine. She was a family friend who spiritually adopted me when I was seventeen, and for forty-five years she was my mentor and friend. When my six children were growing up she was always there, ready to listen to my moans or pray for the baby who wouldn't sleep, the toddler with asthma or the obnoxious teenager. She never gave advice; she just listened, loved and cosseted me and the children with little treats and acts of kindness.

Dorcas obviously gathered many fragile chicks under her comforting wings, and there is usually someone with a 'mother-hen' ministry in most churches. They are never publicly commissioned by the Bishop or listed with the church leaders; they simply mother people. I've even met some brilliantly effective *male* mother hens!

Young parents, single parents and new Christians badly need the steady support of more mature people to love them and be the grandparents their children will remember all their lives.

Could God be asking you to become a 'mother hen' to someone else? Why not ask Him?

Dangerous mother hens

Herodias nursed a grudge against John and wanted to kill him . . .
Finally the opportune time came . . . Herod gave a banquet . . . When
the daughter of Herodias . . . danced, she pleased Herod . . . He
promised her. . . 'Whatever you ask I will give you' . . . She went out
and said to her mother, 'What shall I ask for?' 'The head of John the
Baptist,' she answered . . . The (executioner) . . . beheaded John . . .
and brought back his head on a platter. He presented it to the girl, and
she gave it to her mother.

Mark 6:21–28

The Bible contains some awful mothers, but Herodias beats the lot!
This was her daughter's big moment, and she should have asked for
something that would have benefited her future life; instead, her controlling mother used her to fulfil her own goal – revenge. But when we
point an accusing finger at someone else, three fingers point back at
us! Do we sometimes try to live out our lives through other people?
We've all heard of parents who never became footballers, ballerinas
or musicians who force their children to do it for them. Michelle's husband
died when her children were teenagers; ten years later she told me, 'I
used the kids as emotional props; I focused on them and never built
a life of my own. When I realised what I was doing I had to let them
go and fill the void with God Himself.'

I have also seen spiritual 'mother hens' who control and manipulate
their 'chicks', i.e. older Christians who 'take on' a new Christian or a
young mum and, instead of fulfilling a normal discipling, mentoring
role, totally dominate their life in order to satisfy their own desire for
power and control.

Think about your various relationships and ask yourself, 'Who controls
me, and whom do I control?'

A mother in Israel

March on, my soul; be strong!

Judg. 5:21

I really needed that sentence the day I first 'discovered' it. I was in the middle of one of those horrible times of discouragement and uncertainty. God had given me a job to do but so many frustrating things kept happening that I was beginning to wonder when He was going to start helping me do it! Then, right in the middle of my moans, there it was – 'March on, my soul; be strong!' Obviously God was not going to wave a magic wand and make life easy. I had to command my own inner self to get up and get on with it – regardless of the obstacles.

The words were originally spoken by Deborah, a prophetess who had learned to listen to God's voice. She won so much respect through the wisdom He downloaded through her that she became Israel's leader, which was amazing in a male-dominated world!

Her greatest gift was inspiring people to do far more than they ever dreamed possible. Israel had been under enemy occupation, their national infrastructures were crumbling and morale was so low that no one had the will to fight. Then 'Deborah arose, a mother in Israel' (Judg. 5, 7). Far from being a soothing, cuddly mum she raised an army, defeated the enemy and brought peace to the nation for forty years. In the middle of doing all that I wonder how often she had to speak those words to herself!

The phrase 'Mother in Israel' was used by early Methodists to describe women who inspired others in their homes and communities to turn to Christ and helped their faith in Him to grow.

Lord, however frustrating life may be, help me remember that you simply called me to reveal your love to other people today.

God the Mother

Surely I have calmed and quieted my soul, like a weaned child with his mother

As a mother comforts her child, so will I comfort you; and you will be comforted . . .

Can a mother forget the baby at her breast and have no compassion on the child she has borne? Though she may forget, I will not forget you!

Ps. 131:2, ESV, Isa. 66:13, Isa. 49:15

I love that final verse! It always reminds me of the incessant screaming of my fourth baby. The only way I coped was by carrying him all day on my back, papoose-style, where he invariably slept 'resting between my shoulders'. The debate about whether God is male or female always irritates me because He can be everything we need Him to be at different stages of our life. He uses familiar human relationships to model the infinite variety of His love; He tells us He wants to be our father, friend, husband, lover, brother, boss and king. Today's verses show us He can also mother us with the gentle, tender side of His love. It is often during bereavement that we most need this facet of His love, but we have to choose to let Him comfort us. Over the last few years I've lost several of the most important people in my life. While I want to allow God to fill the gaps they have left, sometimes I think, 'He isn't enough! I can't see, feel or hear Him!' It is easy, then, to search for new human relationships to fill the vacuum, often with disastrous consequences. So I quickly pray, 'Lord, you promised to comfort those who mourn, so I *choose* to run to you for that comfort.' Then I find He either floods me with peace or sends someone to cherish me on His behalf.

Lord, I want to be like a baby kangaroo, hidden safely in your pocket. I give you permission to carry me wherever you want us to go; I rest myself inside your protection and grace.

A mother to Jesus

Whoever does God's will is my brother and sister and mother.

Mark 3:35

When Old Testament writers finished describing the adventures of the kings they usually added two things: whether they pleased the Lord or did evil in His sight, and the name of their mother. Obviously mothers play a vital part in their children's spiritual development, and psychologists tell us that good mothering is crucial to healthy child development. So I often wonder what was so special about Mary that she was chosen, above all other women, to care for Jesus. She must have been a very remarkable woman. So the story behind today's verse is hard to understand unless we realise that the brothers of Jesus did not, at first, believe He was God. When He became massively popular they said, 'He's out of his mind' and set off to 'take him away' (Mark 3:21). Perhaps Mary did not know their intentions. They could not get to Jesus because of the crowds and He did not go out to them because He knew exactly why they had come! Instead He said something many of us find strange. We are all happy to be his servant, friend, sister/brother or child, but we are mystified when He calls us His 'mother'. How can we 'mother' Jesus?

My oldest son seemed totally self-reliant in his successful career and happy marriage. I felt I'd completed my job as a mother, but when his baby son was seriously ill he wanted me there in the hospital beside him, just to sit there keeping him company – and to *mind* for him.

Prayer, on one level, is asking God to do things for us or for others; a deeper layer of prayer simply keeps Him company, as a mother might sit with a grieving son, actually sharing the pain He feels as He looks at a suffering world.

Failure isn't final!

I am the LORD . . . I am with you and will watch over you wherever you go, and I will bring you back to this land. I will not leave you until I have done what I have promised you.

Gen. 28:12–15

I love Jacob! Yes, I know he was a cheat, a liar and a coward, but deep inside he yearned to know God and receive His love and approval. Grandparents can have a profound influence, so perhaps Abraham told little Jacob that God had promised to bless the whole Earth through his descendants, and Jacob grew up longing to be heir to that promise – and to enjoy the wealth that went with it!

Rather than asking for God's help, Jacob tried to get what he wanted by trickery and found himself running for his life from his father's wrath and his brother's death threats. For an anxious person like Jacob it would have been terrible to leave his home for a strange land, but his greatest grief, that first night alone in the hills, was his belief that his mistake had cut him off from God for ever.

But it was that night, at Jacob's lowest point, that God let him see right into heaven and promised to be with him always. When God sees that a person really longs to know and love Him, however many faults that person has, He begins to draw them gently towards His heart and slowly changes them into the person He wants them to be.

When we have a special God-encounter we can think, 'I'll never fall away again,' but Jacob fell many times, and so do we! It is not the absence of falls that makes us successful in God's eyes, but how quickly we get up again.

AUGUST 29

No easy options for God-chasers

Because I, your God, have a firm grip on you and I'm not letting go. I'm telling you, 'Don't panic. I'm right here to help you.'

Isa. 41:13, The Message

After twenty years in exile Jacob became very wealthy, and settling down to enjoy his large family must have seemed attractive. Prosperous middle age is often a dangerous time for God-chasers. Many start their Christian lives full of enthusiasm but their zeal gets lost under the pressures of work, family life, money worries and relationship problems. Yet Jacob always had the uncomfortable feeling that God wanted him back in the Promised Land as the heir to Abraham's spiritual inheritance. That meant facing the terrifying brother who had vowed to kill him. Fear had always tempted Jacob to run away from conflict, angry people or difficult situations. Yet, because of that deep yearning for God, he finally set off.

It is tough to keep on pressing into God when giving up on Him would make life so much easier. Is your faith and desire for God facing you with upheaval and loss or involving you in unpleasant clashes? Perhaps you have always been an 'avoider', wriggling your way out of situations you find unpleasant or threatening. Maybe, like Jacob, God is forcing you to face your worst fear.

Jacob's crunch came when he reached the border of his homeland and heard that his brother was marching a small army in his direction. He must have wondered seriously whether going forward to claim a deeper relationship with God was going to be worth the risks. Is the same issue bothering you? Could you echo the words of Brother Lawrence, when he said:

My goal is God Himself. At any cost, dear Lord, by any road.

Wrestling with God

*So Jacob was left alone, and a man wrestled with him till daybreak.
When the man saw that he could not overpower him . . . the man
said, 'Let me go, for it is daybreak.' But Jacob replied, 'I will not let
you go unless you bless me.'*

Gen. 32:24–26

Who was this mysterious stranger who sprang at Jacob out of the
darkness? Jacob fought for his life, but at dawn he realised his an-
tagonist was God himself. Could they have been wrestling over the
issue of control? Jacob had given his life to God twenty years before,
but now he was faced with the question, 'Is my life mine to enjoy as
I please, or do I really want to stick by my resolve to let God have it,
right down to the last detail?' Perhaps that is a fight we all have with
God quite often.

Jacob was fighting his own fears but it was also a battle of faith.
God had promised Jacob His presence and care, so the issue that night
was, 'Can I trust God to keep His word and protect me and my family?'
Faith and fear are constantly at war inside each of us.

The wimp that Jacob had once been would have given in and crept
away defeated, but instead he fought on until dawn broke because he
wanted God's blessings more than anything else in life.

Because he won through, God changed the horrible name that his
father had given him, Jacob, which means 'supplanter' (schemer, swindler
and cheat), and gave him the name 'Israel', which means 'prince who
persevered with God'.

Perhaps it was this change of identity that gave Jacob the courage to
meet Esau and go on to found a great nation. Do you need God
to change your name?

Are you a good leaner?

Who is this coming up from the wilderness, leaning upon her beloved?
Song of Songs 8:5, NKJV

Beside me, as I write, is a pottery hand with the figure of a child leaning all her weight against it as she rests her head in the hollow of its palm. It is not a great work of art, but I love it. When I'm faced with a sudden decision or I feel low or panicky I remember it as I cup my left hand and lean my right hand into my palm, like that little girl. The gesture feels like a wordless prayer which always makes me feel safe.

During a tough time of my life a friend sent me today's verse and added, 'When you eventually emerge from your desert, you'll rely on God more than ever before, because all this time He's been teaching you to lean.' She was right; when we have no option but to lean on Him, that is when we find how trustworthy He really is!

The apostle John was a very great leaner. Whenever we read about him in the Gospels he is always as close to Jesus as possible, and he was actually 'leaning back against Jesus' during that last supper (John 13:25).

Some people are very good 'leaners' but they lean on the wrong person – themselves! Proverbs 3:5 urges us to 'Trust in the LORD with all your heart and lean not on your own understanding'. Leaning on other people isn't smart either. Once, when enemies threatened God's people, they put their faith in their ally Egypt.

'Don't lean on them for support,' they were told, 'They are like a wobbly walking stick that will only splinter and cut your hand' (2 Kgs 18:21, my paraphrase).

Please, Lord, give me the wisdom to lean on the right person.

Threat of doom

The LORD says, 'I have ended the threat of doom and taken away your disgrace.'

Zeph. 3:18, GNB

We were sitting on a park bench, eating sandwiches. We were strangers but realised we were both attending the nearby Christian conference because of our badges. The sun shone and I remarked happily, 'Life's good, isn't it!'

She replied nervously, 'Whenever things are going well, I suddenly feel sure a terrible disaster is about to ruin everything for me or my family. I know it's irrational but I almost dread letting myself feel happy!' We naturally began to talk and, before we went back to the church, I showed her today's verse and asked the Lord to lift off her that 'threat of doom'.

Two years later we happened to meet again.

'Your prayer started me on a journey,' she explained. 'I wanted to find out *why* I could never trust God to protect me, so I had some regular prayer ministry. I adored my father and for long periods he was delightful, but then suddenly he would go off on a drinking binge and turn violent and abusive. He could wreck the entire house and trash everything we had. For some odd reason I always felt his rages were my fault. Perhaps I'd been naughty in some way I didn't understand? I guess I grew up always thinking disaster was what I deserved so I was bound to cause trouble and misery to those I loved. I needed to accept that God was not like my father; He is always the same, never stops loving me and doesn't punish me by letting bad things happen to my children! Now at last I can relax in His love.'

Is some childhood memory spoiling your relationship with God?

Walking to heel

I will lead the blind by ways they have not known, along unfamiliar paths I will guide them; I will turn the darkness into light before them and make the rough places smooth. These are the things I will do; I will not forsake them.

Isa. 42:16

'Lord, I can't cope!' I admitted early this morning. 'There's too much to do today; decisions to make, people coming for counselling, conflict to sort out with colleagues, emails, phone calls!' I could feel the butterflies in my tummy rapidly mutating into bats as I looked down at my blind spaniel, Stella. She had sneaked up onto my armchair beside me and was fast asleep like a warm cushion tucked under my elbow.

'It's all very well for you,' I told her acidly. 'You have nothing on your mind but staying as close to my heels as you possibly can all day long. That's your only concern.' Then suddenly I felt the Lord say, 'Staying as close as possible to *my* heels all day should be *your* only concern too. Why don't you let me lead you through today, one job at a time? If you really knew how much I love you, you would be as carefree as Stella!'

Fanny Crosby depended on God just as completely as Stella depends on me – and Fanny was also blind. She poured out her devotion to the Lord in many wonderful hymns, and here is my favourite.

All the way my Saviour leads me;
what have I to ask beside?
Can I doubt His tender mercy,
who through life has been my guide?
Heavenly peace, divinest comfort,
here by faith in him to dwell!
For I know, whate'er befall me,
Jesus doeth all things well.

Fanny J. Crosby (1820–1915)

Love that keeps us alive

For God so loved the world that he gave his one and only Son . . .

John 3:16

My dog Phoebe is nearly sixteen now; she has been my constant companion and together we've shared many wonderful walks and cosy fireside evenings. Now, however, her once-glossy coat looks rather scruffy and she no longer leaps effortlessly over the stile. Yet she still trots along beside me, tail up, ready for anything. I spend a fortune on geriatric dog food, pills and potions because I love her so much I would give anything to keep her alive and well – just a little bit longer. As we were walking down the lane together this morning, Kipling's poem about dogs forced its way into my head: 'Brothers and sisters, I bid you beware of giving your heart to a dog to tear.' One day Phoebe and I will have to make that dreaded trip to the vet and life will be rather desolate for a while after that.

'If love could keep you alive, old girl,' I told her, 'you'd live for ever.' Then I suddenly realised that it is love that will keep *me* alive for ever! God *so* loved me that He couldn't bear the thought that one day I wouldn't exist and our friendship would cease, so He gave all He had to keep me right up close to Him for all eternity. He did the same for you, too. He values the friendship He has with each of us so highly that He would give anything and everything to keep it going for ever. Wow!

Thank you, Jesus, that you would rather die than live without me!

Clean exercise books

See, I am doing a new thing! Now it springs up; do you not perceive it?
Isa. 43:19

This time of year always reminds me of going back to school after the summer holidays. Moving up to a new class, perhaps, or even a new school with a new uniform. I actually loathed school so I hastily reject all those memories, but I did love being given new exercise books. All last year's blots, crossings-out or rude comments from teachers had been thrown away; now all I had before me were endless clean, blank pages waiting to receive the brilliant compositions I was determined to produce that year.

Fortunately we don't have to wait a year to make a new start with God; He gives us a new exercise book every morning: 'Therefore, if anyone is in Christ, he is a new creation; the old has gone, the new has come!' (2 Cor. 5:17).

It is so important to remember that we have a God who loves New Beginnings, especially when life feels empty or merely a repetitive grind. Unfortunately God doesn't always change our circumstances, but He really can change the way we feel about them. Rather than being *under* our circumstances He wants us to expect Him to give us all kinds of gifts and blessings *in* the circumstances! And to expect new ones every day!

Sometimes He takes away that which is most precious so that into the void of a life that is utterly broken He may pour the glory of His indwelling love.
Dr Alan Redpath (1907–89)

A new challenge

The word of the LORD came to me, saying, 'Before I formed you in the womb I knew you, before you were born I set you apart' . . . 'Ah, Sovereign LORD,' I said, 'I do not know how to speak; I am only a child.' But the LORD said to me, 'Do not say, "I am only a child." You must go to everyone I send you to and say whatever I command you. Do not be afraid of them, for I am with you and will rescue you,' declares the LORD. Then the LORD reached out his hand and touched my mouth and said to me, 'Now, I have put my words in your mouth.'

Jer. 1:4–9

Is the Lord calling you into a new chapter of your life? Asking you to take on some new role or sending you to a new place among strangers? Perhaps you feel a bit daunted, and you're wondering how you'll cope? Jeremiah probably felt like that too, but all God needed was the 'yes' in his heart – He did the rest!

When I started out in public ministry I felt like jelly – until I met an old lady called Isabel Macdonald. She founded a worldwide organisation which has blessed thousands of young women, the Girl Crusader Union. I told her how I felt and she quietly replied, 'Our only qualification for service is to know our own utter inadequacy, and to know and rely on His total adequacy.' That little sentence turned my jelly into steel.

God calls no one to a special ministry of service for Him without providing the resources by which that ministry can be accomplished. And remember this – no matter the task ahead of you, it is never as great as the power behind you.

Selwyn Hughes

Exceptional in the ordinary

They found him in the temple courts . . . listening to them and asking them questions. Everyone who heard him was amazed at his understanding . . . When his parents saw him . . . His mother said . . . 'Your father and I have been anxiously searching for you' . . . Then he went down to Nazareth with them and was obedient to them . . . And Jesus grew in wisdom and stature, and in favour with God and men.

Luke 2:46–52

Brian and Steve were brothers who both dreamed of becoming missionaries abroad, but when their father died in 1950, leaving their mother and two little sisters, Brian felt he should stay behind and run the family business to provide a home for them. Even though he never enjoyed what he did, he was so successful that for many years he totally supported Steve in Africa, and built him a hospital, a school and a theological college.

It is easy to picture Jesus surrounded by huge crowds, performing amazing miracles and taking Jerusalem by storm when he rode in on a donkey. Actually the largest part of his life was spent in obscurity, in a backwater town, supporting His siblings after Joseph died by running a small business.

He knows exactly how it feels to get up every morning and plod through the same boring routine. Remembering that helped me during the eight years when I was confined to a wheelchair. I loved Oswald Chamber's book *My Utmost for His Highest* and heavily underlined this paragraph:

> We do not need the grace of God to stand crises, human nature and pride are sufficient . . . but it does require the supernatural grace of God . . . to go through drudgery as a disciple, to live an ordinary, unobserved, ignored existence . . . It is inbred in us that we have to do exceptional things for God, but we have not. We have to be exceptional in the ordinary things.

The white toadstool

When I look at the night sky and see the work of your fingers – the moon and the stars you set in place – what are mere mortals that you should think about them, human beings that you should care for them? Yet you made them only a little lower than God and crowned them with glory and honour.

Ps. 8:3–5, NLT

For lots of reasons I felt rather flat and low as I went with the dogs round the fields this morning. It was a vile morning, forcing me to realise that summer is nearly over. It was raining so hard I couldn't see through my glasses, and I felt cold, wet and tired. Then, suddenly, right there at my feet, I saw a pure white toadstool rising gracefully out of a rotting tree stump. The slender stalk looked too frail to hold up its witch's hat with the curly brim. Yet there it stood, bravely defying the lashing rain and wind.

'Jesus made this for me to find,' I thought. 'The mind that created every detail of the universe loves me, cares about me! He knew I'd need some cheering up this morning.'

I'm so sorry, Lord, that when I start thinking gloomy, negative thoughts I walk about your world as if my eyes were closed and I miss the lovely little surprises you leave ready for me to find. Help me, for the rest of my life, to look at your world with the eyes of a child.

Lost hope?

May the God of hope fill you with all joy and peace as you trust in him, so that you may overflow with hope by the power of the Holy Spirit.

We continually remember . . . your endurance inspired by hope in our LORD Jesus Christ.

Rom. 15:13, 1 Thess. 1:3

Jemma's life had been thoroughly bent out of shape by chronic illness. She'd had to leave college, give up the sport she loved and watch many of her friends drift away.

'I've lost hope!' she told me angrily. 'I really believed God would heal me, but in three years, nothing has changed!'

'I remember feeling exactly like that,' I told her, 'while I was waiting for God to heal me. But everything changed when I realised I'd been putting my hope in the wrong thing. I didn't have to believe for healing, I just needed to believe in Jesus – Himself. Once I realised how totally He loved me and wanted the best for me, I could relax and leave myself in His hands while I focused on knowing Him as a friend and companion.'

'But He healed you in the end,' protested Jemma.

'Yes, but not until I'd learnt to put my hope in *Him* instead of in healing.'

Paul tells us that it is our hope 'in our Lord Jesus Christ' that brings endurance and 'joy and peace as we trust *in Him*'.

Lord, help me to put my hope for this life, and the next, in you, and you alone. I belong to you; use me or not as you want, send me out or leave me here; all I want is to please you as often as I possibly can every day.

Joy despite everything

For you have been given the privilege of serving Christ, not only by believing in him, but also by suffering for him.

Phil. 1:29, GNB

Imagine you are in hospital, wired to drips and machinery because of a serious heart condition; the doctors tell you that you could die at any moment. While you are trapped in that bed visitors bombard you with bad news. Work colleagues tell you how others are criticising you and destroying all you've built up over years, and your family worry you with their problems and arguments. Suppose, as you lie there in that difficult situation, you decided to write to some old friends from the past. The Greeks used to say, 'Everyone reveals his own soul in his letters.' Most of us would write about our despair, resentment and self-pity – not to mention doubts about God's love.

I wonder if we could spend a few days looking at the letter Paul wrote in similar circumstances. He was in prison, not hospital, chained to soldiers, not machines, and execution threatened his life, not heart disease – and it was not the situation at the office that was causing him grief but upsets in the churches he had founded. Yet his letter to Philippi is one of the most joy-filled books in the Bible, full of peace and contentment. Everything in his life seemed to be going wrong, yet he possessed an inexhaustible supply of supernatural, inner joy that was not linked to his outward circumstances. I hope that, as we read his letter, we'll discover his secret.

> *Be cheerful no matter what; pray all the time; thank God no matter what happens. This is the way God wants you who belong to Christ Jesus to live.*
>
> (1 Thess. 5:16–18, *The Message*)

Connecting with joy

*I thank my God every time I remember you. In all my prayers for all
of you, I always pray with joy . . . being confident of this, that he who
began a good work in you will carry it on to completion . . . It is right
for me to feel this way about all of you, since I have you in my heart.*

Phil. 1:3–7

Imagine you are a diver exploring the seabed. You are safe because
you are firmly attached by an 'umbilical cord' to your support ship.
One of the secrets of Paul's supernatural joy came from knowing he
was joined to Jesus – being 'in Christ' is a phrase he used often. When
we are completely connected to Jesus, all His qualities, such as joy,
can pass into us as if by some mysterious umbilical cord.

Another reason for Paul's joy was his attitude towards other people.
A critical attitude smothers joy. His friends in Philippi had many fail-
ings and problems but, rather than nagging God about them, he simply
trusted Him to work on their weaknesses while he enjoyed remembering their strengths.

The Philippian church was facing terrible persecution so Paul must
have been worried, because he loved them, but worry also stifles joy.
I love the way he says, 'I have you in my heart.' Recently, while I was
speaking at a conference, I had bad news about my son. I was too
busy to pray at length, so I wrote his name on a pebble and carried
it in my breast pocket – the nearest I could get to my heart! I still
remember the stab of joy I experienced every time I remembered God
was carrying him in His heart too.

Rather than praying for those you love today, think of one of their
qualities, then thank God for it.

Joy is a choice

Now I want you to know, brothers, that what has happened to me has really served to advance the gospel. As a result, it has become clear throughout the whole palace guard and to everyone else that I am in chains for Christ.

Phil. 1:12–13

Paul, stuck on death row, chained to a Roman soldier, with many of his friends working against him, could have been forgiven for feeling miserable, but today's verse shows us why he maintained his joy. It is the angle from which he viewed his situation that determined the way he felt about it.

Rather than seeing his imprisonment as the end of his mission to evangelise the Roman world, Paul realised that he was chained, night and day, to soldiers from the crack regiment of the Roman army. They were his captive audience for hours at a stretch so he could tell them about Jesus until they believed in Him. Then, as they were posted all over the world, they could carry the Good News far and wide!

Paul could also see that friends who had once left him to do all the preaching had suddenly discovered they could preach about Christ too, and so his imprisonment was spawning many new evangelists (Phil. 1:14).

One week I visited two friends in different hospitals, when both were recovering from cancer operations. One was full of fears and grumbles, the other looked radiant as she told me how God was using her situation to reach others in the ward. Joy has nothing to do with our outer circumstances but everything to do with the way we view them. Paul says 'I *will* . . . rejoice' (Phil. 1:18b); he actually *chose* joy and *decided* not to feel worried or sad.

Lord, whatever happens to me today, use it for your glory.

SEPTEMBER 12

Joy-robbers

*Make my joy complete by being like-minded, having the same love,
being one in spirit and purpose. Do nothing out of selfish ambition . . .
consider others better than yourselves. Each of you should look not
only to your own interests, but also to the interests of others.*

Phil. 2:2–4

Paul knew that good relationships bring joy, yet he heard about squab-
bles and power struggles in the Philippian church. He doesn't say, 'You'll
destroy my joy if you keep on quarrelling.' He says, 'You'll increase
my joy by unity.' No one can take our joy away; we have to let them
– that's our choice. However, other people can add more joy on top of
the joy we already have.

Paul was writing to a beleaguered church. Twelve years before, they
had seen him stripped and brutally flogged in their marketplace,
then flung into a dungeon – just for talking about Jesus. They had
been suffering the same kind of treatment ever since. Churches today
are also beleaguered, not by angry humans but by the powers of darkness (Eph. 6:12). Unseen enemies try to split us, disillusion us and rob
us of our joy. Paul tells the Philippians their only chance of survival
is to stick together; the same applies to us!

Church splits often begin when people start using church activities
for their own ends. Some people love controlling others; they want power
so badly that when they come up against others in church with the same
goal, sparks fly. Others use their church involvements to gain the approval,
respect and admiration they crave, and bitterly resent it when others
gain greater popularity. Paul makes it clear that people like that are
joy-robbers.

Lord, please show me if I'm actually doing some of my church activities
to meet some need of my own.

Joy through imitation

For to me, to live is Christ and to die is gain.

Phil. 1:21

Pride is another joy-smotherer. It is the most destructive sin of all because it makes us feel we don't need Jesus because we are so good at doing everything ourselves. The Philippian church was riddled with pride – and so are many of ours! Some of the Philippians were so busy feeling important that Jesus, and the joy He brings, were excluded. So Paul beseeches them – and us – to keep on remembering just how much He did for us because that soon humbles our pride! He says, 'Your attitude should be the same as that of Christ Jesus: Who, being in very nature God . . . made himself nothing . . . he humbled himself and became obedient to death – even death on a cross!'

My father was full of little sayings that he repeated with irritating regularity. One of his favourites was 'Keep looking up'. It wasn't what we wanted to hear when we'd just flunked a driving test or lost a purse, but it was his way of urging us to keep focused on Jesus. In today's verse Paul tells us that Jesus was his *whole life*. Trying his best to imitate Him meant living a life of total humility. Paul had far more reason than any of us to be proud; he was one of the most gifted and energetic men who ever lived. Yet, because he 'kept looking up', he realised where his abilities came from: 'I can do everything through Christ, who gives me strength' (Phil. 4:13, NLT).

When I survey the wondrous cross
on which the Prince of Glory died,
my richest gain I count but loss,
and pour contempt on all my pride.

Isaac Watts (1674–1748)

Sparkling like stars

Do everything without complaining or arguing, so that you may become blameless and pure, children of God without fault in a crooked and depraved generation, in which you shine like stars in the universe.

Phil. 2:14–15

I guess Paul was sitting by an open window when he dictated those words. It was night and the stars stood out against the dark sky, bright, pure and beautiful. 'Our lives as Christ's followers should be so full of His joy that we stand out in the darkness of this world like those stars,' he thought. Because a star has no light of its own it simply reflects the light of the sun, which is invisible from the Earth at night.

Nothing dampens joy more quickly than grumbling! I used to conduct parties of holidaymakers abroad. Even though we stayed in the same hotel, the success of each week varied greatly. One group could have a marvellous time, enjoying everything, but the next week's party might contain 'grumblers' who grizzled about beds, food and hotel staff until everyone's fun was ruined. Paul knew how infectious grumbling can be, and how fast it wrecks a church – as well as being a bad advert for Christianity.

When the people in your community, who know that you go to church, see the default expression on your face as you walk down the street, would it attract them to Christianity or put them off? I'm not suggesting we wear false grins, but genuine inner joy shows on our faces as quickly as our grumpy thoughts.

O Lord, I'd like my face to be a good advert – not for toothpaste but for you! I know when I whinge and gripe inside it makes me look sour and I so long for people to see Jesus when they look at me.

Joy: the antidote to fear

I want very much to leave this life and be with Christ, which is a far better thing. For what is life? To me it is Christ. Death, then, will bring more.

Phil. 1:23, 21, GNB

When my friend Ruth was given only a week to live she looked radiant, propped up in bed with today's verse framed on her hospital locker. Yet death for many of us is something we dread. It is not always 'the dying bit' that feels frightening, but having to leave loved ones behind. Paul said, 'I am pulled in two directions.' But eventually he, like the rest of us, had to trust God to care for the people he loved – even though that is always much harder than trusting Him for ourselves!

Perhaps it is stepping into the unknown that worries us. Yet Jesus tells us so much about heaven that we certainly have nothing to fear. He also promised we don't have to go there alone; He'll come back himself to take us there (John 14:2–3). It was 'for the joy set before Him' (heaven in our company) that He faced death so bravely (Heb. 12:2).

During the last days of Ruth's life she so eagerly anticipated heaven that she looked as if she were preparing for a wedding, not a funeral.

'Give my love to Jesus,' I whispered as I said my final goodbye. I envied her!

Joy was Ruth's antidote to fear, and it was catching. Paul obviously felt the same when he told his friends, 'Perhaps my life's blood is to be poured out like an offering . . . If that is so, I am glad and share my joy with you all. In the same way, you too must be glad and share your joy with me' (Phil. 2:17–18, GNB).

Jesu, Joy of Man's Desiring – thank you for loving me.

He knows what it's like!

I want to know Christ and the power of his resurrection and the fellowship of sharing in his sufferings, becoming like him in his death.

Phil. 3:10

Philippi was an extremely prosperous city. Businessmen, made rich by the nearby gold mines, built mansions near the river, and academics created cool libraries in this centre of medical science. Wealthy citizens bathed in sumptuous Roman bathhouses and reclined in their mosaic dining rooms, tucking into luxurious banquets.

Becoming a Christian in a setting like that was enormously costly; it meant facing the loss of status, livelihood and property as well as torture and death. No wonder Paul told them, 'Knowing Christ isn't just about experiencing His resurrection power; it's also about suffering and dying as He did.'

Perhaps, as he wrote from that prison in Rome, Paul fully expected to share the agony of crucifixion with Jesus, but what does 'sharing the fellowship of His sufferings' mean nowadays? As a teenager I thought it was missing my Sunday morning lie-in! Now, after experiencing many difficult things, I've learnt that it means Jesus understanding how I feel and me realising how things might have felt for Him.

When my friend John lost his leg he was infuriated by hospital staff who tried to cheer him up with remarks about artificial limbs and how easy they were to use.

'They didn't know how it feels,' growled John. 'They even sent the hospital chaplain in to do me good! I hated him on sight – until he pulled up his trouser legs, revealing *two* tin legs. He was my friend for life after that – because he *did* know what it's like!'

Thank you, Jesus, and thank you, Father God, that there is nothing I have to go through that you have not already experienced. Thank you for understanding!

Peace and joy on guard duty

Rejoice in the LORD *always. I will say it again: Rejoice! . . . Do not be anxious about anything, but in everything, by prayer and petition, with thanksgiving, present your requests to God. And the peace of God, which transcends all understanding, will guard your hearts and your minds in Christ Jesus.*

Phil. 4:2–7

Towards the end of his letter, Paul suddenly feels the need to remind the Philippians again that anxiety is the biggest joy-robber of all. We simply can't 'rejoice in the Lord' when our worries are constantly churning around inside us like pebbles in a cement mixer. Paul linked joy and peace very closely here, perhaps because it is impossible to have joy if you do not have peace. Someone once said that peace is joy resting and joy is peace dancing.

The people in Philippi could have felt infuriated with Paul for telling them, 'Do not be anxious.' They faced terrible danger on a daily basis, but they would have known exactly what Paul meant when he said God's peace would 'guard' (garrison) their hearts and minds and save them from worry. The wealthy city of Philippi was kept safe from enemy attack by its thick Roman walls. On top of these fortifications, fully armed, highly trained soldiers kept watch, guarding the Philippian citizens day and night. Paul was saying, 'I'm telling you to be full of Jesus-joy because you know He is surrounding you and your families all the time, like the soldiers on those walls, so you don't have to feel worried in your hearts, or think worrying thoughts in your minds.'

Stop for a moment and allow this supernatural peace to surround you on every side like a protecting wall. Let peace sink into your innermost being, softening your anger, comforting your fears and stilling all your restless thoughts. Sit and enjoy!

Paul's secret

I have learned the secret of being content in any and every situation, whether well fed or hungry, whether living in plenty or in want.

Phil. 4:12

Paul must often have remembered his time in Philippi as he wrote his letter. He'd had two very different lodgings, the luxurious home of a rich businesswoman and the local prison, yet he was equally content in both (Acts 16:14–15, 23–25). During twenty years as an itinerant speaker I've slept in countless beds, some so comfortable I wanted to stay a month – but it was harder to be content on a top bunk or an airport floor. Perhaps the habit of contentment is difficult to cultivate because we are so preoccupied with our outer comfort and convenience that we forget to look inside ourselves to derive our pleasure from the Lord who lives there.

The theologian William Law (1686–1761) said, 'Make it a rule to yourself to thank and praise God for everything that happens to you.' I'm uneasy about that – how can we thank God that our child is seriously ill and in agony? When Paul says 'give thanks in all circumstances' (1 Thess. 5:18) he is not telling us to thank God *for* the circumstances but *in* them. We may not be able to thank God for our child's pain but we can usually find something else to be grateful for in that situation – perhaps the discovery of antibiotics or the cuppa the nurses made us?

Have you ever played Pollyanna's Glad Game? 'It may be raining but I'm glad I've got a big umbrella. My car has broken down, but I'm glad it did so by a garage. My boss may be in a foul mood, but I'm glad it's Friday.' Playing this game when you feel like grouching is a wonderful way of accessing Paul's secret contentment!

Prisoners of hope

*Return to your fortress, O prisoners of hope; Come back to the place
of safety.*

Zech. 9:12, NIV and NLT

Paul was in prison but he was never a prisoner! It is not difficult situations that trap us; it is our reactions to them that form the prison
bars. Psalm 107:10–11 and 13 talks about prisoners like that who are
chained in the deepest gloom, 'for they had rebelled against the words
of God . . . Then they cried to the LORD in their trouble, and he saved
them from their distress. He brought them out of darkness . . . and
broke away their chains' (v. 14). Our spirits can be imprisoned when
we 'rebel' against God by shaking an angry fist at the circumstances
He has allowed. Fortunately He is always ready to save us when we
call to Him for help!

An Old Testament scholar such as Paul would have known
Zechariah's phrase 'prisoners of hope' (9:12). Whenever I read it, I
think of the day I went to tea with my friends Jo and Susie. Their cat
had presented them with five kittens, which had rapidly turned into
teenagers with attitude! In the centre of the sitting room stood a huge
wire cage in which lived a family of gerbils. The kittens swarmed incessantly all over the cage, spitting, hissing and clawing savagely at the
bars. Far from being traumatised, the gerbils took no notice at all, but
happily went on eating, sleeping and playing chase. They could live
happy carefree lives simply because of those bars. A prison holds you
in on all sides and contains you, so being a prisoner of hope means
being surrounded and protected by our unshakeable trust in God's
promises and goodness.

*You hem me in – behind and before; you have laid your hand
upon me . . . Where can I go from your Spirit? Where can I flee
from your presence?*

(Ps. 139:5, 7)

Conkers

Fix your thoughts on what is true, and honourable and right, and pure, and lovely, and admirable. Think about things that are excellent and worthy of praise.

Phil. 4:8, NLT

I have just found the most wonderful conker tree! There it stood – alone among the rich brown furrows of the newly ploughed fields. The ground around it was littered with prickly cases after the storm we had last night, many splitting neatly open to reveal their hidden treasure. Suddenly I shed sixty years and was a child again, as I stuffed my pockets full of these plump beauties. I saw myself, and my brother, stringing them together to make giant caterpillars or having a conker fight. In my memory I 'watched' my sons throwing sticks up into the branches to knock down the precious conkers in the park, and heard again their whoops of joy when they discovered a huge specimen that would surely beat all comers in the playground next morning. (In those good old days children were still allowed to take conkers to school!)

Why would God bother to make conkers so beautifully shiny? I'm sure there is some biological reason but I like to think He made conkers because He loves to see the fun children have collecting them each autumn. I've also wondered whether, if wild flowers were as big as specimen orchids, we would pay a fortune for them at the florist. Perhaps He made them tiny so that most of them bloom for His enjoyment alone (Matt. 6:28–30).

Lord, help me to see the world through five-year-old eyes. Don't let me be so preoccupied with adult concerns today that I fail to see the glorious things you made for the delight of the child who still lives inside me.

The 'loveliness of Christ'

He brought me to the banqueting house, and his banner over me was love . . . My beloved is mine, and I am his.

Song of Songs 2:4, 16, KJV

Outwardly, Mrs Cousins was a dutiful Victorian minister's wife, serving her husband's flock in the Scottish town of Melrose. Inwardly, she was a poet who was fascinated by a man who had been born near her home two hundred years before. His name was Samuel Rutherford and, although he was not famous for his achievements, his remarkable relationship with the Lord makes him a legend. Anne Cousins spent her scanty spare time studying the letters Samuel wrote to his friends, savouring all his little insights into God's love. Finally she wove some of these thought-fragments into her well-known hymn 'The Sands of Time are Sinking', here are some of my favourite extracts:

> *Oh! I am my Beloved's,*
> *And my Beloved's mine!*
> *He brings a poor vile sinner*
> *Into His 'house of wine':*
> *The bride eyes not her garment,*
> *But her dear bridegroom's face;*
> *I will not gaze at glory,*
> *But on my King of Grace.*
> *Not at the crown He giveth,*
> *But on His pierced hand;*
> *The Lamb is all the glory*
> *Of Immanuel's land.*

A visiting English businessman who met Samuel Rutherford in St Andrews in 1640 commented that he was a poor preacher but 'he showed me the loveliness of Christ'. Please, Lord, may I show your loveliness to everyone I meet today.

Finishing well

The righteous will flourish like a palm tree . . . They will still bear fruit in old age, they will stay fresh and green.

Ps. 92:12, 14

Yesterday I went with Mary to see her allotment. As we walked between the patchwork quilt of little garden squares we admired some that were bulging with plump autumn produce: huge marrows, juicy tomatoes, prosperous-looking apple trees and neat rows of greens.

Not all the little gardens were looked after so carefully. Some looked wildly out of control and any fruit that had been brave enough to grow without human help was smothered in weeds.

'It's sad,' remarked Mary. 'When people first take on an allotment they seem full of enthusiasm, reading books, making plans, experimenting, but then they seem to get busy with other things, and there's no time left to tend their strip so it just goes to ruin.'

I couldn't help thinking that Christian life is a bit like that! We can start off so full of enthusiasm, involved in everything that's happening at church, and then suddenly other things creep in. We get busier at work, our family grows, we move to a bigger home so there's more DIY and gardening to do; or we buy a caravan or take up golf!

I vividly remember being squashed into a hall with a hundred other teenagers, listening to an inspiring speaker. We were all on fire for God, ready to die for Him, but a chill came over the place when the speaker said, 'Statistics show that in ten years' time only fifty of you will be following God, and forty years from now He'll only have five of you left.'

Lord, please help me to finish well! I long to go on bearing fruit for you, right up to the end.

Connections

For thus says the LORD God . . . 'In returning and rest you shall be saved; In quietness and confidence shall be your strength.'

Isa. 30:15, NKJV

When I emerge from my bedroom in the morning my two dogs welcome me with ecstatic joy and there follows a daily ritual of tail-wagging and chin-rubbing while I settle into my favourite armchair. They soon flop back to sleep while I enjoy my coffee and Bible.

Throughout the day, while I'm busy at my desk, they'll slump in a patch of shade or curl up by a radiator, according to the weather, but at regular intervals they both come to find me, just to rub my knee with their noses and sit down for a moment at my feet. I give them a stroke or a pat and turn back to my computer. These moments of silent connecting are actually a wordless exchange of love and trust on their part. They don't want anything; they are just letting me know they still there and that they are glad that I'm there too. Then off they go again to relax in their favourite spot.

I've been trying for years to develop the same habit with the Lord. Smiling up at the ceiling is all it takes, but I get so engrossed in what I am doing I often forget Him for hours at a time. One friend of mine tried putting verses of scripture, or hymns, on her loo wall; another sets her mobile to remind her to connect with God on the hour, every hour!

Lord, you have promised to be with me every moment of my life; please help me to acknowledge your presence and respond to it more often.

All-consuming desire

Delight yourself in the LORD *and he will give you the desires of your heart. Commit your way to the* LORD; *trust in him and he will do this: Be still before the* LORD *and wait patiently for him.*

Ps. 37:4–7

Elaine always expected to get married. She was attractive and had all the gifts necessary to make a success of running a happy Christian home. She prayed daily for many years that the right man would come along, but by thirty-five she had become angry and disillusioned. Why had God made her with a desire to be half of someone else and then left her single?

I've met many others who bring their deepest longing to God often and earnestly, trusting in His biblical promises, but the candle flame of their faith soon flickers and dies in the cold blast of disappointment.

I wonder if sometimes the healing, the baby or the new job that we so urgently desire actually becomes so all-consumingly important to us that when we bring our request before God it feels so vast that it obscures His face. In fact, what *we* want has become more essential to us than He is Himself.

So nowadays when I pray, I try to picture myself bringing the situation or the person to Jesus – rather as people did in the Gospel stories – and I lay them at His feet. Rather than focusing on the problem, I look up into His face by faith and wait silently. There may be something He wants me to do or receive from Him first, which He knows is actually more important to my welfare than a quick 'yes' to my prayers.

He really does communicate His desires to us when our first and foremost desire is to please Him and do His will.

Moments of heaven

God bless you and keep you, God smile on you and gift you, God look you full in the face and make you prosper.

Num. 6:24–26, *The Message*

Today, I went down the garden with my three-year-old granddaughter Molly to pick the apples from my funny little tree. Its branches are so low she was able to fill a whole basket to take home to her mummy. Then we went into the field beyond my garden gate and sat in the patch of sunshine munching away together happily; the dogs sat down beside us, watching hopefully for our apple cores. We didn't talk; we just sat – it was one of those moments of stillness and pure delight.

Life often makes me feel as if I'm a hamster endlessly running inside a wheel, but I'm sure God wants to punctuate each day with these 'moments of delight', times when we just stop for a moment and let something funny, beautiful or unusual seep down deep into our inner being. The more we expect such moments, and look out for them, the more often we experience them. Yet I find it so easy to rush through the day with my head down and my mind too full of earthly concerns to make room for these glimpses of heaven.

I love the thought of you smiling at me, Lord. I know I must make you look sad sometimes, but I love it when the clouds of busyness and earthly concerns are parted and we can share together those rare moments of stillness and beauty.

Standing back in faith

At that time Moses was born – a beautiful child in God's eyes. His parents cared for him at home for three months. When they had to abandon him, Pharaoh's daughter adopted him and raised him as her own son.

Acts 7:20, NLT

As soon as I knew I was pregnant I would begin daydreaming about my baby – perhaps the mother of Moses did the same? Yet she knew that if she had a boy he would be instantly drowned in the River Nile (Exod. 1:22). Her only hope was to give birth quickly – before the midwife arrived – so she could hide him. Here's the background to the story.

For three hundred and seventy years the descendants of Jacob had been enjoying prosperous lives as sheep farmers in the fertile Nile delta. Pharaoh had given them the land out of gratitude to Joseph, who had saved Egypt from famine by his brilliant administrative gifts. When a new dynasty seized power Joseph was forgotten and the new pharaoh wanted their lush location as a site for a new city. He also realised that two million Jews could be either a national threat or a cheap, ready-made workforce for his building projects.

In spite of Pharaoh's programme of forced labour and near-starvation, a baby boom scared him into culling all newborn baby boys. Hebrews 11:23 tells us that Moses' parents firmly believed God would protect their child, but trying to hide a noisy baby in a slave's shack soon became too risky. Pushing that little floating cradle out into deep water, and then walking away, must have taken enormous faith in God's power and protection!

Could God be asking you to stand back and leave Him to protect and care for someone you are worried about – as Moses' mother did?

You can always do something

When the princess saw the basket among the reeds, she sent her maid to get it for her . . . When the princess opened it . . . The little boy was crying, and she felt sorry for him.

Exod. 2:5–6, NLT

I wonder if God had already prepared the heart of this princess. Suppose she had been outraged by her father's act of drowning those Israelite babies? She could not save them all, but perhaps she was glad to save one.

You probably know the famous story of the starfish: a freak high tide had landed thousands of them on a beach and then receded, leaving them to die in the hot sun. A man saw a child throwing them back into the sea, one by one.

'What difference can your efforts possibly make?' he asked. As the child hurled the next starfish she replied, 'A lot of difference to this one!'

Do you ever feel overwhelmed when you receive gift appeals from Christian organisations? The little you could give would surely make no difference to such enormous needs. But by saving just one baby the princess eventually saved an entire nation! So who knows what God could do with one small donation?

Pharaoh had many harems all over Egypt and it was not uncommon for foreign children to be brought up and educated with his own numerous offspring. The man God was preparing to free a horde of slaves and turn them into a nation would need a first-class education if he was going to understand and record for posterity all of God's Law for His people (Deut. 31:24).

Lord, help me today to do at least one significant thing, which, with your help, will really make a big difference to someone else.

Paradigm shift

So the LORD stirred up the spirit of Zerubbabel . . . and the spirit of the whole remnant of the people. They came and began work on the house of the LORD Almighty, their God.

Hag. 1:14

Whenever God wants to move me into a deeper relationship with Him or a new sphere of service, He often begins by making me feel discontented with my life, which I had previously found safe and satisfying. Have you ever felt 'stirred up' out of your comfort zone?

For forty years Moses lived as an Egyptian prince. Acts 7:22–23 tells us he was 'educated in all the wisdom of the Egyptians and was powerful in speech and action'. His trained mind and military prowess had probably landed him a plum job in a government department. He might have continued to enjoy this luxurious lifestyle had not something (or someone) mysteriously 'stirred his spirit'. A belated desire to help his own people sent him off to inspect their working conditions. Defending an unpopular ethnic minority was risky, but Moses had obviously experienced a massive shift in the way he thought about his own identity and purpose in life (Heb. 11:25–26).

On paper Moses was perfectly qualified for the job of freeing the slaves. So he set off, brimming with self-confidence, casting himself in the role of 'rescuer'. Unfortunately, he went in his own strength, and failed horrendously because he never prayed about his venture. God cannot use people who rely on their own high-quality gifts and qualifications, because they have so much going for them naturally that they feel they have no need of His help.

LORD, help me remember that your grace is all I need, for your power is greatest when I am weak (2 Cor. 12:9, GNB).

Wilderness experience

Now Moses was tending the flock of Jethro his father-in-law, the priest of Midian, and he led the flock to the far side of the desert and came to Horeb, the mountain of God. There the angel of the LORD appeared to him in flames of fire.

Exod. 3:1–2

Poor Moses must have felt like a total failure and as desolate as his surroundings. Egyptians thought shepherding was the most degrading job of all, so to have to follow his father-in-law's scrawny sheep around the wilderness for forty years would have been deeply humiliating. Yet what felt like failure to Moses was God's training ground. As an Egyptian prince, he could never have led thousands of families through the desert; God knew that job could be done only by someone with years of experience in desert survival.

I always dreamed of doing something special for God but when disabling illness kept me in a wheelchair for eight years I felt God had chucked my life on the scrapheap. Then I gradually began to realise that the things I had wanted to do were not nearly as important to Him as the relationship of love and companionship He was developing with me during my illness. He also taught me things that shaped my future ministry. I believe that's what happened to Moses. He could have spent his wilderness experience wallowing in loneliness, self-pity or remorse, but instead he developed the intimacy with God that characterised him for the rest of his life.

He is not the best Christian . . . who makes the fewest false steps. He is the best who wins the most splendid victories by the retrieval of mistakes. Forget mistakes; organise victory out of mistakes.

F. W. Robertson (1816–53)

Facing the past

Then the LORD said to him, 'What is that in your hand?' 'A staff,' he replied. The LORD said, 'Throw it on the ground' . . . and it became a snake, and he ran from it. Then the LORD said to him, 'Reach out your hand and take it by the tail.'

Exod. 4:2–4

If the Lord had told Moses to go and free the slaves forty years earlier, he would have gone like a shot! Now the very idea of returning to Egypt terrified him. Most people of eighty would relish the comfort of an armchair, but Moses only had his shepherd's crook to lean on; it was his comfort, but also his security – his weapon of defence. Although he might not have enjoyed life in the desert, familiarity equalled comfort and security. The prison you know can feel safer than the prospect of freedom. God was asking him to throw down the symbol of his security and watch it turn into something he feared. Poisonous snakes were life-threatening, and Moses ran! But God wanted to teach him to move towards all the things that most scared him, because by grasping them they could be transformed, by God, into blessings for others (Exod. 4:5, 17).

For years an experience in my past made me too afraid to do things I knew God was calling me to do; 'I'll always have this handicap,' I told myself, 'because of my childhood.' A deep experience of God's inner healing changed all that. God doesn't always remove our fear when we have to do something we are afraid of, but He does help us to 'do it afraid'.

When we give our past to the Lord it no longer has the power to spoil the present.

OCTOBER 1

First port of call

Then Moses went back to the LORD and protested, 'Why have you brought all this trouble on your own people, LORD? Why did you send me? Ever since I came to Pharaoh . . . he has been even more brutal to your people.'

Exod. 5:22, NLT

I can picture Moses, ushered into Pharaoh's throne room – knees knocking but sure of success because God had promised to be with him and show him what to say and do. What a huge shock to his faith when he and his brother were rapidly flung out, with Pharaoh's sneering taunts ringing in their ears. Pharaoh was not impressed by two shabbily dressed octogenarians! He was young, arrogant and ambitious, bent on building monuments to immortalise himself. In order to do that he needed slave labour, so letting the Israelites go free was the last thing he intended!

Have you ever steeled yourself to do something for God, only to fail utterly? When Emma's boss enforced an office procedure that was dishonest, she prayed hard and then felt that God wanted her to express her concern to the boss. His quick talk tied her in humiliating knots and left her determined never to do anything for God again. Then a Sunday sermon encouraged her to try again. This time the boss changed his policy, and actually offered Emma a promotion!

Moses must have felt like running back to the desert when he realised his interview with Pharaoh had *increased* his people's suffering and they were blaming him for having to make bricks without straw.

In the past, when I felt God had let me down, I stopped praying and moaned to my friends. Moses, faced with apparent disaster, turned directly to God himself and told Him exactly how he felt.

Is God your first destination when things go wrong?

Lord, change me!

I will give you a new heart and put a new spirit in you.

Ezek. 36:26

For years I lived with a terrible fear which always used to creep up behind me at unexpected moments. I was sure that if I lost my husband I simply would not cope.

'I don't mind illness or death for myself, Lord,' I used to pray, 'but if I lost Tony I would simply fall apart.' When I *did* lose him it certainly felt like hell – but now I can look back and see how God has used that worst fear of mine to change me in so many good ways.

Moses dreaded having to stand up to Pharaoh but their year-long battle changed Moses from a nervous old failure into one of the greatest leaders of all time.

The people Moses finally managed to lead out of Egypt also needed to change from cringing, servile slaves, dependent on cruel masters, into a free, self-respecting nation who trusted the Lord to meet all their needs. They hated their new life in the desert and often wanted to run back to Egypt; having been in that wilderness myself I have every sympathy for them! Day after day they had to heave their possessions, small children and livestock through nothing but sand, rocks and blistering heat. They were hungry and thirsty and even when God provided miraculous supplies they soon got bored by the lack of variety.

They grumbled at God because they did not realise the desert was all about changing their hearts. If things are not easy for you right now, would you be willing to pray the words of this song?

Jesus, You are changing me . . .
You are the potter and I am the clay;
help me to be willing to let You have Your way . . .

Marilyn Baker (Copyright © 1980 Word Music UK)

The dry old stick

The Amalekites came and attacked the Israelites . . . Moses said to Joshua, 'Choose some of our men and go out to fight the Amalekites. Tomorrow I will stand on top of the hill with the staff of God in my hands.'

Exod. 17:8–9

Those recruits had never fought a battle before! They must have felt terrified – until, high up on the cliffs above them, they saw Moses holding his old shepherd's staff high in the air. They had just seen that stick used to release badly needed water from a rock, and they'd watched Moses hold it out over the sea to make them a pathway to safety. To them it was a tangible symbol of God's power. While Moses kept his stick up in the air, the battle went their way, but when his arms sagged with fatigue the enemy surged forward.

Prayer is not easy either; our minds wander, phones ring, kids wake up, until we give up and do something 'more useful'. Yet Hudson Taylor, who spent his life as a missionary in China back in the 1800s, once said, 'Men can be moved for God by prayer alone.' When the Communists banned Christianity his hard work appeared to have failed completely, yet today the church in China is growing faster than anywhere else in the world. I guess if we once realised just how effective prayer really is, we would give it a much higher priority in our daily schedules.

Moses could actually *see* the effect his prayers were having on the battle but we often pray away without seeing anything change. We just have to go on holding our 'prayer stick' up in the air by faith and willpower.

More things are wrought by prayer than this world dreams of.
Alfred, Lord Tennyson (1809–92)

OCTOBER 4

Triplets

When Moses' hands grew tired, they took a stone and put it under him and he sat on it. Aaron and Hur held his hands up – one on one side, one on the other – so that his hands remained steady till sunset.

Exod. 17:12

A recent survey asked churchgoing Christians what they thought was the greatest threat to spiritual growth. Their answers were: materialism, self-centredness, laziness, lack of forgiveness, sexual lust, gluttony and lying. Actually it is prayerlessness. Another survey showed that most of us pray only once a week in church or in an emergency! Yet it is prayer that changes the world – and us. Samuel Chadwick (1830–1932) was so right when he said that when Satan sees us work he laughs, but when he sees us pray he trembles.

Some of my friends can pray for hours on their own, but I have to confess that I find concentrating terribly difficult – unless I'm praying with other people. I don't mean in prayer meetings, when I'm always scared I'll start at the same time as someone else, but with just a couple of others. During one of the busiest patches of my life I've found being in a prayer triplet a huge help. Two friends and I made a pact to meet for an hour each week to pray for our families and our own personal issues. We trusted each other so it was possible to share our deepest concerns, and we also found that prayer became much easier – as well as more fun! I guess Moses, Aaron and Hur gave the rest of us the idea of prayer triplets; have you ever thought of creating one?

Lord, you said, 'Where two or three come together in my name, there am I with them' (Matt. 18:20). Please help me to find one or two friends I can pray with regularly.

God's recipe for happiness

Mount Sinai was covered with smoke, because the LORD descended on it in fire. The . . . whole mountain trembled violently, and the sound of the trumpet grew louder and louder. Then Moses spoke and the voice of God answered him.

Exod. 19:18–19

The people must have been terrified, but God needed them to see His awesome power because He was about to make a solemn pact with them: 'You live by my rules and you'll be happy and prosperous; disobey them, and misery follows.' That was the deal. God wanted the rest of the world to see that living by His rules resulted in happiness and prosperity, so they would follow Him too.

Here is the recipe for happiness that He gave them: 'Everyone should be free to enjoy his own patch of land, so there's to be no coveting or stealing other people's possessions. Children need the security of two loving parents, so adultery is out – it destroys marriage. Everyone should get along happily with others, so no dishonesty or murder. To avoid family rowing and neglect of the elderly, be good to your parents. Avoid stress; take a day each week to rest and get to know me better. Don't worship images of me; relate to me direct, put me first and everything else will fall into place' (rough paraphrase of Exod. 20:1–21).

It is so easy to dismiss God's rules as negative and restricting, but in fact someone always suffers when we selfishly put our own interests before someone else's. We all frequently break those ten rules in all kinds of little ways, telling ourselves, 'God is kind; He'll understand.' He *is* kind, but Sinai reminds me that He's also holy!

We hear a lot about intimacy with God these days, but are we in danger of reducing God to a sloppy, sentimental Father Christmas figure?

OCTOBER 6

World-changer, difference-maker

When the people saw that Moses was so long in coming down from the mountain, they gathered round Aaron and said, 'Come, make us gods who will go before us. As for this fellow Moses who brought us up out of Egypt, we don't know what has happened to him.'

Exod. 32:1

God was furious! He had done so many amazing miracles to free those slaves; He had promised them a wonderful new life, homes, fruitful farms and peace from their enemies. All they had to do was obey His Rules for Happiness – one of which was never to worship an idol. Yet, rather than wait confidently while He explained His plans for their future welfare to Moses up on the mountain, they panicked, thinking He had abandoned them. 'The Egyptian gods are much more powerful,' they decided and, pooling their jewellery, they created an image of Apis, the bull calf, symbolising fertility and strength. Then they threw a party in his honour, which soon degenerated into a sex orgy (1 Cor. 10:7–8). In a fury of rejection God would have wiped them out – had not Moses interceded for them (Exod. 32:10, 11, 32)!

Intercession is the most important ministry God ever gives to anyone, because an intercessor changes not only the lives of individuals, but also the course of world events. There are certain people I know, and greatly admire, who see prayer as their daily work, and not just a slot in their schedule. It is not a calling that earns human rewards, such as praise and thanks, because few people ever realise how powerfully God uses them.

We are all called to pray for one another and the world, but just a few are given a very special anointing to be world-changers and difference-makers. Would you like to be one of them?

Show me your glory

Now therefore, I (Moses) pray thee, if I have found grace in thy sight, shew me now thy way, that I may know thee, that I may find grace in thy sight . . . I beseech thee, shew me thy glory.

Exod. 33:13, 18, KJV

I long to have the same insatiable desire for God that Moses had; his greatest desire was see His glory and to know Him intimately. For me it is the endless 'busy busy busyness' of life that takes my eyes off my goal.

Exodus 33 tells us that 'Moses used to take a tent and pitch it outside the camp some distance away, calling it the "tent of meeting" . . . The LORD would speak to Moses face to face, as a man speaks with his friend' (Exod. 33:7, 9, 11). Moses had to physically remove himself from all the noise and activity of the huge campsite so he could quieten himself down sufficiently to hear God's voice. That 'stepping away' is the secret of knowing God, but not all of us have a house with a private chapel attached! While Susannah Wesley 'home-schooled' fourteen of her children her 'tent of meeting' was inside the apron she regularly pulled over her head. It is really a question of 'how badly do we want God?'

Carol's husband was not yet a Christian, and when he retired he bitterly resented the time Carol spent with God each day. 'So I asked the Lord to wake me an hour early,' Carol told me, 'so I can pop downstairs and enjoy a pot of tea in His company before my husband wakes up. It is my favourite time of the day.'

Lord, I don't want to be just a 'pew-filler' Christian; I want to live so close to you that I can share your feelings, sense your thoughts and anticipate your plans.

'All in the mind'

The LORD now said to Moses, 'Send out men to explore the land of Canaan' . . . This was their report . . . 'It is indeed a bountiful country – a land flowing with milk and honey . . . But the people living there are powerful, and their towns are large and fortified. We even saw giants . . .' But Caleb tried to quiet the people . . . 'Let's go at once to take the land,' he said. 'We can certainly conquer it!' But the other men . . . disagreed. 'They are stronger than we are!'

Num. 13:1–2, 27–28, 30–31, NLT

'Two men looked through prison bars, one saw mud and the other saw stars.' It is not tough situations that make us feel afraid or miserable, but what we *think* about those situations. One man will see the loss of his job as an irrevocable disaster, while another will view the same event as a challenge – a doorway to new experiences. The first feels depressed and anxious; the second feels confident and positive.

As the people listened to those two, very different, reports, they were faced with a choice. Either they could concentrate on the giants and walled cities and feel discouraged and afraid, or they could think about God's faithfulness and glorious promises and feel excitement and hope. Unfortunately they made the wrong choice, and sentenced themselves to forty more years wandering round the desert.

There is nothing that hurts God more than when we choose to doubt His ability and desire to take care of us. Yet 'giants and citadels' (intimidating people or unsolvable problems) do look terrifying. As we focus on them, they seem to grow larger, but when we focus on God and His promises they shrink.

I've never met a Christian yet who didn't suffer from doubts occasionally, but we can choose either to embrace them or to kick them out.

The final challenge

Climb one of the mountains . . . and look out over the land I have given the people of Israel. After you have seen it, you will die.

Num. 27:12–13, 16–17, NLT

Surely Moses would have been bitterly disappointed not to be allowed to lead the people into the Promised Land? In the past he had successfully interceded at great length, but this time he accepted God's decision without question. Living so close to God, he probably knew instinctively that He wanted acceptance without argument on this occasion.

When bad things hit our lives I'm sure we should never just accept them passively; first we need to ask God to show us if He wants us to pray for release from them, or patience to endure them.

It is not easy to hand over responsibility for something that has been important to us, but Moses' ability to listen to God may have shown him he was now too old for the job. Susan had run the children's work in her church most successfully for years. She was furious when the new minister wanted a younger person to take over. Two years later she had to admit that her successor was doing an excellent job and had been blessed through the challenge. We have to hold the things we do for God in an open hand because He may want to 'grow' someone else through doing the job.

Perhaps there was another reason for Moses' calm acceptance of approaching death. He wanted to be *with* the Master he loved so intimately more than he desired to *serve* Him by leading the people into the Land.

Moses accomplished one of the greatest feats in history yet his epitaph simply reads, 'Moses, whom the Lord knew face to face' (Deut. 34:10). Intimate friendship is God's priority.

Changing clothes

Do not lie to each other, since you have taken off your old self with its practices and have put on the new self . . . Therefore, as God's chosen people . . . clothe yourselves with compassion, kindness, humility, gentleness and patience.

Col. 3:9–12

Colosse lay in a valley by a beautiful river, and when its prosperous citizens became Christians they were probably baptised there. Before they plunged into the water they took off their rich robes to show they were leaving behind their old lives, and as they came up again they put on pure white clothes, which symbolised their new lives as Christians. Paul loved this 'taking off and putting on' simile. He tells us to resist evil by putting on 'the full armour of God' (Eph. 6:10–11), and also encourages us to 'put on Jesus' and wear His qualities and characteristics like royal robes.

When Norman got his first job in the menswear department of a large Oxford Street store, he prayed he would be a good ambassador for Jesus. However, his immediate boss, Smithson, an atheist, made Norman's life miserable by constantly ridiculing his faith and bullying him in front of colleagues and customers. Patience, which means the power to endure whatever comes with a good attitude, was *not* one of Norman's natural gifts! So he pictured himself 'putting it on' each morning. Fifteen years later, when Norman was selling kilts in Scotland, he had a letter from Smithson, who had just been diagnosed with liver cancer.

'You never preached, but there was something different about you. I need a faith like yours right now. Will you tell me how to get it?' Norman caught the next train to London and had the joy of leading Smithson to the Lord.

Please dress me up in your compassion and tenderness today.

Do you believe in angels?

He will give his angels [especial] charge over you to accompany, defend and preserve you in all your ways . . .

Ps. 91:11, AMP

Meg couldn't sleep the night after major surgery – until a fat nurse with frizzy hair and thick glasses sat holding her hand. When Meg woke she described the nurse in detail to the Sister.

'No one like that works here,' Meg was told. One night, alone in my car, I skidded into a snowdrift on Exmoor. A farmer turned up in a Land Rover, pulled me out, towed me to the safety of a gritted road – and then mysteriously vanished.

Angels are watching me as I write this and you as you read; they surround us constantly and the Bible mentions them over three hundred times. I believe we see them more often than we realise because they can take many forms. When I was eighteen and walking alone in a forest, a man began chasing me. I prayed hard, and whistled to an imaginary dog, hoping to scare him off. He soon realised I was bluffing and ran even faster. Then suddenly a huge, vicious-looking dog jumped out of the trees and trotted along at my heels until we reached some houses, and then it disappeared. Elisha saw angels looking like chariot horses, so why not a dog?

Some people develop an unhealthy fascination with angels, and we must remember we are forbidden to worship them (Col. 2:18; Rev. 22:8–9). Our focus must be on God Himself because Satan is not above masquerading as an angel to give us false information (2 Cor. 11:14).

Father God, the universe you created is full of beings I can't see, and mysteries I can't understand. Thank you for making yourself known to me in a down-to-earth human form I can relate to; thank you, Father, for sending Jesus.

Invisible servants

Angels are only servants – spirits sent to care for people who will inherit salvation.

Heb. 1:14, NLT

Mick was driving up the motorway when he heard a deep voice say, 'Turn off at the next exit.' He doesn't have satellite navigation so he was startled enough to obey – and avoided a serious multiple accident. Was it an angel Mick heard? Eve's baby was sleeping safely in her cot, so Eve flopped onto her bed next door. Suddenly she was woken from a deep sleep by acute fear. Rushing in she found her baby blue and lifeless; she had choked on her vomit and stopped breathing. Eve held her upside down and banged her back until the obstruction cleared. When the paramedics arrived they said Eve had been within a minute of losing her baby. Had God used an angel to wake her?

The Bible tells many stories of how God sent angels to intervene in the lives of His friends. When Daniel was flung into a cage full of hungry lions an angel put muzzles on their mouths (Dan. 6:22); Elijah was alone in the desert, suffering from exhaustion and dehydration, so God sent an angel with food and water (1 Kgs 19:5–7). Jesus desperately needed encouragement and company in Gethsemane; because His friends were all asleep an angel was dispatched to care for Him instead (Luke 22:43). When God sees that we urgently need help, I wonder if He first looks for a human to rescue us, and, if no one responds to His nudge, does He have to use an angel instead?

Lord, I'm sorry for all those times when I felt I was too busy or tired to ring, write to or visit someone when you prompted me to do so. Please make me more aware of your voice.

Angels love to worship

Yes, praise the LORD, *you armies of angels who serve him and do his will!*

Ps. 103:21, NLT

Then I looked and heard the voice of many angels, numbering thousands upon thousands, and ten thousand times ten thousand. They encircled the throne and . . . In a loud voice they sang: 'Worthy is the Lamb, who was slain, to receive power and wealth and wisdom and strength and honour and glory and praise!'

Rev. 5:11

Angels love worship! Next time you're in church, remember that angels are there too! The congregation will be doubled because everyone will be accompanied by their own personal angel, who has been guarding them since birth (Matt. 18:10); but if you are *really* worshipping from the heart, instead of just performing the words and music, the sound you make will be so attractive to angels that they will flock from all directions to join in. People have often reported seeing angels dancing with joy in church aisles, on window ledges or in the air among the rafters!

Sometimes when I've been leading worship, I have suddenly felt someone brush past me or move behind me. When no humans are that close I sense that angels are surrounding me (Ps. 34:7).

On the last night of a conference I was running, Jill asked if she could sing Handel's 'Hallelujah Chorus' as a solo, which had been her life's ambition. She had been born seriously deformed and was in a wheelchair, and sadly her little wobbly voice was completely drowned by the piano. Suddenly we became aware of a huge choir joining in, lifting and enhancing her voice supernaturally. I have never heard anything more beautiful!

Angels help us to adore Him;
ye behold Him face to face;
sun and moon, bow down before Him;
dwellers all in time and space.

Henry Francis Lyte (1793–1847)

Angel warriors

The Son of Man will send out his angels, and they will weed out of his kingdom everything that causes sin and all who do evil. They will throw them into the fiery furnace, where there will be weeping and gnashing of teeth.

Matt. 13:41–42

Surely these words of Jesus must banish the ridiculous idea that angels look like fairies or chubby babies? They are fierce warriors!

They have differing ranks and responsibilities, and Daniel tells us that each nation has an angel assigned to it. He also says that Satan has matched them with high-ranking demons to fight them continuously (Dan. 10). Churches have their own angels too (Rev. 2:1), and demons as well (Eph. 6:12).

I ran a retreat in Wales once, which resembled a nightmare! Things kept going wrong: there were major arguments; people were ill or injured. When someone admitted she'd attended satanic rituals in the past I was not surprised that I had been conscious of a dark shape watching us through the windows. On the last morning I got up at four and sat in the chapel, crying out to the Lord to make our last session special. Suddenly 'something' was standing in front of me: it was not the 'dark shape'; he looked like a completely white medieval knight. He rested the tip of his long sword on the floor and leant his head on folded hands as he gripped the hilt. He looked exhausted, bedraggled and battle-worn.

'Who is he, Lord?' I whispered. I 'felt' the Lord reply, 'He has been your angel this week, fighting the powers of darkness who have been attacking you. His battle is won.' Needless to say, we had a glorious final session and saw a major breakthrough in several lives.

Thank you for not leaving us to fight our spiritual battles alone!

Beautiful bride

Husbands, love your wives, just as Christ loved the church and gave himself up for her to make her holy, cleansing her . . . to present her to himself as a radiant church, without stain or wrinkle or any other blemish, but holy and blameless.

Eph. 5:25–27

The Greek town where I was staying was flooded by crowds from outlying villages, eager to enjoy their annual festival. Suddenly I noticed the most beautiful girl I have ever seen; she was totally perfect in every detail – face, figure and hair. Beside her strode her gorgeous bridegroom.

'How wonderful to be young and in love,' I thought. Then I noticed her mother walking behind, and suddenly realised how poignantly fleeting human beauty actually is. Next year when that beautiful girl comes to the festival, she could be concealing a bump under a jumper. Two years later she'd have a baby on her hip, bags under her eyes from sleepless nights, and ugly stretch marks. Five years on she might have three children dragging at her skirts; eventually the lithe figure would bulge and sag, grey hairs would appear and the sun would crinkle her face like a walnut. Arthritis might bow those long slim legs and gnarl her slender fingers and the flashing white teeth would blacken with decay.

Depressing? Yes, but the wonderful thing is that age means nothing to God. He takes us on when our spirits are bent, disfigured and gnarled by sin and over the years He works on us, removing the spiritual bulges, wrinkles and grey hairs as He gradually transforms our inner selves, making them daily more beautiful.

Let us rejoice and be glad and give him glory! For the wedding of the Lamb has come, and his bride has made herself ready.

(Rev. 19:7)

The current of His love

*He (Jesus) had always loved those in the world who were his own,
and he loved them to the very end.*

John 13:1, GNB

One dark night a young man stood on a London bridge, looking down
at the River Thames as it surged below. How easy it would be, he
thought, just to jump and be carried away to oblivion by that current
– life felt completely pointless. Suddenly he was so overwhelmed by a
sense of God's enormous love that Samuel Francis was never the same
again. Whenever he read today's verse and thought about the love of
Jesus, he remembered that night and the surging tide.

Before you read his famous hymn, ask Jesus to speak to you, personally, through just one little phrase. The words may seem old-fashioned
but their message will never be out of date:

> *O the deep, deep love of Jesus, vast, unmeasured, boundless,
>   free!*
> *Rolling as a mighty ocean in its fullness over me!*
> *Underneath me, all around me, is the current of Thy love*
> *Leading onward, leading homeward to Thy glorious rest
>   above!*
> *O the deep, deep love of Jesus, spread His praise from shore
>   to shore!*
> *How He loveth, ever loveth, changeth never, nevermore!*
> *How He watches o'er His loved ones, died to call them all
>   His own;*
> *How for them He intercedeth, watcheth o'er them from the
>   throne!*
> *O the deep, deep love of Jesus, love of every love the best!*
> *'Tis an ocean full of blessing, 'tis a haven giving rest!*
> *O the deep, deep love of Jesus, 'tis a heaven of heavens to me;*
> *And it lifts me up to glory, for it lifts me up to Thee!*

Samuel Trevor Francis (1834–1925)

Dying to live

Unless a grain of wheat is buried in the ground, dead to the world, it is never any more than a grain of wheat. But if it is buried, it sprouts and reproduces itself many times over. In the same way, anyone who holds on to life just as it is destroys that life.

John 12:24–25, *The Message*

The fields round here have all been ploughed and harrowed, ready for the farmer to sow next year's wheat crop, but how do those little grains feel? They lie there in the dark and cold all winter, apparently dead and buried. Do they wonder why the farmer has done this to them, when they thought their destiny was to become a loaf of bread? They have no idea that his purpose was to create a harvest.

I guess we 'die a little' many times during our lives: when we are parted from people we love, lose a job or role, relocate and leave behind friends and perhaps a lively church. While we may be ready to meet a new challenge, we can still feel as if a part of us has died.

This time of year always makes me feel sad, as it was in October that my husband left me after thirty years of apparently happy marriage. I definitely thought my life was dead, but after a time of lying in the cold, dark earth, like a grain of wheat, I did 'come back to life', and God has produced a harvest by helping me to reach out and encourage many others in similar situations.

If part of you has died, keep watching for God to begin stirring your spirit back to life and sending up those new green shoots of hope. He will, if you are willing to let Him.

The bonfire

Anyone who builds . . . may use a variety of materials – gold, silver, jewels, wood, hay, or straw. But on the judgment day, fire will reveal what kind of work each builder has done. The fire will show if a person's work has any value. If the work survives, that builder will receive a reward.

1 Cor. 3:12–14, NLT

I've just made an enormous bonfire! Clippings from the hedges and shrubs made a heap the size of a caravan yet all that vegetation, which had taken so many years to grow, disappeared in less than an hour.

It made me realise that one day, our life's work will burn like that! St Paul tells us that everything we have ever done for the Lord will be tested by fire. All the church activities we organised, sermons we preached, people we helped – everything will be assessed. This is not to discover whether we can go to heaven or not, but simply so that good work can be rewarded. Paul describes some of the things we do for God as 'wood, hay and straw', which of course burn rapidly and disappear fast. These are the things we *appeared* to do for God but actually did because we just wanted to feel needed or important, to control others, to make them dependent on us, or to gain their respect and admiration. On the other hand, Paul describes the work we do simply for the pure love of God as precious stones, gold and silver, which will survive the flames.

If God waited until all our motives for serving Him were totally pure, of course, He could never use any of us, but He wants us to try to make pleasing Him the reason why we do anything and everything.

Lord, you see all the various things I do for you; please show me why I do them: am I working for my own benefit or for yours?

Name change

You'll get a brand-new name straight from the mouth of God . . . No more will anyone call you Rejected . . . Ruined. You'll be called Hephzibah (My Delight).

Isa. 62:2–4, The Message

The word 'name' doesn't just refer to what people call you; it can also mean 'identity' or 'reputation'. You can 'make a name for yourself' by success, or 'get a bad name' for dishonesty. We can also call ourselves names like Stupid, Not-Good-Enough, Useless, Unattractive, Boring, Defective. These name labels were usually stuck on us in the past by parents, teachers and other family members. They became our secret identity, and no one else knows they exist. Children so easily see themselves through the eyes of the adults who surround them and, once labelled, they find it hard to see themselves any other way.

For years I felt I had the word 'Failure' written on my forehead; one day I mentioned this to a friend, who promptly showed me the verses at the top of this page.

'Why don't you ask God to rip that nasty name badge off?' she suggested. 'Then let's ask God to tell you what *He* calls you.' As we waited in silence a beautiful name floated into my head. It was the last thing I would ever have dared to think up, so the God who changed the name 'Simon', meaning a wobbly reed, into 'Peter', a rock, had obviously changed my secret name too. Revelation 2:17 tells us; '*To him who overcomes . . . I will also give him a white stone with a new name written on it, known only to him who receives it.*'

I will change your name. You shall no longer be called
Wounded, outcast, lonely or afraid.
I will change your name. Your new name shall be
Confidence, joyfulness, overcoming one;
Faithfulness, friend of God, One who seeks my face.

D. J. Butler (Copyright © 1987 Mercy/Vineyard Publishing†)

Name-dropping

You can ask for anything in my name, and I will do it, so that the Son can bring glory to the Father. Yes, ask me for anything in my name, and I will do it!

John 14:13, NLT

When I was once asked to speak at an outreach event in a stately home, the owners kindly invited me to stay the previous night. While I was taking an early morning walk in the park, an irate gamekeeper told me, 'We don't allow the public in here!' Feeling terribly embarrassed I explained nervously, 'Lord "Blank" *did* say I could walk here . . .' My name-dropping worked like magic, because a name does not only mean an identity; it also equals power and authority. The signature of a multi-billionaire on a cheque could change your life; the Queen's name at the bottom of a document gives her ambassador royal privileges in a foreign land. The most powerful name of them all is so familiar to us that we sometimes fail to appreciate its value. We finish our prayers by gabbling 'In Jesus' name, Amen' without realising the immeasurable authority that lies behind His name.

Is there someone you are really worried about at the moment? When you bring them before God's throne in prayer, remember whose signature is at the bottom of your petition!

At the name of Jesus every knee shall bow,
Every tongue confess Him King of glory now.
'Tis the Father's pleasure we should call Him Lord,
who from the beginning was the mighty Word.

Name him, brothers, name Him, with love as strong as death,
But with awe and wonder and with bated breath:
He is God the Saviour, He is Christ the Lord,
Ever to be worshipped, trusted, and adored.

Caroline Maria Noel (1817–77)

Grab me, God

When you call on me, when you come and pray to me, I'll listen. When you come looking for me, you'll find me. Yes, when you get serious about finding me and want it more than anything else, I'll make sure you won't be disappointed.

Jer. 29:12–14, *The Message*

Mr Luff was ninety when I was twelve, yet he probably influenced my life more than anyone else.

'Seek the Lord, Jen,' he would tell me every Sunday when I met him at church. 'Seek Him for Himself, not for what you want Him to do for you.' As the years have gone by I've noticed that there are numbers of Christians who are involved in church activities and enjoy Sunday services but who don't know what it means to thirst for God, yearn for Him, seek Him for Himself alone. God is an important part of their lives but not their entire reason for living. In this poem, I think Russ Parker sums up everything that Mr Luff was trying to tell me all those years ago:

Wild Spirit of the living, breathing God, come and get me,
Come and grab me, come and get a hold of me.
I don't want to manage without you any more.

Wild Spirit of the living, breathing God, do your deep work
Do our best work, do what's in your heart to do,
I don't want the thin, unchallenged life any more.

Wild Spirit of the living, breathing God,
Don't go, don't leave, don't be the unseen observer, silent listener,
I don't want to be safe but sorry any more.

Wild Spirit of the living, breathing God,
Send your Spirit, send him more powerfully, send him now.
I don't want to be anywhere else any more.

Russ Parker, from *Wild Spirit of the Living God* (Eagle, 2007)

Jungle hazards

Commit your way to the LORD, trust also in Him, and he will do it.
Ps. 37:5, NASB

David Livingstone was convinced God had sent him to introduce the people of the uncharted African interior to Christ. He was often lost in the jungle, sickened by the slave trade, plagued by poisonous insects, harassed by wild beasts and weakened by illness and pain. He may even have wondered whether the job was worth the effort anyway. We may not have to contend with all that as we struggle to serve the Lord, but other Christians can be just as annoying as mosquitoes or as intimidating as lions! David Livingstone managed to keep going by doggedly repeating today's verse five times every day. In 1856 he finally became the first European to cross Africa; and he even discovered the Victoria Falls!

'Committing your way to the Lord' means rolling every job and activity that make up each day over onto Him in utter abandonment to His loving care. That word 'abandonment' always reminds me of something I saw once in Marks and Spencer. A little boy of about three was shopping with his father, earnestly discussing which slippers he should buy for his mum's birthday. A few minutes later they must have got separated, and I saw the child dashing up and down the aisles, lost and panicking. When he finally caught sight of his father, running towards him, he flung himself into those outstretched arms and was lifted right up into the air as the two of them shared their mutual relief and delight. That, to me, is abandonment.

Sometimes, Lord, the job you have given me to do would be so much easier if you would only make life, and people, just a little bit easier. But, instead of grumbling, I choose to run into your arms.

Just suppose . . .

Do you not know? Have you not heard? The LORD is the everlasting God, the Creator of the ends of the earth. He will not grow tired or weary, and his understanding no-one can fathom.

Isa. 40:28

Suppose you were in the stock exchange, surrounded by frenzied dealing. Brokers gazing into their computer screens, phones clamped to their ears, totally ignore the scruffy-looking man who is shouting at them through a megaphone.

'I've got a message for you from God,' he raves, but no one even looks up. 'No computers will work anywhere in the world, and there'll be no phones, TV, radio or electricity – until God says so!' When all the screens go blank and the lights go out, would they listen to the intruder or describe the ensuing chaos as a 'natural disaster'?

King Ahab faced much the same scenario. Like many countries today, his society had dismissed God as 'old-fashioned'. When he married Jezebel, a priestess of Baal, everyone thought worshipping her god was far more fun than obeying Jehovah. Baal liked them to party under the stars, with dancing and sex. Because their economy, and defence, depended on good harvests and well-fed animals, they even sacrificed children to him to make sure he sent good weather.

Then, one day, a stranger appeared at court saying, 'Jehovah-God says it won't rain again until He says so!' (1 Kgs 17:1, paraphrase).

No one took any notice, of course, and Elijah had to run for his life – but his challenge has thundered down the centuries. You and I still need to face it today: 'If we believe God controls the universe, why don't we trust Him?'

Lord, you could destroy planet Earth at any moment. Forgive me for my lack of awe at your greatness, and my ingratitude for your mercy.

Just you, me and us two

Jesus said, 'Let's go off by ourselves to a quiet place and rest awhile.'
Mark 6:31, NLT

In my family, extroverts were praised for being 'good, outgoing Christians' whereas introverts were dismissed as 'moody and unsociable'. So for years I tried to be the life and soul of every party, until I realised that constantly being with people drained me. I needed plenty of time alone in which to recharge my batteries. It was such a relief to realise God made me the way I am because He likes me that way! I guess Elijah was introverted while his colleague Elisha was quite the opposite. Elijah would not have been daunted when God told him to escape from the fury of Ahab and Jezebel and hide alone for months in the mountains (1 Kgs 17:2–7). The things God taught Him during that period of 'aloneness' would prove invaluable in his later ministry.

One of my father's little sayings was 'Just you, me and us two'. He was a very busy man but he always gave me and my brother time with him on our own. Among other excitements, he and Justyn watched Tower Bridge open for a tall ship, and I got lost with him in a Scottish forest. These treats sealed our relationship with him, which might otherwise have been rather distant; they were special simply because they were 'Just you, me and us two'.

Whether God created us extrovert or introvert, I believe we all need to carve out time to be alone with Him and give Him our undivided attention. Just half a day a month can revitalise our lives.

If you are never alone with God it is not because you are too busy, it is because you don't care for Him, don't love Him and you had better face the facts.

A. Ghazzali

Alone against evil

Ahab summoned everyone in Israel ... to Mount Carmel. Elijah challenged the people: 'How long are you going to sit on the fence? If God is the real God, follow him; if it's Baal, follow him. Make up your minds!'

1 Kgs 18:21–22, *The Message*

Have you ever walked along a busy street looking into the faces of people coming towards you? Because they think no one is watching them, it is easy to see the stress, sadness and resentment they usually hide underneath their masks. When my grandmother was a child, people in Britain still lived by Christian values, but few do today. Have you ever longed to go on national TV and ask, 'If the permissive society hasn't brought you happiness and security, why don't you come back to Christ?' Elijah did exactly that, but not on TV! He came out of hiding to discover that even the drought hadn't turned the people's hearts to God, and Jezebel was systematically exterminating anyone who was still faithful to Him (1 Kgs 18:13). So Elijah summoned the nation to a mountain-top confutation. If you don't know the story, give yourself a treat and read 1 Kings 18.

It takes enormous courage to stand up for God all on your own. Perhaps you often have to do that? You might be the only Christian in your family, workplace or social network; people around you all live by totally different standards. By nature you may prefer to 'merge in' and not look different, but that would mean compromising the ideals of your faith. It is easy to think, 'What difference can a minority group of one possibly make?' But one person and God are always a majority, so don't lose heart.

Fire from heaven did not convince Elijah's audience, but his unwavering example during the rest of his life brought many to faith.

Failure

*Jezebel immediately sent a messenger to Elijah . . . 'By this time
tomorrow you'll be . . . dead.' Elijah . . . ran for dear life.*

1 Kgs 19:2–3, *The Message*

They say, 'There is a tide in the affairs of man which, taken at its
flood, leads on to fortune,' but Elijah missed the boat completely! Had
he stood up to Jezebel while everyone was still talking about his
miraculous success at Carmel, surely he could have swung the nation
back to God? God would certainly have protected him from Jezebel's
venom. Instead Elijah vanished, leaving people to dismiss Carmel's
miracle as a convenient thunderstorm.

Poor Elijah, he felt that his work had been wasted and he'd let the
Lord down badly. Lots of us have felt like that too! Convinced that
God could never use him again, Elijah just wanted to die (1 Kgs 19:4).
Intimidation, control and manipulation were the tools of witchcraft
that Jezebel used against him, and, rather than asserting God's
authority over them, Elijah gave in. The enemy usually attacks most
fiercely when we are tired. Elijah had staged a mass evangelical rally,
executed hundreds of Satanists (1 Kgs 18:40) and sprinted seventeen
miles (18:46); no wonder he was exhausted! Yet, when our own
human resources are finished, there is always a moment when we can
choose to turn to God for His strength and courage – or take the self-
preservation option and run away. I've made the wrong decision more
often than Elijah, but God has always been able to do amazing things
with us failures!

Elijah could have stayed lying defeated under his bush in the desert.
Instead he got up and staggered off to find God on His holy mountain
(1 Kgs 19:8). Making straight for God and flinging ourselves onto His
mercy is the only way out of the black hole of failure.

Changing negatives into positives

The LORD said, 'Go out and stand on the mountain in the presence of the LORD' . . . After the earthquake came a fire, but the LORD was not in the fire. And after the fire came a gentle whisper.

1 Kgs 19:11–12

It took Elijah forty days to walk to Sinai (Horeb); it took me only one day in a minibus, but the journey through that bleak desert still felt endlessly long. As Elijah trudged through lifeless sand and bare rocks his feelings must have matched his surroundings. Depression makes everything seem colourless and barren. It can also feel as dark as the cave where he eventually crawled for shelter (1 Kgs 19:9). Elijah desperately wanted to connect with God after his terrible failure, but depression often makes God seem far away. He had to listen very carefully to catch that reassuring whisper.

Depression can be caused by stress, grief, physical illness or chemical imbalance, yet Christians are quick to put it down to unconfessed sin or lack of forgiveness. Fortunately there were no amateur psychiatrists to plague Elijah; God was his companion and He knew exactly what was needed. Among other things it was Elijah's wrong thinking that was causing his despair (1 Kgs 19:14). God needed to change his negatives into positives by telling him he wasn't the only one left who believed, and God still had plans for him (1 Kgs 19:15, 18).

If you are feeling down, list some of the thoughts that go round endlessly in your head. Ask yourself if they are true in the light of God's promises. Then write the positives beside your list of negatives.

Sorry, Lord, that I'm constantly telling myself I'm useless and worthless. You tell me I am precious and honoured in your sight and that you love me (Isa. 43:4), so I'm replacing my negative lies with your positive truth.

VIPs

Calling the Twelve to him, he sent them out two by two . . . These were his instructions: 'Take nothing for the journey except a staff – no bread, no bag, no money in your belts.'

Mark 6:7–8

Do you have a VIP (very irritating person) in your life? Someone God has chosen to work closely with you, but whom you are finding difficult because you are total opposites? I suspect that Elijah was maddened by his young apprentice and companion, Elisha. God restored Elijah's ministry as prophet and teacher and sent him down Mount Sinai with the name and address of a young man He had chosen to be his companion. Left to himself, Elijah would never have chosen Elisha! He was a rich man's son who loved people and parties (1 Kgs 19:20–21), while Elijah was a homeless vagabond, solitary, sombre and serious. Yet God needed them both to demonstrate two sides of His character to people who had forgotten what He was like. Elijah showed them His power and judgement; Elisha modelled His love and mercy. He also demonstrated that He cared about the ordinary details of daily life, such as a lost axe head and a single mum's debts.

God often puts opposites together so that their different personalities and gifts can complement one another. Could God have matched you with your personal VIP for that reason? When Jesus sent His disciples out to preach and heal, He sent them off in twos. I've often wondered who had to put up with Peter – and Thomas. Perhaps they went together, in which case they would have done each other a power of good!

Lord, I bring you my VIPs and ask you to change my heart towards them. Open my eyes to see in them the qualities I lack so that together we may serve you better.

Green for danger!

Resentment kills a fool, and envy slays the simple.

Job 5:2

King Ahab fancied growing his own veggies and his neighbour had the perfect plot. Ahab made a fair offer, which was turned down because it was against God's rules for Naboth to sell his inherited property. Ahab went to bed and sulked while Jezebel set about having Naboth framed and lynched. Unfortunately God can see everything we try to hide secretly in our hearts, and no sooner had Ahab hurried onto his new property to plan his autumn planting than God sent Elijah to prod his conscience. God didn't bother to send Elijah to Jezebel because she was not one of His people – but Ahab was! God has higher standards for us.

Of course we would *never* behave like Ahab – or would we? When Trish and I were both young mums, her house was much larger than ours, and she had a tumble dryer and a dishwasher. Worse still, she kept her figure and mine sagged, and she had all kinds of amazing spiritual gifts while I was a mouse in the corner. I loved spending time in her comfortable house but secretly I resented all she had. One day I was reading Mark and realised Jesus puts envy on a par with 'sexual immorality, theft, murder and adultery' and a few other nasties (Mark 7:21–23). Horrified, I had to ask Jesus to yank this thing out of my heart like a dentist pulling a rotten tooth. It took a while but eventually my relationship with Trish became better than ever before.

Lord, please show me if there are any 'Green Spots' lurking in my heart. Help me be content with what I have and who I am in you.

Ask and you will receive

Elijah said to Elisha, 'Tell me, what can I do for you before I am taken from you?' 'Let me inherit a double portion of your spirit,' Elisha replied.

2 Kgs 2:9–10

For ten years Elisha had been Elijah's apprentice, travelling with him, listening as he preached, and watching him perform miracles and establish numerous training colleges for would-be prophets. He carried the luggage and stood at the back of the crowd, doing the only thing he was good at, chatting to people about God. When both men realised it was time for Elijah's promotion to heaven, Elisha must suddenly have realised he might have to step into his master's role, and I suspect that made him feel daunted. Beside this spiritual giant, he would have felt down to earth and plain ordinary!

Just before the famous chariot of fire parted them (2 Kgs 2:11), Elisha, with intense longing in his heart, asked his master one last favour. He wasn't arrogantly demanding to be twice as powerful as Elijah had been; he just wanted to inherit an oldest son's portion (Deut. 21:17). 'I want God's power to surge miraculously through me, as I've seen it do through you,' was his passionate request.

Do you have someone whose spiritual gifts, ministry or relationship with God you deeply admire? While it is never right to compare ourselves with others (God loves us the way we are), it is never wrong to want to be the best for Him. Too many Christians are content with being mediocre. Paul urges us to 'desire spiritual gifts' (1 Cor. 14:1), and Jesus says, 'Everyone who asks receives' (Luke 11:10).

Is it a gift of healing you long for, or the ability to pray more effectively, or do you yearn for the confidence to speak out for God? Ask Him – He's listening!

The crunch

Then [Elisha] took the cloak that had fallen from [Elijah] and struck the water with it. 'Where now is the LORD, the God of Elijah?' he asked. When he struck the water, it divided . . . and he crossed over.

2 Kgs 2:13–14

Elisha was being watched by fifty students from Jericho's theological college (2 Kgs 2:15) as he stood nervously on the far bank of the surging river. They wanted to know whether he had been chosen by God to replace his master, Elijah. The old prophet only had to touch the water with his cloak for it to form an instant ford (2 Kgs 2:8). A prophet's cloak symbolised his authority and power under God (1 Kgs 19:19), but how could Elisha be sure of God's anointing? There is only one way to discover that!

Stepping into God's miracle dimension takes a lot of courage. Have you ever wondered whether it was *really* God who gave you that word for someone, or whether He *really* wants you to pray confidently for this person's healing? Elisha would have looked a fool if nothing had happened, but he struck the water anyway. We will never move in the gifts of the Spirit unless we are willing to make a lot of mistakes. Ask God to put His prophet's cloak round you every morning as you dress, if you yearn to experience His supernatural power in your life.

The first thing that most of us face, when we dare to live supernaturally, is criticism. The men from Jericho clashed with Elisha by suggesting Elijah had just been caught in a whirlwind and might be lying injured somewhere (2 Kgs 2:16–17). Elisha was now looking at the world from a heavenly perspective, so he *knew* Elijah was safely with God.

People who move deeper into God's invisible world are always misunderstood; are you willing to deal with that?

Nothing in the house

Elisha replied . . . 'Tell me, what do you have in your house?'
'Your servant has nothing there at all,' she said, 'except a little oil.'

2 Kgs 4:2

The woman at the door was so broken by grief that Elisha hardly recognised her. She was the wife of one of his trainee prophets, but her husband had died; they had borrowed money to pay for his education and now their creditors meant to take her two little boys as slaves while she was doomed to die of starvation. Tragically, she told Elisha she had nothing left at all. Sometimes that is exactly how we feel. When we look inside our 'internal house' we find we've lost our joy, hope, confidence, sense of purpose and will to live, and God probably appears to have gone too!

Then the widow remembered: 'I do still have a little oil.' In the Bible, oil always represents the Holy Spirit and, once we have asked Him into our lives, He always remains. Sometimes we feel so full of worry, despair, busyness or even sin that there is not much room left inside our 'house' for Him, but there is always a 'little oil' left on the bottom shelf.

'Go and borrow jars from your neighbours,' Elisha told the widow, 'and start filling them with the oil you have.' Miraculously she soon had so much to sell that her debts were paid and her sons were free.

It would have taken faith and determination to face her neighbour's nosy questions or snubs; she could have given up after collecting the first jar! When we are in the empty place, we have to rouse ourselves to *want* God again. Staying at home and drifting on in our dreary vacuum can feel safer than making the effort go out and live in the real world again.

Please, Lord, fill my house with oil again!

The slave girl and the king

Even after Jesus had done all these miraculous signs in their presence, they still would not believe in him.

John 12:37

King Joram lived around the corner from Elisha. He constantly heard about Elisha's amazing miracles and witnessed some (2 Kgs 3:1–20), yet he implacably refused to believe. Hundreds of miles away in a foreign country lived a slave who had far more faith. She worked in the home of Naaman, general of Israel's enemy army. She had been kidnapped by a gang of his soldiers, but, surprisingly, that had not made her hard and bitter. She had once met Elisha, and seen God's power working through him; looking into his kind eyes she may have thought, 'If God looks like that, I'm going to serve Him – always.'

One day she found her mistress devastated. Naaman had developed leprosy.

'If he could see Elisha in Israel, he'd be cured,' she said bravely (2 Kgs 5:3). Suppose Naaman had come home, after that long journey, disappointed? He'd have taken his rage out on the slave who had made him look silly in front of his enemies. Would you risk your life for your belief in God's supernatural power?

When his most powerful enemy rode up to Joram's palace, demanding to be healed, the king had a panic attack and ripped up his best suit – he never thought of Elisha!

'Tell your visitor to pop round here,' came the message from the neighbour Joram loathed. 'Shame about your suit!' (2 Kgs 5:7–8).

Sadly, miracles never convince anyone – unless they want to be convinced. Accepting God's absolute power means obeying Him absolutely, and those who want to be their own boss can always dismiss a miracle as a 'hoax' or mere coincidence.

Do you live your life expecting to see God's power, or have doubt and apathy robbed you of your birthright?

Finding God's love

And I pray that you, being rooted and established in love, may have power . . . to grasp how wide and long and high and deep is the love of Christ, and to know this love that surpasses knowledge – that you may be filled to the measure of all the fullness of God.

Eph. 3:17–19

Our human bodies cannot live more than a few days without water, but love is just as crucial to our survival. The 'real us', the invisible part which thinks, feels and desires, was designed to be 'oiled by love', just like a car's engine.

Sadly, many of us never learn the art of giving and receiving love, because our parents either failed to love us or found it hard to show us that they did. Others only seemed to love when we were 'good' or achieving well. So we grow into adults who are constantly hungry for the love we've always craved, searching desperately for it in relationships that often go wrong, because we demand too much or find it difficult to love in return.

Even when two well-adjusted people come together in a perfect relationship, still there is bound to be disappointment because no human can ever give us all the love we crave, however hard they try.

God – who *is* love – created us like Him with this desire for love because He wants to pour His love into us and feel our love responding in return. He longs to heal our damaged idea of what love really is and to show us how it feels to be loved completely and unconditionally. This process begins when we are willing to forgive those who failed to love us well.

Lord, help me to open myself to your love like a daisy unfolding its petals to the sunshine.

God's unconditional love

But when the kindness and love of God our Saviour appeared he saved us, not because of righteous things we had done, but because of his mercy.

Titus 3:4

A friend, who happened to be a GP, stunned me some years ago by saying, 'You're always working yourself ragged serving God; it looks to me as if you're trying to earn His love.' As a child I had wonderful parents but they were always doing important things somewhere else and I grew up thinking God must also be more interested in other people than in me. Perhaps I have always tried to attract His attention by my constant activity. The glorious fact that He loved me just because I was *me* had never sunk from my head into my heart.

Being a doctor, my friend gave me 'medicine' to cure my problem, telling me to take it three times a day. I had to repeat, 'There is no one in the entire world that God loves more than He loves me. There is no one more important to Him than I am. There is nothing I could ever do that would make Him love me any less. There is nothing I could ever do that would make Him love me any more.' I felt an idiot muttering that as I did the washing up, but gradually the prescription began to work.

Maybe someone gave Rick Warren similar medication because I once heard him say, 'When I get up in the morning, I sit on the side of my bed and say, "God, you didn't put me on earth to fulfil a To-Do list. If I don't get anything else done today, I want to know more of your love, and to love you better in return."'

Please, Lord, replace my faulty thinking with your truth.

God's never-ending love

Though the mountains be shaken and the hills be removed, yet my unfailing love for you will not be shaken nor my covenant of peace be removed, says the LORD, who has compassion on you.

Isa. 54:10

'I often think I'll wake up one morning and find God's gone.' The person who said that also told me her father had left her mother when she was five. When we lose a parent in childhood or suffer a lot of rejection as adults we often have a nasty feeling God may desert us too. Yet the one thing we can always cling to is the everlasting quality of God's love. He never withdraws His love, however badly we fail Him.

Recently I went for a wintry walk on a beach where we used to take our six children when they were small. Happy memories flooded over me – but with the joy came a dreadful sense of loss. My husband has gone, our children have grown up and scattered all over the world, and now I walk alone.

'Ouch, Lord!' I said out loud through my tears. Then I realised I was *not* alone. He shared all those memories. He had been there with us, enjoying those summer days, sandcastles, beach fires and chilly swims. My family may have gone far away, but He will never leave me.

St Paul suffered horrendous rejection and many awful experiences of loss and pain, yet he was still convinced that nothing 'will be able to separate us from the love of God'. If only we shared his convictions, few things in life would ever worry us again.

Lord, help me to get my head round the comforting fact that I will never have to face anything in this life or the next without your love to surround me.

God's forgiving love

The LORD is compassionate . . . he does not treat us as our sins deserve . . . For as high as the heavens are above the earth, so great is his love . . . as far as the east is from the west, so far has he removed our transgressions from us.

Ps. 103:8–12

'It's my punishment,' a young mum told me, as she held her severely handicapped baby. 'I injured a child in a car accident once, and I always knew God would punish me.' As a Christian she had asked God's forgiveness many times for careless speeding and she knew Jesus had been punished in her place, yet she still felt she had to be punished too.

There is no sin that is too bad for God to forgive; the only 'unforgivable sin' is the one we refuse to confess. Yet there are so many Christians who feel like second-class citizens in their churches because of mistakes in their past, or secret habits they can't kick. Whenever they are asked to help with some church activity a little voice whispers, 'If people knew all the things you've done, they wouldn't want you near them!'

I used to be plagued like that, and one day I was driving to speak at a meeting when 'my voice' started pointing out all my past sins. As I began confessing them all to God – yet again – I had the distinct impression that He yawned. He was tired of hearing about stuff He'd long since forgiven and forgotten. In His eyes I was as pure, innocent and perfect as Jesus Himself, simply because of the cross. The impact of that was so great I had to pull off the road to weep copiously.

Lord, help me to understand what your death on that cross really means to me.

God's compassionate love

*In all their distress he too was distressed, and the angel of his presence
saved them. In his love and mercy he redeemed them; he lifted them
up and carried them all the days of old.*

Isa. 63:9

When I first noticed this verse I had been in hospital for months. One
evening when the drugs trolley was late and pain was becoming unbearable, I suddenly thought of Jesus sitting comfortably in heaven and I
snarled, 'It was all very well for you; you only had to hang on the
cross for six hours – my pain goes on continuously!' I am convinced
that He replied, 'My suffering will go on until the last of my children
are safely home, because I live in each cell of your physical bodies. I
feel all your pain as you feel it; I also feel the emotional pain of your
broken hearts and the distress of your troubled minds. Please don't
think I have separated myself from you.'

Later, when the painkillers had worked, I scrawled those words
inside my Bible, and then I found today's verse.

Compassion is different from sympathy or pity. Sympathy feels *like*,
pity feels *for*, but compassion feels *with*. Sympathy sucks us down into
someone else's suffering and gets us so involved that we can easily
drown in it with them. Pity looks on helplessly, but compassion feels
and cares so greatly it remains sufficiently objective to do something
to help. Jesus did not stay in heaven feeling pity for us, nor did He
allow sympathy to bring Him to earth to be swamped by human misery.
His compassion led Him to suffer and die in order to make heaven
possible for us – the place where sickness, pain, death and tears are
banished.

Thank you, Lord, for feeling with me and then dying for me.

God's patient love

The LORD your God is with you, he is mighty to save. He will take great delight in you, he will quiet you with his love, he will rejoice over you with singing.

Zeph. 3:17

On my granddaughter Hannah's fourth birthday she was up at six, opening presents. She took a big chocolate cake to nursery school and later ten little friends arrived, complete with party frocks and more parcels. Suddenly the excitement of the day was just too much, and Hannah exploded! She howled so loudly that her friends gaped in awed admiration. The patience of most of us adults was exhausted by then, but my son-in-law scooped Hannah up, screaming, kicking and tearing at his hair, and carried her into the garden. Sitting with her on his knee, still protesting, he sang to her until she nestled happily in his arms with her head on his shoulder. He had 'quieted her with his love'.

Perhaps most of us have days when life suddenly seems too much and we long for a reason to scream and kick. Have you ever noticed how everyone *else* seems to be in a bad mood on days like that?

When my six children were small my mother, who had Alzheimer's, lived with us. Whenever I reached 'screaming point' I would run to my room and fling myself face down on the bed, picturing myself lying before God while He poured His love all over me, quietening me down. Thirty seconds was enough – heaven knows what disasters might have occurred if I had stayed away longer!

Today's verse says that God delights in us to such an extent that He sings over us. Being loved like that makes even a terrible day feel manageable!

This is what the LORD says . . . As a mother comforts her child, so will I comfort you.

(Isa. 66:12, 13)

At home in God's love

Make yourselves at home in my love. If you keep my commands you'll remain intimately at home in my love. That's what I've done – kept my father's commands and made myself at home in his love.

John 15:9–10, *The Message*

Recently I visited a lady who told me she hasn't spoken to her husband for ten years.

'He lives upstairs, and I live down here,' she explained. 'We share nothing at all.' When you live with someone because you love them, you usually share everything you have: thoughts, irritations, pleasures, disappointments, finances, skills, energy – everything. Jesus is asking us in today's passage to live with Him in that intimate way. Naturally that includes obeying His commands, but it also means learning to share ourselves with Him at the deepest possible level.

I went for a drive once with a friend who kept muttering away to herself: 'Pulling out to overtake high-sided van . . . slowing down to give learner driver space . . . indicating right.'

'Sorry,' she said. 'Since I took the advanced drivers' test I can't kick the habit of commentary driving.' Surely the habit of referring constantly to God can be learnt too?

Experts say we talk to ourselves inside our heads at the rate of several thousand words a minute, so surely it must be possible to direct those words towards God. I am trying to train myself to tell Him before I start each tiny job of the day, and then to thank Him when it's safely done. It's not really 'praying without ceasing'; I'm simply thinking in His presence.

Let the day be full of little prayers, to me, little turnings towards me. The smiles of the soul at one it loves.

The Two Listeners (c. 1932)

I can't pray for more than five minutes, but I can't live for more than five minutes without praying.

D. L. Moody (1837–99)

Radiating God's love

Dear friends, since God so loved us, we also ought to love one another. No one has ever seen God; but if we love one another, God lives in us and his love is made complete in us.

1 John 4:11–12

I was travelling on the London Underground at the height of the rush hour. All day I'd been in a church full of happy Christians, but how different were the faces that surrounded me now! They looked stressed, bored and devoid of hope. Probably the only contact most of them had with Jesus – who came to give them peace and joy – was to use His name as a swear word. He must long for people like that to know how much He loves them, but the only way He has of connecting with them is through you and me.

So do we all have to start preaching on the Underground? No way! My bedroom radiator feels ice-cold at night, but once the central heating boiler has rumbled into action, hot water begins to trickle into it and I know I can safely get up and dress beside its cosy warmth. It is not the radiator itself that warms me, but the water inside it. When we are filled with the Holy Spirit we can introduce people to Jesus simply by 'radiating' the warmth of His love to everyone we meet. By nature, we might be cold and unloving, but it is *His* supernatural love that touches them.

Jesus, it was not what you said that impressed people most, it was the love they saw in your eyes, your smile, the way you treated them; these were the ways you showed them what God's love is like. Please fill my heart with that same love and help me to 'radiate' it to everyone I encounter today.

The new me

We grow weary in our present bodies, and we long to put on our heavenly bodies like new clothing. For we will put on heavenly bodies; we will not be spirits without bodies. While we live in these earthly bodies, we groan and sigh . . . we want to put on our new bodies so that these dying bodies will be swallowed up by life.

2 Cor. 5:2–4, NLT

Taking the dogs to the woods yesterday was misery! A bad back and a sore ankle made me feel ninety.

'November!' I muttered crossly as I shuffled through the soggy brown sludge that had once been gloriously coloured autumn leaves. A rustle suddenly made me look up into the bare branches to see a squirrel eyeing me curiously. He was not a romantic red 'Squirrel Nutkin', just the ordinary grey kind that people dismiss as tree rats – but I was captivated by his grace and beauty. He was almost flying as he leapt effortlessly from tree to tree and swarmed up and down the trunks. His agility and balance were breathtaking. 'Oh for a body like that!' I thought, and then realised that I'll have one some day! God has it waiting for me to put on the moment I step into heaven – and it won't be trees I'll be jumping about in – but mountain peaks!

I believe that if we could only see beforehand what it is that our heavenly Father means us to be, – the soul's beauty and perfection and glory, the glorious and lovely spiritual body that this soul is to dwell in through all eternity, – if we could have a glimpse of THIS, we should not grudge all the trouble and pains He is taking with us now, to bring us up to that ideal, which is His thought of us.

Annie Keary (1825–79)

Visual aid

You have not given up. But this is what I have against you: you do not love me now as you did at first.

Rev. 2:3–4, GNB

Last month we looked at two prophets who performed mighty miracles to capture people's attention, but God spoke through Hosea's life and experiences to remind them of His love.

During a time when Israel had turned away from the Lord, Hosea was a travelling preacher with such a close relationship with God that they could share their feelings with each other on an unusually deep level. When Hosea fell in love with a girl called Gomer, he felt sure it was God's will for them to marry, even if his mother probably had her doubts!

Perhaps the couple were happy at first. Hosea would come home from a preaching tour with his saddlebags full of presents, revelling in Gomer's pleasure, but after their first baby was born things began to change. She grew discontented, her tenderness was gone and Hosea's company and gifts bored her. Nothing he did pleased her and he suspected she found other men more exciting. Hosea took his pain to God, who told him, 'That's how I feel about my people. The love they used to have for me has evaporated like morning dew' (Hos. 6:4).

The more we love someone, the greater their capacity to hurt us! Do you think God is enjoying His relationship with you at the moment? Can He revel in the way you delight in all His gifts and blessings, or are you always grumbling and never satisfied? Are your times with Him a mutual delight or do you see them as a dull part of your daily routine, and is being in church no longer stimulating?

Could God be speaking the poignant words of today's verses to you?

Praying the thorn hedge

*Therefore I will block her path with thornbushes; I will wall her in so
that she cannot find her way. She will chase after her lovers but not
catch them . . . Then she will say, 'I will go back to my husband . . . for
then I was better off than now.'*

Hos. 2:6–7

Gomer was soon enjoying a string of affairs, which made Hosea feel
so miserable he called her two next babies 'Unloved' and 'Rejected'.
He kept on forgiving his wife, and continued to provide her with a
home, food and clothes, but she was never satisfied and in the end she
left him to live with wealthier men.

Everyone in Israel watched to see how this well-known prophet
would react. Husbands had the right to stone their wives to death for
adultery, but Hosea never gave up hoping she would come back; he
knew God felt the same about His people (Hos. 11:8) so he continued
to pray for Gomer.

I found today's verses very helpful when my teenage daughter left
home and appeared to be making a terrible mess of her life in London.
I used to picture myself constructing Hosea's thorn hedge around her,
asking the Lord to put a barrier between her and all her harmful relationships and activities. One night, when all her luck had run out, she
was walking the streets alone and penniless.

'God, if you love me,' she prayed, 'like Mum always said you do –
show me.' Two girls stepped straight up to her, saying, 'We felt God
telling us to tell you He loves you.' They took her home, cared for her
and brought her back to the Lord.

Are you praying for someone who seems to have turned their back on
God? Hosea probably had to pray his thorn-hedge prayer for years, so
keep going; prodigals do return!

The unforgettable sermon

The LORD said to me, 'Go, show your love to your wife again, though she is . . . an adulteress. Love her as the LORD loves the Israelites . . .'

Hos. 3:1

Hosea had spent years going round Israel's towns, sharing his story and saying, 'God wanted to be a loving husband to you, His people, but you rejected His love and put your trust in idols. My wife broke my heart but you have broken God's heart by your desertion.'

When Gomer's youth and looks were gone, and her rich boyfriends abandoned her, she was hauled, destitute, to the slave market. It must have caused a colossal stir when Hosea, the famous preacher, bought her for an amazingly high price (Hos. 3:2). What, they wondered, would he do with this wife who had betrayed him? Stone her, or beat her to a pulp and then use her as slave labour for the rest of her life? Instead, Hosea tenderly covered her nakedness with his own cloak and carried her home to care for her as his honoured wife. The crowds were astounded!

What a brilliant way to illustrate Hosea's sermon on God's forgiveness and mercy! Actions always speak more loudly than words when we are trying to tell people about God. He would have had everyone's attention when he told them, 'God sees you as the wife He loves and He also wants you back. He says, "I'm going to start all over again. I'm taking her back out into the wilderness where we had our first date, and I'll court her. I'll give her bouquets of roses. I'll turn Heartbreak Valley into Acres of Hope. She'll respond like she did as a young girl"' (Hos. 2:14–15, *The Message*).

Lord, as I smile at the people I meet today, may they see your love and compassion looking at them through my eyes.

The walls we hide behind

God's name is a place of protection – good people can run there and be safe.

Prov. 18:10, *The Message*

'When I look at you,' a neighbour once told me, 'I wonder if there is a real person inside your wall of candyfloss.' I was horrified – but she made me think. I grew up in a Christian conference centre and my parents were spiritual superstars; wanting to please them, I tried to be a perfect Christian – always smiling sweetly. The 'real me' often felt frightened, unlovable, hurt and frustrated, but candyfloss always hid all that. My neighbour's comment led me to ask God to demolish those self-protective layers.

Some people who have been badly hurt as children build thick, granite walls, which say, 'No one will ever hurt me again'; others create misty walls that they call shyness, because they would rather be invisible than rejected. 'Clown walls' often conceal sad hearts.

No one dared cross Judith; an angry prickle-hedge was her protection. Jane, on the other hand, made herself walls of sticky glue, hoping to 'catch' anyone willing to take care of her, because inside she felt like a lost child. Sharon, one of Jane's victims, had developed the 'efficient professional' wall. She wanted to solve everyone's problems and organise their lives. Perhaps a sense of worthlessness made her want to be needed and admired?

God wants us to be real – through and through. I've realised that forgiving those who caused us to develop our walls is the dynamite that demolishes them. Yet we can feel very vulnerable without them. When I'm temped to crawl back inside my candyfloss I remember today's verse and run for cover inside God.

Why am I afraid to tell you who I am? Because if I do, you may not like me, and who I am is all I have.

John Powell (From *Why Am I Afraid to Tell You Who I Am?* Fount, 1999)

What drives you?

For the love of Christ controls and urges and impels us.

2 Cor. 5:14, AMP

Another honest friend asked, 'Why can't you just sit and *be* instead of doing-dashing-making-talking; what drives you?'

As I asked the Lord that question I remembered my mother saying, 'Don't just sit there! Do something useful.' Because I yearned for approval I allowed those words to build an internal engine. Instead of going 'brum-brum' it goes 'I must keep busy'.

Other people are driven by engines that go, 'I must succeed . . . I've got to have someone to love me . . . I've got to be in control . . . I must look attractive . . . everyone must notice, respect, need or approve of me.'

Most engines are built in childhood: Tammy's angry father caused her to create an engine that says, 'I mustn't cause trouble . . . don't rock the boat.' Her sister built a different engine, which goes, 'I must be strong, mustn't show my feelings.' Phil has an immaculate house and garden. 'Something inside me makes me want to be perfect,' she told me. 'Perhaps it's because I was revolted by my messy mum, but now,' she added sadly, 'perfectionism is ruining my marriage.'

Just trying to stop being busy, perfect or successful doesn't seem to work. I discovered I needed a totally new engine, not a repair job. We all need goals, but God wants us to set our sights on pleasing Him, not on meeting our own needs. It changed my life to realise I didn't have to keep achieving or doing something useful in order to be a special person. I *am* special, simply because God thinks so, regardless of my achievements (Isa. 43:4).

Jesus, be the centre . . . Be the wind in my sails . . .
Be the reason that I live . . . Jesus, be my vision . . . Be my
  guide – Jesus.

Michael Frye (© 1999 Vineyard Songs UK[†])

Neglected garden

Don't stare at me because . . . the sun has darkened my skin. My brothers . . . forced me to care for their vineyards, so I couldn't care for myself – my own vineyard.

Song of Songs 1:6, NLT.

King Solomon's new bride feels embarrassed in front of the grand ladies of his court because of her unfashionable suntan.

'I couldn't help it,' she protests. 'I was so busy running round after other people that I didn't have time to look after myself.' Does that sound familiar? Many of us are ruled by the constant demands of small children, elderly relatives, draining friends or a workaholic boss.

During a busy patch of travelling and speaking I suddenly realised my times with the Lord had become nothing more than preparation for the next meeting; and phone calls, letters and emails from needy people seemed more important to me than enjoying His company. I remember looking out at my neglected garden one autumn and thinking my spiritual life must look like that: nothing but blackened stalks and shrivelled leaves of plants that had been beautiful once.

Our first and greatest responsibility is to tend our love relationship with the Lord and give it priority each day. That is the first commandment, but we so often put the second commandment in its place and love our neighbours *more* than we love Him. When we do that all we can offer them are our own limited resources, which soon run dry. When our priority is to spend time in the secret place, enjoying God for Himself, it is His life that flows out of us to bless everyone we encounter.

Lord, help me to balance my time, my energy and my priorities, keeping you always at the centre of my existence.

The God of all comfort

You turned my wailing into dancing; You removed my sackcloth and clothed me with joy.

Ps. 30:11

Today always feels gloomy to me, not just because November is a dismal month in England, but also because it's the anniversary of my mother's death. It always takes longer to get over grief than we think it will – and a great deal longer than other people think it should!

Today's verse reminds me of Isaiah's words (61:1–3), which Jesus later made His mission statement: 'He has sent me to bind up the broken-hearted . . . to bestow on them a crown of beauty instead of ashes.' I remember being so proud of myself for not crying at my mother's funeral, but in Bible days they wailed as loudly as possible. They didn't just wear black ties – they covered themselves in ashes and old sacking. Weddings were different too; no one bought an expensive hat – they danced for joy with flowers in their hair! Can God *really* comfort people so completely that it feels like the difference between a funeral and a wedding? Yes, but He needs our co-operation.

Three years after Karen's husband died she was still incapacitated by grief. Her doctor urged her to 'let her husband go and move on with her life', but holding on to her misery was Karen's way of keeping him close. One day her vicar reminded her that Jesus promised to comfort those who mourn (Matt. 5:4), but added, 'That only applies to people who *choose* to let Him.' While it felt too much for Karen to 'let her husband go', she finally managed to give him to Jesus by placing his photo under the cross in the vicar's study. That was the moment when she began to live again.

Praise be to the . . . Father of compassion and the God of all comfort.

(2 Cor. 1:3)

Enjoying a worry session

Be still before the LORD *and wait patiently for him. The meek will inherit the land and enjoy great peace.*

Ps. 37:7, 11

'Our curate's far too meek and mild,' I overheard someone complain. Calling someone 'meek' nowadays is like saying they are a wimp! Moses and Jesus were both described as 'meek' but they were anything *but* wimps! They were strong and courageous, yet totally submitted to God the Father in everything. When Jesus said the meek are blessed (Matt. 5:5), He was referring to a quality that is totally opposite to arrogance, pride and self-assertion. In the language of His hearers, meek would describe a powerful war horse that was totally under the control of its rider. These days we prize self-confidence, but its roots are in pride, which says, 'I can manage my own life; I don't need God's help.' Pride like that is a dangerous illusion: God did not design us to be self-sufficient. Yet there are areas in all our lives where we secretly want to take control. In this psalm David urges us to trust God to provide everything we need, and then to sit waiting for Him to act on our behalf. Ouch! That is extremely difficult, especially if you are a born worrier and a bit of a control freak. Someone said to me once, 'You must really enjoy worrying because you do it so often!' I could have killed her! All the same, the very best antidote to worry is to allow God to take control of every place in us where we are not being meek. Then we'll 'enjoy great peace', which is far more pleasant than 'enjoying' a prolonged worry session!

Some people bear three kinds of trouble – the ones they've had,
the ones they have, and the ones they expect to have.

Edward Everett Hale (1822–1909)

Layers of intimacy

As a bridegroom rejoices over the bride, so will your God rejoice over you.

Isa. 62:5

She was sixteen, with braces on her teeth and spots on her chin. Her walk to school led past a massive tower block, which she knew was the headquarters of a worldwide corporation, founded by a brilliant man, still in his thirties. She often looked up at the gleaming monument to his genius and wondered what he was like. One day she saw a limo arriving at the main entrance and the great man himself emerged. For one second their eyes met.

'One day I'll work for him,' she promised herself. Five years later, as a junior trainee, she scarcely ever glimpsed 'the Boss', but slowly she hauled herself up the company ladder until she finally became his PA. Their relationship was distant and professional but gradually they began sharing the occasional leisure activity, and a platonic friendship developed. The story ends predictably with wedding bells, but can you see how their relationship developed in stages – just as ours does with God?

We first become aware of Him as a distant creator, and then we realise He wants us to see Him as our Father. (Unfortunately that image didn't fit into my parable!) As we mature we want not only to receive from Him but also to give, and He becomes the master we long to serve. Later still we realise that Jesus calls us friends not just servants (John 15:15), and some of us move even closer as we discover all the verses in both the Old and the New Testaments where He calls Himself our husband and bridegroom. God so badly wants us to understand how close He wants us to be to Him that He gives us all these different human relationships as models.

How do you most easily relate to God?

The perfect husband

For your Maker is your husband.

Isa. 54:5

For years I saw God as an exacting master whom I could only please by endless Christian activity. Then, during a long illness, I realised my company was more important to Him than my service. Being God's friend felt great but, when my husband left, after thirty years of apparently happy marriage, God showed me He wanted more than my friendship.

I had never lived alone before and was terrified of the dark; sleep was difficult for weeks as I lay worrying about unpaid bills, a leaking roof and an ailing car. The last straw was a mouse in my bedroom! I took refuge on the lounge sofa, where I found a card on which a friend had written, 'Take a look at Isaiah 54.' Obviously a husband was *exactly* what I needed at that moment: a rich and generous one who would take care of bills, DIY – and mice, but who would also satisfy my deep ache for love and acceptance. Could God *really* be offering me that kind of personal tenderness and intimate care? I knew He was giving me the choice of either trusting Him over every tiny detail of my existence or continuing to feel afraid and alone for the rest of my life. After a struggle I finally copied today's verse onto a piece of paper, which I headed 'Marriage contract'; I signed my name and stuck it on the fridge. Since then it has astonished me to see how many practical and emotional needs God has met – even the mice have mysteriously disappeared!

You may be a man, or you could already have a perfect husband, so seeing God in this light may not appeal; but could He be asking you to take a step further into His heart?

Sea billows

He has sent waves of sorrow over my soul; chaos roars at me like a flood . . . May the LORD show his constant love during the day, so that I may have a song at night.

Ps. 42:7–8, GNB

On 22 November 1873 there was a terrible shipwreck in the Atlantic. Horatio Spafford, a Chicago lawyer, had just waved his wife and four little girls off on a ship for England – where he soon hoped to join them. The family needed a holiday badly. Two years before, a huge fire had devastated the city of Chicago, which Horatio had helped to build. Regardless of the fact that he had lost most of his money, and his only son, Horatio had worked tirelessly to help the homeless and injured. How must he have felt when he heard news of the wreck? Only his wife survived – all the little girls were drowned.

Catching the next boat, he sailed for England; perhaps, as he watched the huge Atlantic waves surging repeatedly against his ship, he felt they were like the 'billows' of sorrow that kept on swamping his soul. Yet, because of God's miraculous grace, during that voyage he was able to write one of the best-loved hymns of all time. He wanted the world to know that it *is* possible to survive even the biggest 'waves of sorrow'.

Sometimes we manage to survive one major tragedy surprisingly well, but when, like Horatio, we are hit by several terrible losses in close succession, only by asking God for His amazing grace in abnormally large quantities can we hope to keep our faith afloat.

When peace, like a river, attendeth my way,
When sorrows like sea billows roll;
Whatever my lot, Thou hast taught me to say,
It is well, it is well with my soul.

Horatio Spafford (1828–88)

Look up!

You lift my head high.

Ps. 3:3, *The Message*

Recently several things have been getting me down badly. As I opened an old prayer journal to check something for this book, a little card fluttered out. The handwriting told me it was from my close friend and prayer partner, Violet, who died twelve years ago. She could not have known that her message would be *exactly* what I needed to hear so many years later.

'Dearest Jen, Let Him cup your chin in His hand, and lift your head until you are gazing straight into the love and beauty shining in His face.' Suddenly I realised I have not *wanted* to look up at His face lately. I've felt too upset with Him, so I've been looking down at my problems instead.

I once met an old man called Ivan when I was speaking in the Ukraine. He had been imprisoned for many years by the Communists for pastoring a church, and tortured when he refused to stop telling other prisoners about Jesus. Once, after a terrible beating, lying face down on his cell floor, he felt like giving up. When he heard someone behind him say, 'Ivan, lift up your nose,' he obeyed, dreading more violence. 'Ivan,' the voice continued, 'lift up your head.' As he did so he saw Jesus Himself smiling down at him.

Phoebe, my greatly loved dog, is now too old for long walks in the woods, so she simply sleeps at my feet while I work at my computer. Occasionally she looks up and her brown eyes say, 'I love you and trust you completely.' If only I would just keep looking up at the Lord like that!

Really knowing God is not about what we do for Him; it is just that look which connects us on the deepest level of all.

Yearning for intimacy

O God, you are my God, earnestly I seek you; my soul thirsts for you, my body longs for you, in a dry and weary land where there is no water. I have seen you in the sanctuary and beheld your power and your glory. Because your love is better than life, my lips will glorify you. I will praise you as long as I live, and in your name I will lift up my hands.

Ps. 63:1–4

There are two people I particularly want to meet in heaven because I love the intimacy with God that they both enjoyed.

Widowed and childless in her twenties, Anna longed to spend her life perpetually in God's presence, so for eighty-four years 'she never left the temple but worshipped night and day' (Luke 2:37). I suspect King David wished he could also spend his life in uninterrupted enjoyment of God in His temple. He says, 'This is what I seek: that I may dwell in the house of the LORD all the days of my life, to gaze upon the beauty of the LORD and to seek him in his temple' (Ps. 27:4).

When David wrote today's psalm he was feeling sad because his exile in the desert meant he could no longer visit God's house (Ps. 63:2). Yet it was *while* he wandered in that desert that he discovered he could glorify, praise and pray wherever he happened to be (Ps. 63:3–4).

Lord, you didn't call me to live a cloistered life, like Anna, where I could focus on you without interruption. I'm constantly surrounded by people and activity, but I long for you just as she did. Help me to train myself, as David did, to be aware of you continually – with me in the centre of all my busy everyday activities.

Oh God, why, why, why?

How long, O LORD, must I call for help, but you do not listen? Or cry out to you, 'Violence!' but you do not save? The wicked hem in the righteous, so that justice is perverted.

Hab. 1:1–4

Have you ever felt exasperated with God? Maybe you prayed for something long and hard, only to be met with stony silence? Or have you wondered how God can watch murder and injustice and not *force* people to keep His laws?

When I had my worst-ever 'fall-out' with God, the soothing assurances of Christians merely irritated me; I needed someone who had felt the same – but survived their faith crisis. Habakkuk came to my rescue.

He had prayed for years that God would send revival to His people, who had turned away from Him yet again. When nothing changed, Habakkuk fired the same angry questions at God that I was asking. God told him that rather than sending revival He was sending the Babylonians (Hab. 1:5–9) to destroy their land and carry them off as slaves. It was the last thing Habakkuk wanted!

God had also failed to comply with my prayers; instead, He'd done the exact opposite. Habakkuk's book begins with anger but finishes with joy (Hab. 3:18); I wondered what caused the change.

First, Habakkuk took his confusion and pain and climbed a high tower to be alone with God (Hab. 2:1). It is easy to withdraw from Him when He disappoints us, but going off alone with Him gives us the chance to view our problems from His angle.

I didn't have a convenient tower, so I went on a silent retreat instead. God gave me no answers but showed me I needed to let go of all the grudges I was holding against Him. So I listed them, wrapped the paper round a rock, and chucked it into the sea.

Jigsaw pieces

You can't condone evil! So why don't you do something about this?
Why are you silent now? . . . Evil men swallow up the righteous and
you stand around and watch!

Hab. 1:13, *The Message*

Can we really let our anger out at God as Habakkuk did? When we
doubt His love and care we insult Him painfully, but He prefers honesty
to silence! When my son Duncan was angry with me he shouted until
he felt better, and then hugged me and said sorry. His brother Richard
went quiet for days when he was angry, shutting himself in his room
– excluding me from his world. Duncan's furious accusations hurt me
far less than Richard's lengthy rejection. God is big enough to take
our outbursts, but, like Job after all his rudeness towards God, we do
need to ask forgiveness (Job 42:3, 6).

God promised national disaster instead of the spiritual revival
Habakkuk wanted, so Habakkuk was furious, because he could only
see a few pieces of the 'jigsaw', while God could see the whole picture.
God knew that Nebuchadnezzar would reduce Jerusalem to heaps of
smoking rubble and drag away her inhabitants as slaves. Yet He also
knew that, during their seventy years of exile, they would turn back
to Him, and go home to rebuild a nation firmly based on His laws
(Jer. 29:14). Because we don't know the future we often think, as
Habakkuk did, 'God's getting it wrong.' God *is* a God of love, but
He is also a God of justice. He had made a bargain with His people:
'You keep my rules and I'll protect you – break them at your peril.'
God warned them so often but they habitually broke His rules.

If you thought of God as an overindulgent father who never carries out
His threat of punishment, could you respect Him?

Out of the dark night of the soul

Though the fig-tree does not bud and there are no grapes on the vines, though the olive crop fails and the fields produce no food, though there are no sheep in the pen and no cattle in the stalls, yet I will rejoice in the LORD. I will be joyful in God my Saviour.

Hab. 3:17–18

Habakkuk's protests were finally silenced when God gave him an experience of His awesome glory and power (Hab. 3:2, 4, 12–13). Although Habakkuk must have realised he might die in the invasion – or in the inevitable famine which would follow the destruction of farmland and livestock – still he skipped from his tower full of joy. He had gone up there thinking God must be either powerless or uninterested, only to discover what He is actually like. When we catch a glimpse of that, all our questions seem irrelevant!

I came out of my 'tower' (retreat) realising that God really *was* all I needed. Human sources of happiness and fulfilment – such as money, loving relationships, success, being needed and appreciated, health, appearance, fitness or a beautiful home – all these were too precarious to be my security because they can so easily be lost. In my journal I rewrote Habakkuk's song of joy like this:

'Though my computer crashes, losing weeks of vital work, though no one asks me for Christmas, if it rains every day of my holiday or I write off my new, uninsured, car; if my bank account is badly overdrawn, the new vicar disbands my house group, my best friend dumps me, the dog dies, the house burns down and I lose my job, yet I will choose to believe God is right in the middle of the mess with me – completely in control and committed to getting me through. So I accept His gift of supernatural peace and joy in spite of EVERYTHING!'

'Go in the strength you have'

When the angel of the LORD *appeared to Gideon, he said, 'The* LORD *is with you, mighty warrior.' 'But sir,' Gideon replied . . . 'the* LORD *has abandoned us and put us into the hand of Midian.' The* LORD *turned to him and said, 'Go in the strength you have and save Israel.'*

Judg. 6:12–14

Vividly I remember the day when I realised the thing I feared most was my own inadequacy. I firmly believed in God's promises, as well as His desire – and ability – to help me meet all life's challenges; it was my failure to summon enough faith to grasp His assistance that I dreaded. It was Gideon who helped me.

I guess he also feared his own inadequacy, not only because he was born anxious and diffident, but also because he felt impotent in the face of enemy oppression. The Midianites swept down at every harvest time to steal crops and livestock, leaving severe famine in their wake. Gideon was hiding in the hills when he noticed a tired traveller resting under a tree. When the man addressed him as 'mighty warrior' Gideon probably snorted – he felt more like a wimp! However, as they talked it dawned on Gideon that this might be God Himself, in human form. The command to 'Go in the strength you have and save Israel' horrified him because he knew he had no strength at all; but the Lord was saying, 'It's *my* strength you have – so use it!'

Although Gideon's faith was never strong (he often had to ask God for tangible signs to confirm His promises – Judg. 6:17, 36–37, 39), he needed to realise that God was bigger than his own fear of failure. I had to learn that too!

Help me, Lord, to stop concentrating on my lack of faith, and focus instead on your faithfulness.

Home-made wedding dresses

'Let us rejoice . . . For the time has come for the wedding of the Lamb, and his bride has prepared herself for it. She has been given clean shining linen to wear.' (The linen is the good deeds of God's people.)

Rev. 19:7–8, GNB

St Peter once met a lady called Dorcas, who was greatly loved for all the kind little things she did for people (Acts 9:36–41). I told you about the 'modern Dorcas' (August 23) who helped so much when my children were very small. She was always leaving cakes, jam or little toys on my doorstep. It was not until her funeral that we discovered just how many people she had secretly helped, nurtured and encouraged.

Today's verse shows how highly God values little acts of kindness, even if no one else notices them. Jesus makes it clear that how we act during our earthly life affects our eternal reward (Matt. 16:27); but He also warns us that if we want His reward, rather than man's approval, we need to keep very quiet about what we do (Matt. 6:2).

Peter also met a woman who was very different from Dorcas. Sapphira's reward was everyone else's admiration, so with her husband she pretended to give away their entire fortune – when actually they kept some back in case God let them down. Peter spotted their deception and they dropped dead (Acts 5:1–10).

Fortunately the same doesn't happen to us when our super-Christian masks fall off abruptly when we get home from church and turn grumpy, or talk on the phone in a syrupy, spiritual voice, then ring off and growl, 'Stupid old fool!' Isn't it tempting to remark casually, 'When I was spending my hour with God early this morning . . .'

Please help me care more about the beauty of my future wedding dress than my present reputation.

Stabbed by joy

For the eyes of the LORD range throughout the earth to strengthen those whose hearts are fully committed to him.

2 Chr. 16:9

This morning a thought came to me that was so beautiful I felt as if I'd been stabbed by joy! My dog Phoebe is now very old and frail and needs a lot of extra fussing, special food, frequent short, slow walks, extra warmth and lots of strokes. At the moment I have three dogs, because my son has left his huge young Labrador with me while he works abroad – and of course, there is little blind Stella. I was feeling a bit guilty that Phoebe and her special needs are absorbing an unfair amount of my 'doggie time', while the other two, who are strong and healthy, are being a bit neglected. Then I suddenly thought how very different the Lord is! When we need His extra special help and reassuring blessings, He gives them lavishly, but never at the cost of His stronger children. His eyes are also on them constantly, enjoying their every triumph and achievement while never taking His eyes off those who appear to need much more of His care.

As Phoebe lies beside me I constantly find myself talking to her, using the comforting little phrases I've always used to encourage her over the years. Now, however, she is stone deaf and perhaps she wonders why I never speak to her any more, just when she most needs to hear my voice. I felt another stab of joy when I thought of all the things God says to me constantly, but my humanness blocks up my ears.

O Lord, Your tenderness –
melting all my bitterness!
O Lord, I receive Your love.

Graham Kendrick (Copyright © 1986 Thankyou Music*)

A 'yes' in my heart?

He will be great and will be called the Son of the Most High.

Luke 1:26–38

For a moment, just stop and imagine you were Mary; how would you feel if an angel suddenly showed up and told you that God wanted to plant Himself in your body (Col. 1:19)? It is a mind-blowing idea, but that is exactly what God does for each of us when we ask Him to come and live inside us by His Holy Spirit. Mary willingly opened herself to His divine seed even though she risked her future happiness and even her life by doing so (Joseph could have had her stoned to death – Matt. 1:19). It cost Mary a lot to carry the glory of God's presence in her body, because that seed did not stay small and hidden. As the months went by the life inside her grew and developed, and her body had to expand in order to make space for it. Soon that life was no longer a secret but was obvious to everyone who saw her. She nearly lost the man she loved and might well have jeopardised relationships with family and friends.

Some of us like to keep the life of God in us small and secret, particularly on weekdays! But the challenge of Advent is: how willing are we to open ourselves to more and more of Jesus until His presence in us is obvious to all? Are we willing to carry the glory of God everywhere we go, every day of the week? Will God find an unqualified 'yes' in our hearts, as He did in Mary's?

> O Holy child of Bethlehem,
> descend to us, we pray;
> cast out our sin, and enter in;
> be born in us today.

Phillips Brooks (1835–93)

Immanuel

The virgin will be with child and will give birth to a son, and will call him Immanuel.

Isa. 7:14

Choosing a name for a baby can be surprisingly difficult, but it must have been even more so in Bible times when the meaning of a name was much more important. One poor woman, who went into labour when Philistines killed her husband and stole the ark, called her baby Ichabod, 'God's glory has departed'. After a terrible labour another woman called her son Jabez, 'Pain-giver'. They called Jacob 'Supplanter' because he was born clutching his twin's heel (Gen. 25:26) – and he certainly lived up to his name.

Mary and Joseph had no choice over names for their baby; the angel told them it would be Jesus but, because He is the greatest king of all time, He was given many other names too, each of which reflects a different facet of His character. Immanuel, 'God with us', is my favourite.

Recently I asked a Jewish lady how she saw God.

'I have a gas ring in my flat,' she replied. 'I love to watch its flames dancing in a circle – blue, red, orange. If that circle of flaming energy could be magnified billions of times over until it surrounded the entire universe, then that is how I see God.'

That is a magnificent description, but too vast for most of us to relate to; God had to show us His love in a form we could understand. We needed to see His love in action, such as when He touched a filthy leper, stopped to heal a blind beggar in the gutter, gave back self-esteem to a prostitute or comforted a crying child on His lap.

Thank you, Immanuel, that there is nothing I will ever have to face without you right there beside me!

Saviour

You are to name him Jesus, for he will save his people from their sins.

Matt. 1:21

Poor Joseph must have felt a positive kaleidoscope of emotions when he saw an angel: terror; but also relief, because now he could believe Mary's story; joy that at last the long-awaited Messiah was coming, but confusion over the angel's words. He expected the Messiah to save His people from the *Romans,* not their sins!

Joseph's land was occupied by a ruthless military dictatorship, which forced high taxes and foreign laws on his people. Surely God would want His Messiah to set them free from such cruelty? But God had a far bigger agenda than simply to provide His people with a few years of comfort on Earth; He wanted to provide a way for them to live with Him for ever (John 3:16).

Have you got any 'Romans' in your life – things that restrict you and make life difficult, such as an unhappy marriage, illness, awkward teenagers, a stressful job or lack of money? We want a Saviour who has the power to change these circumstances and make life pleasant again, and we feel frustrated when the Jesus we encounter says, 'Come up here and look with me at the Big Picture. See all the good things I want to do for you *through* the problems you face; I want to purify your heart, cleanse you from your wrong attitudes, change the way you see people, and give you my supernatural strength and peace.' During His life on Earth, Jesus watched many people turn away because He was not the kind of 'Saviour' they wanted (John 6:66).

Lord, you know all about my Romans! I'd love you to kick them out of my life, but, until you do, please save me from my bad reactions to them.

Christ

You are the Christ (Messiah), the Son of the living God.

Matt. 16:16

Most people are happy to talk about 'God as they see him', and admit they pray sometimes to a higher power. They will even concede that Jesus was a historical character with revolutionary ideas, brilliant teaching skills and a flair for healing, but they would disagree heartily with Peter when he called Him Christ.

'Christ' is more than a name – it is a title, and a far greater one than 'Prince', 'Lord' or even 'King'. It is the Greek version of the Hebrew word 'Messiah', who was someone the Bible makes clear would be no mere human – but God incarnate (Isa. 9:6; Jer. 23:5–6). If Jesus had been just a good man surely He would have corrected Peter when he called Him Christ? Instead He praised him.

Yesterday I was watching a science fiction film with my grandson. When the hero was in a tight corner he called on the power of a mysterious life force by invoking its name. Clouds of fireworks and swirling smoke soon got him out of trouble. That fictional story made me realise that we have the right to invoke the most powerful force in the universe, by calling Him by His full name and title – JESUS CHRIST OF NAZARETH, SON OF THE LIVING GOD. Unlike the hero in the film we don't have to shout; He even hears our silent screams for help. The next time you find yourself in a tense situation, invoke that name and title under your breath. You may not see fireworks but He will definitely intervene on your behalf.

Please help me never to forget how awesomely powerful you really are!

Lamb of God

Here is the Lamb of God who takes away the sin of the world!
                                                            John 1:29, NRSV

I have to confess I don't find it easy to relate to Jesus as a lamb! We adopted a newborn orphan lamb once, called Percy. He looked sweet but smelt horrible and ruined my kitchen rug! As I've reflected on the name 'Lamb of God' I see it was His destiny that gave Jesus this name and certainly not His appearance. The baby depicted in school nativity plays and on Christmas cards was actually born with one aim in life – to die. Was that why the Wise Men were prompted to include myrrh for embalming the dead among their gifts?

Before Jesus came, when a Jew realised he had sinned, he chose a calf, kid or lamb to be punished by death in his place. He would put his hand on its head as a symbolic way of transferring his sin onto the animal, which then paid the ultimate penalty. Finally the priest would sprinkle the man with the dead animal's blood as a sign that he was free.

God never liked all that slaughter (Ps. 51:16) but He loved justice too much to let people get away with sin, which always hurts innocent people. Sin *must* be punished, but God loves the sinner as well as the 'sinned against'! So all these lambs became a prophetic picture of what Jesus would one day do when He allowed Himself to be sacrificed for the sin we all commit.

Jesus, perhaps after thinking all that through, I can relate to you as a Lamb after all; but please help me to be as willing as you were to sacrifice myself and my plans for other people – especially the awkward ones!

Lion of Judah

See, the Lion of the tribe of Judah, the Root of David, has triumphed.
Rev. 5:5

I've just been watching the first film of 'The Chronicles of Narnia' with some of my grandsons; it usually appears on TV at this time of year, and the story invariably reduces me to tears. C. S. Lewis was certainly inspired when he chose a lion, the king of beasts, as a symbol of Christ. Mr Beaver's classic remark, 'Of course he isn't safe; he's a lion!' has been quoted in countless sermons to illustrate how impossible it is to domesticate God or predict what He might do next. Whenever I see people being blessed by the Lord I always remember Mr Beaver's other famous quote: 'Aslan's on the move!'

As a child in Sunday school I used to love singing, 'The Lion of Judah shall break every chain and give us the victory again and again!' I was always being picked on in the school playground because I was painfully shy and timid. So I used to sing that song to myself while I imagined Jesus walking round beside me, like an invisible lion, growling protectively at anyone who was horrid to me. Try it next time you feel intimidated; it's a glorious morale-booster.

The term 'Lion of Judah' was a prophetic name for the Messiah. When the patriarch Jacob staged a deathbed scene with all his twelve sons in attendance, he prophesied over them in turn, telling Judah he was a lion whose descendants would rule for ever (Gen. 49:9–10). Judah's direct line included David, and of course Jesus Himself, who will rule the entire universe for eternity.

Lord, you are not only a gentle lamb but also a fierce lion. The contrasts in your vast personality are too much for me to comprehend! All I can do is worship you.

Almighty

I am the Alpha and the Omega . . . the Almighty.

Rev. 1:8

Can you picture a lonely prisoner in his cell? His mind is full of memories of the past – but the worst one returns often. He is standing by a cross, watching his best friend die in agony. Suddenly this terrible memory is replaced by something amazingly different! He gasps as a vision of the future floods his mind with glory. He sees the friend, whom the world had rejected, coming back again surrounded by angels and golden clouds. This time no one could ignore Him, and the soldiers who callously tortured him quake in terror. As the Holy Spirit pulls back the curtains of time, John glimpses the carpenter, who had been his friend, gloriously transformed, enthroned for ever in heaven.

At this time of year, which the church has christened Advent, we are not only preparing our hearts for the coming of the baby in a manger; we are also focusing our eyes of faith on the *second* coming of our King. This amazing event was not just an old man's imagination – it is *real* (1 Thess. 4:16–17)! Most of us probably wish we could have been in that Bethlehem stable on the first Christmas Eve, but nothing is going to stop us being present the next time Jesus comes!

He came down to earth from heaven,
who is God and Lord of all;
And His shelter was a stable,
and His cradle was a stall:
with the poor and mean and lowly
lived on earth our Saviour holy.

And our eyes at last shall see Him
through His own redeeming love . . .

Cecil Frances Alexander (1818–95)

Bread of life

Then Jesus declared, 'I am the bread of life. He who comes to me will never go hungry.'

John 6:35

I've just been to a friend's pre-Christmas lunch. Instead of all the usual seasonal fare she had baked a batch of homemade bread, which we devoured, still hot, with soup and cheese. We all agreed there is nothing more satisfying than bread. Jesus was in Capernaum when He called Himself 'the bread of life'. The fishing port was jam-packed with people who had been with Him the previous day on the far side of Lake Galilee. He had fed thousands of them with just five small loaves and two fish (John 6:11). Now here they were pestering Him for another free lunch (John 6:26).

'I came from heaven to give you so much more than food,' Jesus told them sadly. 'I long for you, and the millions who follow you, to embrace me – not just my teachings, but the supernatural and eternal life that is in me. The only way you can have this life is by taking me right into yourselves, so I become part of you, just as bread does when you eat it.' They simply could not understand, and many rejected Him in disgust that day (John 6:66). The apostles stayed (John 6:68), and after His crucifixion they remembered how Jesus had given them bread during their last supper together, telling them it symbolised His body broken for them (Luke 22:19). Then at last they understood.

Lord, give me today my daily bread (Luke 11:3). Not just the practical, outside things, but fill me all over again with your energy to get things done; nourish my spirit so your life grows and matures in me; come into this aching hunger I have for love and security and satisfy me with yourself.

Bright Morning Star

I, Jesus . . . I am the bright morning star.

Rev. 22:16, NLT

'Oooh! It's so dark!' I gasped. I was eight years old and it was five o'clock on an ice-cold December morning. My father was scraping frost from his car.

'See if you can find the Morning Star,' he suggested. I had never been up early enough to see it before and was amazed by its bright-ness. As we set off on a long drive to deliver presents to distant friends my father explained, 'Before clocks were invented sailors, watchmen and farmers always knew it was nearly dawn when the Morning Star appeared, so they called it "Star of Hope".'

The message about joy, peace and goodwill that the angels gave to the shepherds seems rather strange! Ever since then there has been very little joy or peace – you only have to watch the news to know how terrible life on Earth can be – at least for some people.

Christmas seems to underline how unfair things are! Some children have masses of presents, others have none; we 'pig out' on Christmas Day while others die of starvation; some people are surrounded by loving families while others sit alone, forgotten or unwanted. God is often accused of being unfair but Jesus never promised us anything but trouble in this life (John 16:33), although He *did* promise to make everything fair in the next! Because of the birth (and death) of Jesus we can confidently look forward to an eternity of nothing but joy and peace. However, the angels actually promised peace and goodwill *on Earth* (Luke 2:14, KJV). Although our lives down here may be outwardly difficult, we can still experience a foretaste of heaven in our hearts.

Star of wonder, star of night,
star with royal beauty bright . . .
guide us to Thy perfect light.

John Henry Hopkins (1857)

Dayspring

The Dayspring from on high has visited us; to give light to those who sit in darkness and the shadow of death.

Luke 1:78–79, NKJV

What a lovely name, 'Dayspring'! Not only is Jesus called the Morning Star that announces the dawn – He *is* the dawn! Most of us who live in the northern hemisphere find the nights very long and dreary at this time of year. We struggle off to work in dark, damp discomfort wondering if we are succumbing to flu! But this morning the dawn was magnificent; gradually the navy sky was painted in great lavish brush strokes of scarlet and gold as the sun made his appearance – looking like a huge red rubber ball. The shadows that seemed so black and menacing were quickly dispelled. As I walked the dogs through the frosty fields I thought of Malachi 4:2: 'The sun of righteousness arises with healing in its wings.'

The sun is the centre of the universe; it gives energy, causes growth, dispels illness, kills harmful germs, heals wounds, banishes damp and cold and brings back colour to a dull, grey world. Jesus is not only the Son of God but also an even greater power than the rising sun itself. When we invite Him into our personal world He banishes the dark shadows of fear and doubt and becomes our power source, grows us as people, heals our inner wounds and warms our cold hearts. Perhaps, at this moment, you're depressed, grieving, ill or exhausted. Ask the 'Dayspring from on high' to shine into all your dark, painful thoughts and feelings and give you His dawn light.

Who paints the skies into glorious day?
Only the splendour of Jesus.
Who storms the prison and sets men free?
Only the mercy of Jesus.

Who Paints the Skies into Glorious Day by Stuart Townend
(Copyright © 1995 Kingsway's Thankyou Music*)

Rock

Since you are my rock and my fortress, for the sake of your name lead and guide me.

Ps. 31:3

God is often described as our 'rock' in the Old Testament, but it is Paul who says 'that rock was Christ' (1 Cor. 10:4). Before dynamite was invented, large outcrops of rock were immoveable and indestructible. People who journeyed through deserts used them as navigation points to guide them safely through the constantly shifting sand. These rocky 'fortresses' which are such a feature of the wilderness also provided shade from the blistering sun and a place to hide from enemies.

Life can change as rapidly as a desert landscape! In my work as a counsellor people often tell me how totally disorientated they feel because their lives have changed suddenly. Even 'good' changes can be difficult to handle, such as getting married, moving house or having a first baby. This is because there is generally some degree of loss involved in every change, and this is why most of us find change so disconcerting. Yet, for all of us, life involves change – and successful living depends on our ability to adapt.

In the middle of any major life readjustment, sometimes Jesus is our one permanent, fixed point of reference – our unchanging Rock and a familiar place in which to hide. If we keep our eyes fixed on Him, He will show us the way to navigate through the upheaval and protect and shelter us while we are vulnerable.

Jesus once told a story about a man who built his house (i.e. his life) on shifting sand dunes and another who built on solid rock. Only one of those 'houses' withstood the storm.

When you're through changing, you're through.

Bruce Barton (1886–1967)

Glutton and drunkard

John the Baptist came neither eating bread nor drinking wine, and you say, 'He has a demon.' The Son of Man came eating and drinking, and you say, 'Here is a glutton and a drunkard, a friend of . . . sinners.'

Luke 7:33

Jesus was given these unkind names simply because He loved hanging out with people and sharing jokes, food and wine. When He was challenged by religious leaders for going to a party with some rather undesirable characters, He replied, 'I have not come to call the righteous, but sinners to repentance' (Luke 5:32). Christmas provides an excellent opportunity to throw a party and invite neighbours and work colleagues; a good party can often make it easier to ask them to carol service or the next Alpha Course.

Yet some Christians definitely feel they should not be involved at all with the partying side of Christmas because following Jesus is all about self-denial and being serious. Actually Jesus Himself was full of fun; He invented laughter and decided that babies should smile before learning to do anything else! People flocked after Him because they found His humour, love of life and infectious joy both attractive and refreshing. So if you are dreading the office party or the 'Staff Do', ask Him to lend you some of His joy, not just to get you through the evening but to bubble over onto others so they are attracted to the Jesus inside you.

Here is a biblical description of a celebration which somehow gives us all permission to have fun this Christmas: 'Nehemiah said; "Go and celebrate with a feast of rich foods and sweet drinks, and share gifts of food with people who have nothing prepared. This is a sacred day before our Lord. Don't be dejected and sad, for the joy of the LORD is your strength"!' (Neh. 8:10, NLT)

DECEMBER 13

The Good Shepherd

I am the good shepherd; I know my own sheep, and they know me, just as my Father knows me and I know the Father.

John 10:14–15, NLT

Once I was asked to the Royal Garden Party at Buckingham Palace – but only to accompany an illustrious relative. All the same, I hired an impressive hat!

'The Queen will *love* that,' murmured my awestruck granddaughter. Afterwards I did not like to tell her that there were four thousand other guests between me and the Queen, who was so far away in the distance that she could not possibly have seen me – or my hat!

My uncle in Scotland probably had about as many sheep as the Queen had garden-party guests. He certainly didn't know his sheep individually either; to him they were just numbers painted in red on their woolly sides. Nor did they know him; they were controlled by dogs and men on quad bikes. So I could never understand why Jesus called Himself the Good Shepherd until I went to rural Turkey. Shepherds there are still very similar to the shepherds Jesus would have known. The flocks of sheep and goats are very small; the shepherd, who is usually an old man, stays with them all the time, watching over their safety and anticipating their every need. He knows each by name and they follow him around like pet dogs.

That is the kind of shepherd Jesus was talking about. Unlike the Queen and my uncle, He longs for me to feel personally precious and vitally important to Him. I am not one of a vast, nameless crowd of guests or flock of sheep; He knows how many hairs grow on my head and exactly what I'm thinking!

The All-Powerful Ruler of the Universe knows me intimately! Wonderful!

Wonderful Counsellor

For a child is born to us, a son is given to us. The government will rest on his shoulders. And he will be called: Wonderful Counsellor . . .

Isa. 9:6, NLT

One of the first things they taught us as trainee counsellors was never to get too emotionally attached to our clients or allow them to become dependent on us, and *never* to permit any kind of contact between appointments. I'm so glad Jesus isn't that kind of cold, clinical counsellor! He likes to hear me talking *any time*; He longs for me to depend on Him and never gets bored when I repeat myself. That makes Him an exceptionally wonderful counsellor!

Now, after many years of experience as a counsellor, I still often think, as I listen to a client's terrible story, 'There's no way I can possibly help this person!' Then, with a huge sense of relief, I hurriedly turn to Jesus, 'in whom are hidden all the treasures of wisdom and knowledge' (Col. 2:2). I can safely step back to let Him take over. I always feel closest of all to Him when I'm sitting watching the way He gently sorts out complex problems or mends broken hearts.

Most humans react to tough experiences in one of two ways; some talk out all the pain and confusion to as many of their friends who will listen sympathetically, and then find themselves a psychotherapist or a life coach as well. Others merely grit their teeth and crawl off into their private cave to hide. These 'cavemen' usually take a lot longer to recover, but Jesus longs to be invited into their cave alongside them, to share their pain. He also longs for the 'chatters' to turn to Him before downloading all their distress onto everyone else.

I will praise the LORD, who counsels me . . .

(Ps. 16:7)

Nazarene

He will be called a Nazarene.

Matt. 2:23

Of all the names given to Jesus, 'Nazarene' is quite the most derogatory! In the AD 30s the 'in crowd' who lived around Jerusalem dismissed Galileans as unspiritual, uneducated bumpkins. The King of Glory not only allowed Himself to be born in a stable, He became a refugee and then grew up in a 'deprived area'. When Nathaniel said, 'Can anything good come out of Nazareth?' (John 1:46) he was stating a popular belief but also saying a Nazarene could never be the Messiah because the prophets named Bethlehem as His birthplace. Many other people rejected Jesus because of that misunderstanding, so the name 'Nazarene' cost Him dear.

Nazareth itself rejected Him more harshly than any other town. When He preached His first sermon there they were so angry they tried to kill Him (Luke 4:16–29) and when He later returned as a celebrity their scepticism made it impossible for Him to perform miracles (Matt 13:54–58).

Being misunderstood and despised are two of the worst forms of human suffering, especially when it's people close to us who are doing the despising. It was Jesus' own brothers (John 7:5), cousins and childhood friends who turned on Him in Nazareth.

Is there someone in your life who looks down on you or rejects you? You are not alone; the man they called 'Nazarene' knows just how you feel. Paul tells us that if we really want to know Jesus we need to be willing to go through the same things that He faced (Phil. 3:10).

Lord, I hate it when I'm disapproved of or criticised. Please help me to realise it's only your opinion of me that matters.

The Word

His name is the Word of God

Rev. 19:13

Alan sat in his wheelchair beside the huge model railway his father had built for him. Trains whizzed through tunnels, stopped at stations and raced over bridges – there was no control panel in front of Alan, he could not have used one; there was just a microphone pinned to his jersey.

'Train stop! Train reverse!' I was amazed to realise it was Alan's words alone that controlled his model world. Watching him made me appreciate the enormous power of God's Word, which created the entire universe! 'Then God said, "Let there be light"; and there was light' (Gen. 1:3).

By calling Jesus 'the Word', John tells us that He was the visible, touchable, audible power of God (1 John 1:1). Throughout His life on Earth the words Jesus spoke brought people life (John 6:68); they were also powerful enough to still a storm (Mark 4:39), knock flat the soldiers who came to arrest Him (John 18:6), and kill a fig tree instantly (Matt. 21:19).

Our words may not be as powerful as His, yet they actually have the ability to build or demolish. An encouraging, appreciative comment builds someone's confidence, while unkind, negative remarks damage their self-image. Words can lodge in the memory and continue to do good or harm for many years. Because Jesus is the 'Word' He is the only one who can heal us from the effect of other people's negative words and wipe them from our minds; but have you ever stopped to ask Him to heal the scars *your* words might have left on the souls of other people?

Lord, I explode so easily, and say things I regret. Please control my words; use them to bring peace and hope instead of hurt.

Teacher

Jesus said to her, 'Mary.' She turned towards him and cried out in Aramaic, 'Rabboni!' (which means Teacher).

John 20:16

'Teacher' is my least favourite name for Jesus because teachers frighten me! When I was a nervous dyslexic child, a bullying, vicious teacher made me too terrified to learn anything. If you have wonderful memories of brilliant teachers you probably often call Jesus 'Teacher', but I've only just realised that I never have. Of course I *want* Him to teach me – how would I cope without His wisdom? So perhaps I ought to start using that name more often, but first I would have to make a conscious decision to accept that Jesus is a good teacher who will always be patient and encouraging. I have forgiven my bad teacher many times over, but maybe I need to do it yet again?

Just before he died, C. S. Lewis wrote a letter to a friend, telling her about the awful teacher who had blighted his childhood. Apparently he had forgiven him in the past and thought the job was finally complete, but suddenly the terrible memories had returned to haunt him and he realised he had to start the process of forgiveness all over again.

Has someone in your past ruined a name for you? Every time you hear it you cringe because it reminds you of a person who treated you badly. I have a friend called Eva who could never say the Lord's Prayer or address God as 'Father' because her human father had been so cruel. One day she realised she needed to redeem the name 'Father' by choosing to see God as the kind, loving, accepting father she never had. Forgiveness was the tool she used.

Forgiveness is not a feeling; it is an act of the will.

Selwyn Hughes (From *Every Day With Jesus*)

Light of the world

I am the light of the world. Whoever follows me will never walk in darkness, but will have the light of life.

John 8:12

For me, this time of year always means light: twinkling street decorations and glowing shop windows, candles and Christmas-tree lights – light everywhere, even in the gloomiest weather. Jesus called himself the Light of the World very early one morning as He stood in the temple. The courtyard would have been blazing with the light of massed candles for the feast of tabernacles, yet He was surrounded by a very dark situation. A woman, caught in the act of adultery, lay at his feet, publicly humiliated and facing execution. Adultery and divorce were surprisingly common in those days and probably just as painful as they are today. Jesus would have hurt for everyone involved but He was also upset by the darkness in the hearts of those men who were willing to use a family's agony for political advantage. It was indeed a very dark world into which Jesus stepped in order to save us from the pain we constantly inflict on one another.

For the Christmas Eve service our vicar asked us all to bring a candle in a jar. He had built a huge bonfire in the churchyard and we all had to light our candles from the flames and carry them home to put on our window ledge for the rest of the night.

'Jesus is the source of all light,' the vicar told us, 'so take His light into the world.'

Your faith may feel as small and wobbly as a candle flame but remember it takes only one tiny candle to banish darkness from a huge room (Matt. 12.20).

Please, Lord, help me to be your light-carrier wherever I go today.

Prince of Peace

And he will be called . . . Mighty God, Everlasting Father, Prince of Peace.

Isa. 9:6

Every year I think, 'This Christmas I'm *not* going to get stressed out!' but I soon forget that resolve as I hurtle through my 'To-Do' list. I have a cousin who always 'did' Christmas on a grand scale, until she became so sick of all the pressure that she declared she would delete it from her calendar. So, with no presents, cards, decorations or festive food to buy, she and her husband could afford to go abroad and lie in the sun! A month later I asked if she had enjoyed her peaceful break.

'No,' she admitted ruefully. 'We rowed the whole time. I discovered peace isn't external; it's internal!'

The Prince of Peace spent most of His earthly life surrounded by people who were often quarrelsome, demanding or downright hostile. He was constantly busy and pressured, yet He was full of peace because He carried it about with Him in His heart and never let the outside world steal it away. He says to us once again this Christmas, 'My [own] peace I now give and bequeath to you. Do not let your hearts be troubled . . . [Stop allowing yourselves to be agitated and disturbed and do not permit yourselves to be fearful and intimidated]. . .' (John 14:27, AMP). His kind of peace does not depend on the absence of strife. He wants us to inherit His *internal* peace, but we must choose to accept our legacy. Peace is not a warm fuzzy feeling that floats down automatically; you have to decide to grab it with both hands. I just hope I remember that when I start hitting the ceiling next week because the roast potatoes have burnt, or everyone's left me to wash up alone!

Peace, be still.

(Mark 4:39, NKJV)

Son of David

A blind man was sitting by the roadside begging. When he heard the crowd going by, he asked what was happening. They told him, 'Jesus of Nazareth is passing by.' He called out, 'Jesus, Son of David, have mercy on me!' Those who led the way rebuked him and told him to be quiet, but he shouted all the more.

Luke 18:35–39

This blind beggar had more faith than the crowds who scornfully dismissed him. They thought Jesus was merely a prophet from Nazareth, but the blind man recognised Him as the Messiah. For hundreds of years people had been expecting a descendant of David who, like him, would rule with justice and wisdom (Isa. 11:1–5). God told David that a member of his family would reign for ever, and many prophets repeated the promise. Some religious leaders doubted whether this Son of David would be more than a highly gifted human king, but Jesus told them they were wrong (Matt. 22:42–46). While He was descended from David through His mother, His father was God Almighty.

The blind beggar realised Jesus was no mere man, and was convinced He had the power to heal him. His faith outshone that of most of the people of his nation and nearly all of its religious leaders! Because we know his name (Mark 10:46) and he is mentioned in three Gospels, I think he must have followed Jesus immediately he was healed (Mark 10:52), and later became a well-known member of the early church.

Sometimes in our churches, disabled or elderly people are overlooked and undervalued, but when you get to know them you often discover they have far greater faith than more prominent members of the congregation or even the 'up-front brigade'.

Jesus, Son of David, creator of life and eternal ruler of the Universe, have mercy on me today.

Faithful

I saw heaven standing open and there before me was a white horse, whose rider is called Faithful and True . . . His eyes are like blazing fire, and on his head are many crowns.

Rev. 19:11–12

I always enjoy running quiet days – events where people can find space to focus on God; of course I would never plan one at this time of year, as everyone's too busy! Often I start by asking people which of the qualities of Jesus they love most. Invariably 'faithfulness' comes top of the list. We all have a crucial need to be loved but we can never be certain that human love will be permanent. This time of year, those of us who are getting older tend to look back to Christmases long ago and remember the love shown to us by long-dead grandparents and parents and then, more recently, by friends or spouses who are no longer with us. However glad we may feel to have been loved like that once, we often miss their love most at Christmas. The tender love that our hero with the white horse has for each one of us will last for ever. It feels almost unbelievably wonderful to know that there will never be a day, or night, when we will not be loved to the uttermost by a love that we can never ever lose. Here's one of the Bible's many promises about that love: 'For great is His love towards us, and the faithfulness of the LORD endures for ever' (Ps. 117:2).

Here is another promise for anyone who is feeling a bit apprehensive about Christmas. 'Because of the LORD's great love we are not consumed, for his compassions never fail. They are new every morning; great is your faithfulness.' (Lam. 3:22–23).

DECEMBER 22

Alpha and Omega

Behold, I am coming soon . . . I am the Alpha and the Omega, the First and the Last, the Beginning and the End.

Rev. 22:12–13

'I'm sick of babies!' muttered a five-year-old boy. 'Baby Jesus at school. Baby Jesus at church. He's even outside Marks and Spencer's! I don't want Jesus to be a baby; babies *smell*!' He was entitled to his opinion, but as we focus on worshipping a baby we mustn't forget who He really is! If you are not too stressed by Christmas, sit back and enjoy some of the things the Bible says about Him.

'The LORD formed me from the beginning, before he created anything else . . . I was the architect at his side. I was His constant delight, rejoicing always in His presence.' (Prov. 8:22, 30, NLT)

'And when He brought His firstborn Son into the world, God said, "Let all of God's angels worship Him" . . . to the Son He says . . . ". . . you laid the foundation of the earth and made the heavens with your hands. They will perish, but you remain forever. They will wear out like old clothing. You will fold them up like a cloak and discard them like old clothing. But you are always the same; you will live forever"' (Heb. 1:6–12, NLT).

'For by him all things were created: things in heaven and on earth, visible and invisible, whether thrones or powers or rulers or authorities; all things were created by Him and for Him. He is before all things, and in Him all things hold together . . . so that in everything He might have the supremacy. For God was pleased to have all His fullness dwell in Him' (Col. 1:16–19).

Jesus, I worship you for what you were, what you are and what you will be.

Man of Sorrows

He was despised and rejected by men, a man of sorrows, and familiar with suffering.

Isa. 53:3

It may seem odd to call Jesus 'Man of Sorrows' right in the middle of the festive season, but Christmas is an extraordinary time when we can hit phenomenal heights of happiness but difficult things can plunge us abnormally low. Illness, bereavement, loneliness, poverty, rejection – they all seem worse at a time when we think we *ought* to feel happy and excited. The Ghost of Christmas Past conjures up vivid memories which only seem to remind us of the special people who are no longer there, or the traditions we used to enjoy.

The first Christmas after my husband left, none of my six children could cope with a Larcombe Christmas without him, so they made other plans. I walked aimlessly through our village, past all the lighted windows where families were having fun together – but I was alone. I felt suicidal, but I suddenly remembered something my friend Sheila had once said soon after her husband died.

'You never get over sorrow, but you do get through it, and right at the very heart you meet the Man of Sorrows Himself.' During that Christmas I realised how perfectly Jesus understood how I was feeling, because He had been through so much Himself; He wanted me to let Him share my load of sadness. Isaiah tells us that 'He has . . . carried our sorrows' (53:4), but letting Him have mine was a major struggle because feeling sorry for myself was the only comfort I had left. What a relief when I finally shifted all those angry, hurt, desolate feelings onto Him!

If you are finding Christmas painful this year, don't forget you have the Man of Sorrows right there beside you!

Son of Man

The Son of Man came not to be served but to serve.

Matt. 20:28

Before He came to Earth Jesus enjoyed unlimited power and the ability to be everywhere at once, yet He chose the restrictions of a human body by becoming the Son of Man in order to win our friendship.

He could have floated down to Earth accompanied by massed bands of angels, plus thunder and lightning; instead He chose to be squashed unceremoniously inside the womb of a peasant girl; covered in blood, he was squeezed out into a cold, inhospitable world. Then he was hastily immobilised by strips of rag and placed in an animal feeding trough – surrounded by stinking dung and disgruntled livestock. Why? Because He wanted to identify with the most disadvantaged of the race he had created and show us all how much He loves us. The hands that 'flung stars into space' were reduced to gripping His mother's finger; the eyes that could see every detail of all the billions of galaxies He had made were swollen shut by birth trauma. The voice that had called everything into existence could only bawl with hunger.

He wanted to help ordinary working people to understand intricate concepts by using illustrations that they could relate to instantly; things like bread-making, sparrows, house-cleaning, a mother hen, and a farmer sowing seeds. It must make Him sad when we exclude Him from the nitty-gritty areas of our life, only talking to Him at set times in stilted language and going to worship Him once a week in grand buildings, accompanied by special music. He became the Son of Man so that He could be with us in the middle of our mess.

Thank you that you, the King of Heaven, should become the Son of Man!

DECEMBER 25

King of Kings

The blessed and only Ruler, the King of kings and LORD *of* LORDS.
1 Tim. 6:15

British monarchs in historical times were born surrounded by astounding pomp. All the important relations, senior court officials and church dignitaries, dressed in their grandest robes, would crowd the queen's bedchamber. Other VIPs waited in anterooms; foreign ambassadors queued with expensive gifts, while huge crowds assembled outside the palace gates. The moment a son was born, loud peals of bells announced the good news from every church tower in the country, cannons fired and everyone cheered.

There were no church bells or cheering crowds for the King of Kings; only a smelly animal shelter, filthy straw and a few shepherds. No one else in the busy little town noticed Him, wanted Him or even bothered to make room for His arrival. Yet all heaven was ripped open with pure joy as the angels danced and sang in the skies overhead.

My parents bought their first TV set in time for the Queen's coronation; watching the sheer glory of the spectacle flooded me with awe! All those silken robes, furs, diamonds, gold; the music and symbolism – how I loved it; but the best bit was when the peers of the realm came to pay homage. It was so moving to see these men in coronets, red velvet and ermine, kneeling before their monarch, who put her hands round theirs as they vowed lifelong obedience to their liege lord.

Perhaps today we all need to come to that stable and renew our vows of allegiance to the most powerful ruler in the universe, our everlasting King!

All hail the power of Jesus' name!
let angels prostrate fall;
bring forth the royal diadem,
and crown him Lord of all.

Edward Perronet (1726–92)

The Truth

Jesus answered, 'I am the way and the truth and the life. No-one comes to the Father except through me.'

John 14:6

I once wrote a book for children telling the Christmas story, describing the stable graphically, talking about the animal poo, rats running along the rafters and spiders weaving webs underneath them. My proof-reader was incensed.

'You can't publish this!' she protested. 'It wasn't like that!' In her mind the stable resembled the beautiful candlelit crib scenes she had enjoyed in church since childhood, or the pretty, sentimental Christmas cards she loved to send. Perhaps we all have our own mental pictures of that first Christmas, but they are not always very accurate.

When I visited Bethlehem I realised the limestone rock on which it's built is full of alcoves and caves. I'd always pictured an English-type wooden stable, but Jesus was far more likely to have been born in one of these natural rock shelters. The manger was probably a lump of limestone with a hollow chiselled out of it. I have always respected shepherds for the skilled and responsible job they do, but in those days they were considered the 'lowest of the low'. Yet God chose to announce the birth of His Son to people despised by others.

I used to think angels resembled fat babies without nappies, or anorexic teenagers with wings. When I actually saw one looking like a huge, fully armed warrior I realised how wrong I'd been!

Lord, if I have a distorted picture of who you were and are and your claims on my life, service, finances and possessions, please shine Truth into my fog-filled mind.

The Vine

I am the true vine . . . Remain in me, and I will remain in you.

John 15:1, 4

For some people, today could feel like an anticlimax, when indigestion sets in, the children play up, teenagers become obnoxious and Granny drives everyone up the wall.

Many people, such as schoolteachers and those who play key roles in church activities, can find the run-up to Christmas spiritually exhausting. By the time one vicar had sprinted through carol concerts, crib services, nativity plays and midnight communion, he said he would scream if he heard anyone mention the word 'Christmas' again!

Even if we have not been involved in organising Christian activities, the last few days may have been a frenzied whirl for most of us; and the human reaction to all this can be a desire to 'switch God off' and forget Christianity for a few days. We feel that if we 'stay connected' to 'the Vine', Jesus will start telling us to 'do something' when all we want to do is *nothing*.

I sense that Jesus just wants us to rest in His love today. That does not mean sitting still in contemplative prayer; we'll probably be far too busy for that, but it is actually possible for our spirits to lie down and rest in God while our bodies get on with being active. The TV blares, teenage music thumps, Granny complains and the baby grizzles – but, inside, you can be connected to Jesus as effortlessly as a branch growing from the tree trunk.

Please, Lord, show me how to 'remain' in you today so all your loveliness can seep into me continuously like sap from the vine. Give me your rest right down deep in my soul.

Holy One

You disowned the Holy and Righteous One . . . You killed the author of life, but God raised him from the dead. By faith in the name of Jesus, this man whom you see and know was made strong.

Acts 3:14–16

It was the power of the *name* of Jesus that healed the crippled beggar by the temple gate. Peter must often have seen supernatural power pouring through Jesus and dramatically changing lives; now, by using His name, that same power was available to him. He began to tell the amazed crowd who watched the healing all about Jesus, calling Him 'the Holy One'. No one could have been a better witness to His holiness than Peter. It is easy to think church leaders or evangelists are wonderfully holy people, but we'd probably change our minds if we had to live with them! Peter actually spent three years living and working with Jesus – and still described Him as holy!

Perhaps it was that awesome holiness of Jesus that first struck Peter. It caused him to feel so sinful that he flung himself down on his knees in his own fishing boat and begged Jesus to go away (Luke 5:8)! Instead, Jesus began the process of pouring his holiness into Peter.

When we give ourselves time to think just how holy Jesus really is, our reaction will probably be the same as Peter's, particularly if we have just been tripped up, yet again, by the sin that so often lands us in the mud. Jesus never gave up on Peter, in spite of his frequent falls, and He won't give up on us either.

Holy One, my head is full of TV junk, my body is sluggish with over-indulgence and I'm thoroughly irritated with everyone. Please detox me by your Holy Spirit.

The Way

Thomas said to him, 'LORD, we don't know where you are going, so how can we know the way?' Jesus answered, 'I am the way . . .'

John 14:5–6

Stella, my blind spaniel, manages remarkably well to navigate herself along our favourite path through the woods. She has become so confident now that she runs ahead of me, without her lead. Because the path is so familiar, she avoids the tree trunks which could give her a nasty headache if she ran into them at full tilt.

This morning, however, our path was covered by four inches of fluffy white snow. It covered all Stella's landmark smells and totally disorientated her – even my footsteps were oddly muffled, so she had to keep her nose as close to the back of my boots as she possibly could.

After a while I realised she wasn't behind me any more; looking round, I saw that a particularly chewy stick had distracted her.

'*Stella*!' I yelled. She wanted to bring the stick with her but it was far too big. She had to choose between staying to enjoy her stick and risking being lost in a strange new world, or abandoning it to run back to me as fast as she could.

In a few days' time we will all be faced with the fresh untrodden path of a new year with all its unknowns and new challenges. Jesus is the Way, so our only hope of navigating safely through it is to keep our noses as close to His boots as possible. His promise is: 'I will lead the blind by ways they have not known, along unfamiliar paths I will guide them; I will turn the darkness into light before them and make the rough places smooth . . . I will not forsake them' (Isa. 42:16).

Please, Lord, let nothing distract me from following you closely through the coming year.

The Resurrection and the Life

Jesus said to her, 'I am the resurrection and the life. He who believes in me will live, even though he dies.'

John 11:25

As we move towards a new year, many things will be left behind. The person we have been is dying so that the new one can emerge. Probably most of us are quite glad about that!

My garden felt dank and dismal this morning when I was raking autumn leaves onto the compost heap. Those leaves had been such a joy when they first appeared in the spring, and during hot summer days they had formed a shady canopy for many a barbeque or quiet cup of tea on the swing-hammock. Now they look brown and lifeless, but new leaves are already forming inside the bare twigs on the trees. As I leant on my rake I pictured how the garden will look next July!

As we move through our lives we do have to allow areas of them to die in order to make room for new things. Not just the bad habits and negative thinking but also good things have to go in order to make space for the best.

It is Jesus himself who will bring these new qualities, gifts and attitudes into our lives during the coming year. The wonderful names He called Himself when He spoke to Martha have echoed with hope down the centuries.

Which areas of your life would you most like to leave behind permanently? And what new things do you think Jesus might like to 'plant' in you next year?

My Father, during the coming year 'I want to know Christ and the power of his resurrection (Phil. 3:10).

DECEMBER 31

The Door

I am the Door; anyone who enters in through me will ... live ... I came that they may have and enjoy life, and have it in abundance [to the full until it overflows].

John 10:9–10, AMP

What a promise for the new year ahead! Jesus wants us to enjoy living life to the full so that His abundant life can overflow to everyone we encounter. Our outward circumstances might be grim, because life with the Lord does not mean immunity *from* difficulties but peace and joy *in* difficulties. He promises to 'make the Valley of [Trouble] a door of hope' (Hos. 2:15).

Jesus called Himself 'the Door' just after He said He was the Good Shepherd. He may have taken a walk out into the hills around Jerusalem and sat down to watch the shepherds who raised the thousands of lambs needed for temple sacrifices. He often illustrated His teaching with examples from real life, so perhaps when He called Himself 'the Door' He was pointing at one of the circles of stones in which sheep spent the night. These shelters had no doors to keep out robbers or predators, so the shepherd himself lay down in the gap to keep his sheep safe. In the Exodus story, which was a prophetic picture of what Jesus did for us on the cross, it was the blood of the lamb, painted on the doorposts, which gave protection to the people inside (Exod. 12:23).

My front door not only protects me when I'm safe inside, but each time I open it, I step out to a special adventure. Jesus is our 'Door of hope' for the new year.

I have placed before you an open door that no-one can shut. I know that you have little strength, yet you have kept my word and have not denied my name.

(Rev. 3:8)

Contents by Date

Series on Hearts

Series on King David

Series on King David (continued)

Series on King Solomon

Series on Hands

Series on Abraham

Series on Paul's Secret of Joy

Series on Moses

Themes

Intimacy with God and our Love for Him
January 16, January 28, February 20, February 22, February 23, February 26, March 2, March 15, March 19, March 21, March 25, April 2, April 10, April 11, April 23, May 6, May 18, May 19, June 12, June 13, June 18, July 19, July 26, August 10, August 12, September 2, September 3, September 7, September 21, September 25, October 15, October 21, October 24, November 8, November 9, November 17, November 20, November 24, December 13

God's Love
November 3–10, February 14, February 22, February 23, February 24, February 26, March 7, April 21, May 8, May 12, June 14, June 17, June 22, June 23, June 26, July 2, July 22, July 23, July 25, August 3, August 22, September 3, September 21, September 23, October 16, November 3, November 4, November 13, November 14, November 21, December 2, December 21, December 24

Angels
March 28, July 9, September 23, October 11, October 12, October 13, October 14, December 3

Dependence on God: His Protection, Help, Strength, Promises, etc.
January 1, January 6, January 9, January 27, January 28, February 4, February 9, February 15, February 20, March 8, April 22, April 23, May 6, May 19, May 24, May 27, June 4, June 22, July 2, July 3, July 5, July 8, July 11, July 20, August 1, August 14, August 18, August 20, August 31, September 2, October 22, November 15, November 16, November 19, November 21, November 28, December 1, December 3, December 11, December 29

Understanding Grief
March 6–18, May 13, November 18, November 22

Walking through Hard Times

January 4, January 5, January 8, January 10, January 11, January 12, January 14, January 17, January 23, January 29, February 1, February 2, February 3, February 5, February 14, February 28, March 2, March 4, March 5, March 8, March 11, March 22, March 23, March 26, April 5, April 6, May 7, May 17, May 20, June 4, June 11, June 29, July 15, July 28, July 29, August 13, August 26, September 16, October 9, October 17, October 27, November 23, December 4, December 14, December 19, December 23

Grappling with Fear

March 10, April 26, April 30, June 5, August 29, August 30, September 1, September 15, September 17, September 30, October 2, October 26, November 28

Surviving Failure

June 26, August 28, September 29, October 1, October 26

Coping with Change and Upheavals

February 8, March 22, March 23, March 26, June 25, June 29, July 4, July 17, August 3, August 9, August 11, September 4, September 5, October 2, December 11

Difficult Relationships

April 26, April 27, April 28, May 25, August 24, September 12, October 28, November 13

Handling Anger

March 3, March 12, March 13, May 3, May 4, May 5, May 16, May 21, June 16, August 8, November 26

Forgiveness

March 18, March 31, April 19, April 25, May 4, May 14, May 15, June 29, November 3, November 14, December 16

Inner Healing: Finding God's Healing from Emotional Pain and His Forgiveness for Guilt and Shame

February 5, February 11, February 23, March 2, March 10, March 18, April 16, April 17, April 18, April 19, April 23, April 24, April 25, May 9, May 11, May 12, May 14, May 15, May 16, June 15, June 16, June 17, July 26, August 21, August 24, September 1, September 30, October 2, October 8, October 19, October 27, October 28, October 29, November 3, November 4, November 5, November 6, November 7, November 8, November 14, November, November 15, November 16, November 18, November 28, December 6, December 14, December 15, December 16, December 19, December 23, December 23, December 30

Faith

January 10, January 12, February 6, February 10, February 11, February 26, March 4, March 14, faith March 16, April 2, April 22, April 30, June 25, July 4, July 11, July 29, August 3, August 4, August 11, August 13, September 8, September 19, September 26, October 22, October 31, November 1, November 27, December 20

Faith Crises, Doubt and the Dark Night of the Soul

February 6, March 5, March 6, March 7, March 11, March 12, March 13, March 15, March, April 1, April 29, May 13, June 28, July 6, August 7, September 4, September 8, September 24, October 8, November 1, November 13, November 25, November 26

Spiritual Dryness

January 2, January 29, February 25, June 2, June 27, December 27

Prayer

March 28–April 4, January 7, January 10, January 11, January 15, February 24, February 26, April 20, June 13, July 26, July 28, July 31, August 16, August 27, August 31, September 6, September 7, September 10, September 12, September 24, October 1, October 3, October 6, October 7, October 20, October 30, November 9, November 13, November 24, November 25, November 26, December 8

Heaven and the Second Coming
June 6–10, February 6, February 7, April 7, July 30, September 15, November 11, November 29, December 7, December 9

Dogs: Lessons about My Relationship with the Lord, Learnt via My Dogs
January 5, January 7, February 20, February 21, May 21, June 12, June 14, June 28, August 19, September 2, September 3, September 23, November 23, November 30, December 29

Stories about Famous Christians
January 15, February 2, February 14, February 20, March 1, March 5, May 20, June 19, July 16, July 17, July 30, August 16, August 20, September 21, October 3, October 16, October 22, November 22, December 25

Hymns (and How They Came to Be Written)
February 2, March 1, March 5, April 5, May 20, June 5, June 14, June 19, July 16, August 16, August 20, September 21, October 16, October 19, October 20, November 16, November 16, November 22, December 7, December 9, December 11, December 25

Joy
September 9–17, February 16, February 19, February 27, April 4, April 8, May 6, May 12, June 14, June 20, July 12, August 20, October 13, November 27, November 30, December 9, December 12, December 25

Living the Jesus Way: Discipleship, Relating to Others, Character, Christian Behaviour
January 19, January 31, February 8, February 9, February 15, February 16, February 17, February 18, February 19, March 12, April 12, April 18, April 21, April 22, April 26, April 27, April 28, April 30, May 8, May 10, May 11, May 16, May 24, May 28, May 29, May 30, June 1, June 3, June 21, June 27, July 1, July 7, July 13, July 14, July 15, July 21, July 24, August 2, August 4, August 6, August 8, August 19, August 22; August 23; August 29, September 7, September 9, September 10, September 13, September 14, September

18, September 22, October 5, October 29, November 10, November 15, November 16, November 19, November 29, December 1, December 12, December 18, December 19, December 28

Supernatural Dimension: Gifts of the Holy Spirit, Miracles

April 16, May 26, June 18, July 6, July 9, August 21, September 24, October 11, October 12, October 13, October 14, October 23, October 30, October 31, November 1, December 28

Worship

January 13, April 6, May 1, May 6, May 7, May 26, June 20, July 12, August 17, October 13

Natural World: Illustrations from Animals, Birds and Gardens

July 1–14, March 20–24, January 4, January 5, January 8, January 9, January 10, January 16, February 12, March 17, April 24, May 1, June 11, June 15, June 20, June 21, June 22, July 1, July 18, July 30, August 19, September 7, September 20, September 22, September 25, November 11, December 10, December 11, December 29, December 30

Poems

January 3, January 5, January 6, February 13 June 23, July 30, October 21

Seasonal Themes

New Year:	January 1, December 29, December 30, December 31
Spring:	March 19, April 24, May 1
Easter:	April 7–14
Summer	June 20, June 21, August 2,
Autumn:	September 7, September 25, November 17
Winter:	January 4, January 7, January 8, January 16, December 10
Advent:	December 1, December 5, December 7
Christmas:	December 9, December 12, December 18, December 19, December 25, December 26, December 27, December 31

Serving Christ
January 3, February 13, February 18, February 29, March 1, March 9, April 13, May 2, May 22, May 23, May 24, July 10, July 31, August 4, August 10, August 11, August 15, August 21, August 23, August 25, September 5, September 6, September 27, September 28, October 10, October 18, October 25, November 2, November 10, December 1, December 18

Contents by Series

Bible characters

Noah June 7, July 10

Job March 6–18, July 2

Abraham, Sarah and Hagar August 3–15, January 18, June 25, July 5

Jacob August 28–30, June 26, December 2, December 6

Joseph June 29

Moses September 26–October 9, January 20, January 27, February 15, February 29, March 4

King David April 22–30, May 2–19, January 24, January 25, January 26, February 16, February 19, November 24

King Solomon May 22–June 6, March 19, June 30, July 11

Gideon November 28

Deborah August 25

Elijah October 23–30, July 3

Elisha October 30–November 2, October 28, June 16, September 23

Jonah June 28, July 6

Hosea November 12–14

Habakkuk November 25–37

High Priest Joshua August 21

Mary the Mother of Jesus August 27, December 1, December 2, December 3

Anna November 24

Mary and Martha March 1, April 9, April 10, April 11, April 12, April 13, April 14

Judas Iscariot April 14

Dorcas August 23, November 29

Sapphira November 29

Paul September 9–19

Peter June 15

John December 7

Bible translations

Bible translations used in the text are marked and used with permission as follows:

AMP: Scripture taken from the *Amplified Bible*, Copyright © 1954, 1958, 1962, 1964, 1965, 1987 by The Lockman Foundation. Used by permission.

ESV: Scripture quotations are from The Holy Bible, English Standard Version® (ESV®), copyright 2001 by Crossway Bibles, a publishing ministry of Good News Publishers. Used by permission. All rights reserved.

GNB: Scriptures are quoted from the *Good News Bible* © 1994 published by the Bible Societies/HarperCollins Publishers Ltd. Used with permission.

LB: Scripture quotation taken from *The Living Bible* copyright © 1971. Used by permission of Tyndale House Publishers, Inc., Wheaton, IL 60189. All rights reserved.

Message: Scripture taken from The Message. Copyright © 1993, 1994, 1995, 1996, 2000, 2001, 2002. Used by permission of NavPress Publishing Group

NKJV: Scripture taken from the New King James Version®. Copyright © 1982 by Thomas Nelson, Inc. Used by permission. All rights reserved

NLT: Scripture Quotations from the Holy Bible New Living Translation, copyright © 1996, 2004, 2007 by Tyndale House Foundation. Used by permission of Tyndale House Publishers, Inc., Carol Stream, Illinois 60188. All rights reserved.

†Adm. by Song Solutions Copycare, 14 Horsted Square, Uckfield, East Sussex, TN22 1QG www.songsolutions.org

*Adm. by worshiptogether.com songs excl. UK & Europe, adm. by kingswaysongs.com tym@kingsway.co.uk www.kingsway.co.uk

Do you wish this wasn't the end?
Are you hungry for more great teaching, inspiring
testimonies, ideas to challenge your faith?

Join us at www.hodderfaith.com, follow us on Twitter
or find us on Facebook to make sure you get the latest from
your favourite authors.

Including interviews, videos, articles, competitions
and opportunities to tell us just what you thought about
our latest releases.

 www.hodderfaith.com

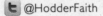 HodderFaith

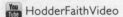 @HodderFaith

 HodderFaithVideo

H

HODDER

WHERE FAITH IS INSPIRED